The Seven Ages

A selection of books by
CHRISTOPHER HOLLIS

Thomas More
Foreigners aren't Fools
Death of a Gentleman
Fossett's Memory
Can Parliament Survive?
A Study of George Orwell
Along the Road to Frome
Eton
The Papacy
The Oxford Union
Newman and the Modern World
A History of the Jesuits
The Mind of Chesterton
Parliament and its Sovereignty

THE SEVEN AGES

THEIR EXITS AND THEIR ENTRANCES

Christopher Hollis

HEINEMANN : LONDON

William Heinemann Ltd
15 Queen Street, Mayfair, London W1X8BE

LONDON   MELBOURNE   TORONTO
JOHANNESBURG   AUCKLAND

Printed in Great Britain by
WESTERN PRINTING SERVICES LTD
Bristol

Contents

1 Mewling and Puking   1

2 Shining Morning Face   16

3 Sighing Like Furnace   68

4 Full of Strange Oaths   119

5 Full of Wise Saws and Modern Instances   158

6 The Lean and Slipper'd Pantaloon   187

7 Second Childishness and Mere Oblivion   228

    Index   235

CHAPTER ONE

Mewling and Puking

I was born on March 19, 1902, on Good Friday as I believe it was in that year, at St Michael's Home in Axbridge—a pleasant little Somerset town which up till the Reform Bill used to return a single member to Parliament. King John hunted in the neighbourhood and his memory is still preserved in an old hall which is known as King John's Hunting Lodge, though there is no reason to think that King John ever had anything to do with it. It lies in the Cheddar Valley, home of strawberries and cheese, and in the days when the little Cheddar Valley branch line still survived, as it did until a few years ago, Axbridge was the next station in the Yatton and Bristol direction beyond Cheddar. St Michael's Home stood up on the hill above the town. It was an old folks' home, founded—I do not know exactly how—by some Anglican charity. It has in recent years passed into the hands of the Cheshire Homes of Group-Captain Cheshire and Axbridge itself is now threatened with transfer from the ancient county of Somerset into the newly created county of Avon.

I was only one year old at the time that we left there and although from time to time I pass through Axbridge—less frequently now that it is completely bypassed than a few years ago when there was no way round it and no way through it except by a narrow road in which there was no possibility of vehicle passing vehicle—I have never since visited St Michael's Home. My elder brother took his name of Michael from it. I cannot imagine that my father's duties there were very onerous, nor the remuneration very munificent. He was then a young and energetic man, full of evangelical zeal and with a first-class university degree behind him. They had a chapel there and doubtless had services twice on Sunday. There was some form of prayers conducted on other days and I am sure he was generous in the offer of his spiritual aid to any who needed it. How far any of them called for such assistance except from time to time to be buried I cannot say. I cannot think that it was very often.

In any event it is clear that the duties of the chaplaincy were not in themselves sufficient to line his purse. He was glad to get other work. He did a certain amount of reviewing for the *Guardian*, an excellent High Church Anglican paper, that had been in its day the organ of the Oxford Movement and which has since, like so many other excellent newspapers, gone out of existence. I cannot think that he made much out of that. Apart from that he went a few days in the week into Wells to lecture at the Theological College. These were days when impoverished clergymen had not yet even dreamed of travelling upon any private machine more lordly than a bicycle. Even the Bishop of Bath and Wells when he called at St Michael's arrived neither by train nor motor car but on a bicycle with his apron pinned up round his middle to keep it out of the mudguards. With the Mendip Hills above it was not easy to leave Axbridge unless one travelled up or down the Cheddar Valley. Along the Valley the journey was easy enough. So it was no difficulty for my father to take a train into Wells after breakfast in the morning and to return, having delivered his lecture, in the evening. How he passed his time during the half of the year when the College was in vacation I cannot guess.

In any event he did not long remain at Axbridge. A place soon fell vacant on the regular staff of the Theological College and he moved to Wells. There we lived for the next four years and there I grew up. . . . Wells indeed has always through all the vicissitudes of my life been my home of homes. For, even before we came to live there, my grandfather was its senior Canon and lived on there until he died well on in his nineties in the middle of the First World War; and, as we shall see, shortly afterwards my father was brought back there first as Canon and afterwards as Bishop Suffragan of Taunton, and he lived in Wells until his death during the Second World War.

I thus grew up in a clerical family. This is less common today with the decline in vocations, but there was nothing at all odd about it in the early years of the century. In my Election of sixteen at Eton, four were the sons of clergymen and that was, I should imagine, a fairly usual proportion to find among any group of schoolboys in a school which catered for the education of scholars. But of course the average schoolboy who was the son of a clergyman was the son of a vicar. He lived in a parish. His father was a clergyman and, it may be, there was a curate or two to help him. But the majority of his neighbours were laymen and the majority of his schoolfellows were not the sons of clergymen. My ambience was different. For the most part the cathedral cities of England are cities of at least a certain secular importance. Wells and, I suppose, Ely are the only two seats of a cathedral that are purely ecclesiastical. The atmosphere of one who grew up in a cathedral close was wholly different from that of the average Englishman who casually enters himself as C. of E. on some official form. In Wells the cathedral was the centre of all life. 'How old is the cathedral?' a tourist one day asked of a townsman. 'Can't say,' he replied. 'It's been there ever since I can remember.'

Wells—a little city with a population at that time of just under 5,000 and now just over 9,000—had a paper works down by St Cuthbert's church in Southover but for all practical purposes it had no reason for its existence except for its cathedral. The episcopal see was placed at Wells by the Saxon bishop Giso because in pre-Norman days the first necessity for a new foundation was water and Wells possessed water from the rivers that ran down underground through the Mendips and came out in the city's springs.

The cathedral dignitaries—the Bishop, the Dean and the four Canons who between them constituted the quinque personae—and the lesser fry, such as the priest vicars, lived around the Liberty, by which, to mark its extra-parochial status, the cathedral was surrounded. Of these ecclesiastics the priest vicars, whose duties were in turn to sing the cathedral services morning and evening and of whom my father was at that time one, were by far the least distinguished. 'Uncle Arthur, is a priest vicar quite the lowest kind of man?' one day asked a cousin of mine after having heard him reciting some of his grievances against his ecclesiastical superiors. 'Absolutely bim-bottom,' said my father. Life rotated round the Bishop who lived in his moated Palace. In the world before 1914 no question of the Bishop not being able to afford to live in his Palace had ever been raised. When we first lived in Wells, Bishop Kennion was the Bishop and a great event in our lives was to go to tea at the Palace on the last day of the school holidays when we always received a bountiful tip from his delightful old Scottish wife. After the war when Bishop Kennion died he was succeeded by Wynne Wilson. Wynne Wilson had been Headmaster of Haileybury and Marlborough and had then become Dean of Bristol, where he had married a member of the Wills tobacco family. This meant that he could afford more easily than others to keep up the large palace. He was a decent old fellow, and it was said that his addresses to young boys preparing for confirmation were of a clear, manly and edifying type. But they bore little sign of being tinged with theology and, for a headmaster, his scholarly interests seemed strangely limited. His main interest was in his games. 'I like to get my golf over in the morning,' he pronounced, 'because then I'm free for bridge after lunch,' or again, 'Personally I must admit that the spiritual side of this job doesn't particularly appeal to me.'

In the middle of the Liberties in the Vicars' Close lived the members of the Theological College—students recently down from the University but training for ordination at the end of what was then a year's course. (Subsequently the course was lengthened.) As a consequence I grew up not merely as a clergyman's son—which was common enough in those days—but in a cleric-inhabited society—in a sort of Trollopean world. I grew up taking it for granted—what between cathedral clergy and the Theological College students—that the natural thing was for a man to be ordained and that to remain a layman was an eccentricity.

I enjoyed greatly the company of the theological students. Their lives were very different from those of Catholic seminarians. They sometimes frequented the town pubs and, when I saw them going in there, begged me not to mention it to my father, to which I readily agreed. Naturally I knew nothing of the details of their curricular studies. My interest was in their cricket and rugby football teams. They also used to come round and play tennis on my grandfather's court and in the summer evenings to play a curious game called bean-bags in my father's garden. We would sometimes go to tea with them in their lodgings in the various houses of the Vicar's Close. The College consisted of about forty-five students. It has, alas, been recently closed down and the students moved to Salisbury. There were four terms in the year— three of them corresponding to the three terms of Oxford and Cambridge and a fourth in the months of August and September. The greater number of the students came directly from completing their undergraduate courses at the University. Occasionally a schoolmaster came to put in the August term. Of such the most interesting was a young laymaster, from Malvern, named Geoffrey Fisher. Lambeth was still far before him. At Marlborough, one of his schoolfellows had been a young man who was a master at my preparatory school at Summer Fields. We exchanged badinage. Fisher asked me to tell him anything that I had learnt from my master and I replied by challenging him to tell me anything that he had been able to teach to his pupils. But my main interest in him lay in the discovery that he had been born in Leicestershire. That year in the county cricket championship it so happened that Leicestershire was the only county that was below Somerset. Mr Fisher was the only person that I knew who supported Leicestershire. It was a great joy to be able to crow over his county's misfortunes.

I knew no doubt in a sort of way that there were such beings as laymen, but such laymen did not come easily my way and I did not expect to meet them. I remember hearing my father say of the changing fashion in dress, 'Of course I very rarely see a layman in evening clothes' and the remark did not seem to me at all peculiar.

In those days Wells was not an easily accessible little place. It had, it is true, two railway stations—one on the Great Western Cheddar Valley line which ran down from Bristol to join the Westbury line at Witham—the other on the Somerset and Dorset branch from Glaston-bury. The Somerset and Dorset line in particular was as tortuous as could be imagined. As one travelled down the Somerset and Dorset main line from Bath to Bournemouth after some twenty miles across the Mendips one reached the little station of Masebury and he who could afford a carriage to meet him could alight there and in three miles down the hill be in Wells. But, if he insisted on travelling all the way to Wells by train, he had to go to Evercreech Junction, there change and take the Burnham line to Glastonbury, change again at Glastonbury and take the little side line to Wells. It took a good hour's extra journeying. Nor was it clear why there were the two stations at Wells, for, coming from Witham and Shepton Mallet up the Cheddar Valley line, one had to pass through the Somerset and Dorset station before reaching that of the Great Western in Tucker Street a quarter of a mile away. In those days of course there were no buses and few people had motors. Today buses abound, the trains have vanished and the problem is the inadequacy of the parking space.

As I say, Wells was an ecclesiastical city and had no other raison d'être. The cathedral authorities lived round the cathedral in the Liberty of St Andrew, but clergymen, though they abounded, were even there a minority of the population. There were, as I say, those who worked in the paper mills down at Southover but the men of the cathedral hardly penetrated into their world. It was a foreign land inhabited, it was rumoured, by nonconformists and other such strange creatures. The clerical families kept almost entirely to themselves and, though I did not suspect as much at the time, there was in fact a considerable atmosphere of hostility between town and gown. The lay tradesmen thought of the cathedral clergy as a stand-offish and unfriendly lot. My father was, I think, in this respect a great deal less stand-offish than the rest of the clergy. We made a number of lay friends from the town. It was mainly on the town cricket ground which we frequented that we made these friendships, but my father never made any objection to them—in which he differed from his more particular colleagues—nor made any demand to inquire who they were. In particular there was a doctor who worked at the sanatorium up on the Mendips. He had two sons, one of whom played for the town second eleven, and his company caused some comment because he was a black man. Why he came to be working in Somerset I have no idea. A black man in rural England was at that time a rarity. He was the first black man that I had ever seen or was to see for many years. My friendship for him was notable. 'You could not have been nicer to me—not even if I had been black,' said with heavy irony a young companion to whom I had stood a bull's eye. But it never occurred to me or to my parents that there was any reason why I should not associate with a black boy, and I was greatly surprised when I heard one of the other canon's sons say, 'I don't think you ought to go about with Mahrab too much.' I could not imagine why.

Naturally in such an atmosphere I was brought up to regular religious practice. We began the day with family prayers—which, I fancy, had been universal in Victorian times and which, now virtually unknown, were still common enough in the first decade of the century. The maids, in their little white caps, trooped demurely in to hear a collect or two, recite the Lord's Prayer and listen to a passage from the Bible. Of course we were regular attendants at the Cathedral. I took this for granted. I doubt if at that age it had ever occurred to me that there were people who did not go regularly to church. I was not at all pious. I of course regularly knelt down and said my prayers morning and evening. They were of a routine pattern—the Lord's Prayer, and God bless Father and Mother and make me a good boy. What I expected to happen as a result of them—how God would set about blessing Father and Mother and, still more mysteriously, succeed in making me a good boy —I had naturally not considered. There were occasions—such as an important cricket match on the next day—when I might entreat Him for fine weather. I do not know what I meant by such entreaties, I certainly did not seriously expect God to change the weather that he had arranged, to suit my convenience. That there might be other people who for one reason or another might want it to be wet the next day I do not imagine that I had ever considered. I do not remember ever having been lectured by my father or hearing in any other clergyman's sermon threats of hell-fire, and in any event it was at that time so wholly beyond my imagination that I should ever die that threats about the after-life would have had small effect on me. There was a lady of some sort of Adventist faith who lived down in the west end of the city near the Great Western railway station. She, it was announced, had one day had a vision in which it was revealed to her that of all the inhabitants of Wells she alone 'and Mr Moggs, the butcher' were destined to be saved. I do not think that I ever met either her or Mr Moggs, but her revelation was often recounted in a spirit of some ribaldry along the Cathedral clergy who thought it highly ridiculous to suppose that their butcher would find greater favour in the eyes of the Almighty than was accorded to them with the special grace of ordination upon them. I did not live in any way in fear of hell-fire. Such threats I did not in the least take seriously. My interest in church services was of a sort that had little to do with piety. Throughout all my childhood, like, I fancy, many other children, I always lived a double life. I was always something else as well as myself. Most frequently I was a county cricketer, playing for Somerset and of course, whenever there was a test match, invariably selected for England. But also, as was natural enough considering the clerical circles in which I moved, I often played at being a clergyman. I conducted services in the nursery, reading Matins out of the Book of Common Prayer, and was almost beyond fault in my knowledge of the incidental instructions of that book—the Prayers for special feasts, the days on which the Athanasian Creed as opposed to the Apostles' Creed was to be recited, the methods of calculating Easter and the rest. Familiarity bred a great liking and, whatever the other benefits, it was a great wrench for me, when I became a Catholic, to be divorced from the Prayer Book. Even in the days when regulations on such matters were a great deal more rigid than they are today, I always took any opportunity that came my way to attend an Anglican wedding or funeral simply for the pleasure of hearing Cranmer's prayers read, and it is a great sorrow to me that, along with the numerous changes of recent years in the Roman liturgy, Anglicans have in the spirit of modernity so largely abandoned their own glories. I would read out to myself in stentorian voice the order of Morning Prayer and was a little irritated when my mother told me that it would not be proper for me to conduct a mock communion service.

I do not know if at that stage I sincerely thought that I would be a clergyman. I remember once saying to my father that that was my ambition and he replied, expressing pleasure but with sensible moderation. My guess is that I only looked forward to being a clergyman in the sense that I looked forward to being a county cricketer or an engine driver. They were mainly characters of the second life which I was leading. I do not think that I ever seriously imagined that I would ever grow up, that these dreams would ever have to meet the challenge of reality.

I of course was told and accepted—or it did not occur to me to doubt —the common Christian story. I could follow the historical account, not knowing of course very well what a Virgin Birth meant, nor able to understand a Resurrection or an Ascension. I remember one day asking my mother, 'Who was Jesus' father?' 'Of course He did not have a human father,' she explained. 'How could He have had one, being God?' I had of course obediently recited and accepted the claim of the Creed that Christ was born of the Virgin Mary but I had no notion what the claim to Virginity meant nor did it occur to me that it provided any reason why He should not have had a human father. The issues about Joseph being a just man who was minded to put her away privily and Mary's claim that she knew not a man had no meaning to me. Equally I had accepted the claims of a Resurrection and an Ascension but had not considered what such claims meant or how they could have happened. I remember at Eton a few years later Hugh McNaghten, a master who was a deeply religious man but something of a modernist, asked us if we could think of Christ going up into Heaven like a balloon. A parent wrote to him to complain that his son was up to an atheist. It was very far from true, but at the same time it is difficult for the most rigidly orthodox, particularly if he does not think of Heaven as geographical, to envisage what exactly did happen at the Ascension. Yet understandably these problems did not trouble me in these early years. In so far as I thought about them at all I took the balloon for granted.

Of the metaphysics of the Christian claims—why, if Adam had eaten an apple which God had forbidden him to eat, that would involve a penalty on all the rest of the human race; why, if Man sinned, it should be necessary for God to die on the Cross to redeem him from that sin —these were problems to which I had no inkling of a clue at that age, nor indeed did they enter my head at all. Indeed the only piece of what I might call direct religious instruction which I at that time imbibed was of a very peculiar sort. We had a young nursemaid. She was, I suppose, only fifteen years old but at that age of five I looked up to her as fully grown, and I ascribed to her enormous authority from the fact that she had an elder brother called Arthur who was a policeman in London and who had, she boasted to me, been in some minor way involved in the Sidney Street shooting which as that moment was bulking so largely in the press. And the lesson that I learnt from her and which I have retained to this day was a *memoria technica* for remembering the order of the books in the New Testament, which succeed the Four Gospels. They run in a jingle. Ac-Rom-Cor-Cor-Gal-Ephe-Phil-Col-Thes-Thes-Pet-

John-John-Jude-Revelation. Such knowledge is a convenience, if a minor convenience. I wonder how many nursery maids of today know the order of the books in the New Testament.

There was one thing which I certainly did not in the least learn during those years, and that was anything about denominational or ecclesiastical party divisions. My father had, as in his position he could not well help having, his theological opinions. But he never spoke of such things to his children and never came near to doing so. When I was some-where in my teens, I discovered an autobiographical fragment of some clergyman who had in his day been one of my father's pupils at the Wells Theological College. This clergyman said something to the effect that he had studied at Wells under 'High Church' tutors. Reading it, I appealed to my mother to know whether my father was a High Church-man. My mother's maiden name was Church and her uncle was the famous Dean of St Paul's of the Oxford Movement and the intimate friend of Newman and Gladstone. Our family traditions were then very much of the Tractarian School but naturally at that age I knew nothing of Tractarianism and nothing of schools of thought, my father's or any-one else's. I did not know that there were such things as denominations. There were, as I grew up believing, three churches in Wells—the three Anglican churches—the Cathedral, the ancient city church of St Cuth-bert—the parish church of what had until recent years been a very exten-sive parish stretching into districts which were now known as Out. St Cuthbert's and far beyond the boundaries of the city—and a modern church in the east end of the city dedicated to St Thomas. Then one day walking down the street that is known as Chamberlain Street which led down from the Liberty to the direction of the Great Western railway station, I saw to my very great surprise on the opposite side of the road a fourth church, St Joseph and Teresa, whose existence had hitherto been kept from me. My father was at that time the Vice-Principal of the Theological College. The Principal was Dr Goudge, later to be a Regius Professor at Oxford and Canon of Christ Church. He was the father of Elizabeth Goudge, the well-known author of *The City of Bells*, with whom under a governess I did my first lessons. Dr Goudge's wife had a few years before had a serious bicycle accident as a result of which she was wholly paralysed and condemned to spend her life on a sofa. In the strange way of children, because she was thus when first I came to know her, I took her condition entirely for granted as a natural con-dition and never considered the suffering it involved, the period of anxiety before it was certain whether or not the condition was irrevocable, the hardship to her husband—still less, it is hardly necessary to say, why they had no further children. I used often to visit Mrs Goudge on her sofa and to talk to her, and it was to her that I took in great excitement the news of my new discovery. 'There aren't just the three churches in Wells,' I told her, 'there's a fourth church in the middle of Chamberlain Street.' She explained to me that there were other sorts of churches that had nothing to do with the Church of England, and for the first time I learnt of the existence of such a body as the Roman Catholic Church. I knew that in the Creed we professed a belief in 'the holy Catholic Church', but it had never before occurred to me to wonder what was the meaning of that phrase. Mrs Goudge explained to me a little, I forget in what terms, but needless to say, I did not derive from her explanation the smallest notion why there were different churches. Going to church was doubtless a good thing, but why it should matter what church one went to I could not guess.

There lived in Wells a titled lady, the widow of an army surgeon who had been knighted. She was an extreme low churchwoman, and when the names of those who had been killed in the war were read out and prayers asked for them she would kneel at the back of the church and at each name shout out 'if repentant'. I thought that very funny but had no notion why she did it.

In 1909 my father was appointed the Vicar of St Bartholomew's Church at Armley in Leeds. Armley is perhaps mainly noted for its famous gaol. It is not one of the more salubrious suburbs of Leeds, that splendid town, rivalling only Swindon according to the excellent judgement of Sir John Betjeman for the title of the most Christian city in England, and it was in Leeds that we lived for the next six years of my life, first at Armley and then at the somewhat more fashionable church of St Michael's at Headingley, in whose parish was the county cricket ground. It is still a great delight to me, whenever I see on television a cricket test match or a battle of the roses at Headingley, to catch a glimpse of this spire of my father's old church standing up over the ground.

After a short time I was old enough to go into the bottom form of the Grammar School and went there for a couple of terms. Only then eight years old, I was the youngest boy in the form and in the school. I resented this and was ashamed when the master, as he sometimes did, held me up as a model to the other boys if I attained a place in the form above any of my elders. I was so ashamed of my youth that I even pretended—without any sort of validity—that there had been a mistake about my age and that I was really a year older than had been imagined. There was in fact nothing to be proud of in my place in form, for we acquired marks by writing down on slips of paper the answers to the questions which we had prepared in Home Work and which the master asked us the next morning. We then handed our slips to our next-door neighbour whose duty it was to mark them as the master read out the correct answers. The boy who shared the desk with me suggested that we should each always mark the other's answer as 100 per cent correct. I agreed and followed this plan. We were never detected, though why it was that the master so lamely accepted such results I cannot guess.

Leeds Grammar School was, and is, an admirable school. My brother stayed there for his full scholastic career and won from it academic success a great deal better than mine. I have no doubt that I would have benefited had I remained there. But it did not happen thus. The school was of course nominally an Anglican school and had, as most schools then did, a clerical headmaster. But its religion did not in the least impinge on my life. We began the day every morning by an Assembly of the whole school and I suppose that on that occasion some prayer was said or hymn sung, but I have no memory of either. All that I can remember of it was as an occasion for the headmaster to make announcements about forthcoming events and on one occasion for very full-throated applause for one of the prefects who had made a century in a match on the previous day. Our home in Armley was right across the city—a good tram ride away from the school—and quite outside the radius of its Chapel. We used to go to the Armley Church, St Bartholomew's. It never occurred to me, any more than it had at Wells, that there could be any question of not going to church on a Sunday. At the same time I was not by then in any way devout. I do not know what future I foresaw for myself but I was not especially interested in clerical affairs, and in a town parish where my father and his curates were the only clergymen in the midst of a population of some 40,000 I was much more in lay company than I had been at Wells. My main interest in the church services was not at all devotional but in conformity to the details of the Prayer Book regulations. I sat one day at the back of the church and explained in great detail and no doubt in my customary loud voice to my younger and then very junior brother what was going on. I was much shocked when one of the sidesmen behind me, no doubt thinking that I was engaged in a brawl, tapped me on the shoulder and said, 'We expect better manners from the Vicar's son.'

Of course I went regularly to church every Sunday, as a rule in the morning. In my parents' catalogue of obligation one had to go to church though it did not matter whether in the morning or the evening. One Sunday I had not for some reason gone in the morning. It was therefore taken for granted that I should go in the evening. But, when half-past-six came that evening the matter slipped my mother's mind and she forgot to send me. I kept silent with a delicious sense of guilt, feeling that I was doing something very delightfully naughty in not reminding her but at the same time comfortable that the guilt was not finally mine. It was only at about seven o'clock and when it was all too late that she suddenly remarked, 'Chris, you haven't been to church today.' I pretended that it had slipped my mind as completely as it had hers.

The curiosity, as I look back at it, of my life at Leeds, as indeed of all my upbringing, was this. As I have said, the only time when I still lived in Wells that I heard of the existence of such a body as the Roman Catholic Church was in the conversation that I have recounted with Mrs Goudge. There was a single resident Catholic priest in the little city, but he was of course wholly submerged beneath the avalanche of Anglican clergymen. The Catholic population was then small, though in recent years it has been considerably augmented by a large Italian immigration. The Catholic priest played no part in the city's general life and indeed I never heard of his existence until, years later, shortly before the Second World War, I happened to be giving a lecture in Winnipeg when I received a letter from an old priest, Father Moreton. He had been in my boyhood the Catholic priest in Wells and had by then emigrated to Canada and lived a lonely life in a gigantic tower some forty miles from that unexuberant city. I discovered that in Wells he used to go and read to my grandmother who at the end of her life and immediately after the First World War was totally blind. Apparently, as inquiries then showed me, they had a considerable friendship but during my boyhood I was never told of this and knew nothing of these visits. The Vice-Principal of the Theological College of Wells, when my father was its chaplain, had also been the man who was afterwards to go over to Rome and to become Headmaster and then Abbot of Downside, Abbot Ramsay. Apparently when the Roman fever struck him he went for a time in retreat to Downside prior to his reception, and my father and he used to meet at some half-way point and go for walks. But again I was never told of this and my father hardly, if ever, saw Abbot Ramsay again after his reception. The Dean of Wells, the learned Armitage Robinson, uncle of the later famous Bishop of Woolwich, was a High Churchman and one of the participants in the Malines conversations. He had many Catholic friends—and particularly at Downside—and used to spend much time there. He and Abbot Chapman, who had succeeded Ramsay as Abbot, used to sit round at Christmas, roasting chestnuts in the fire and eating them. A fervent Low Church clergyman complained to him of a phrase in a hymn that spoke of Our Lady as sitting at the right hand of Our Lord. 'And whom would you propose for the position?' said Armitage Robinson. He never went to bed before about three o'clock in the morning and did not rise again before lunch. The only time that I ever remember him getting up for Early Service at eight o'clock in the morning was when the Archbishop of Canterbury came to stay with him for the weekend.

My father, as I remember him once saying, did not approve of Armitage Robinson's too frequent visits to Downside. Indeed in all these early years I only remember him once admitting to any conversation with a Catholic. He had a story how once—I do not know why—he visited Ushaw and there met the Bishop of Hexham. He was not attracted by him. To make conversation he passed some remark on the tragedy of a bad railway accident in which there had been some fatal casualties and of which the papers were at the moment full. My father said how sad it was. The Bishop did not seem to be in the least interested. The Bishop explained the system of the church boys who were being trained there for the priesthood. My father asked what preparation they were given if they did not find themselves possessed of a vocation. How would they fare in the world? The Bishop at any rate gave the impression that, if they did not care to become priests, he was quite indifferent to what happened to them.

The meeting was not a success. I do not know who was the Bishop of Hexham of the time, but the whole pattern is a great deal clearer to me than it was to my father. The Bishop certainly had no university education. In all probability he had himself in his youth been a church boy and had spent his whole life in clerical circles. He had never come across anything remotely resembling the general reading of an Oxford man—had probably never seen any book except a seminary text-book. His flock with few, if any, exceptions were from working-class families and no better read than he. He was therefore intensely ill at ease—the victim of what it is now the fashion to call an inferiority complex—in the presence of an educated man and an Oxford man. Conscious of his own disabilities he was also conscious of, as he thought, the possession of a divine privilege which the other had not got and which he was under most sacred obligation not to compromise. He was prickly, intensely embarrassed, intensely suspicious, and it was doubtless a great relief to him when he could get away from such a circle and back to the Irish company that he could understand.

In 1908 in a great millenary celebration the grounds of Glastonbury Abbey were made over to the Church of England. The Prince of Wales (later George V) attended the open-air dedication service. So did the Archbishop of Canterbury. My elder brother, then eight years old, was of those detailed to bear his train. A very large concourse of bishops from all over England and Scotland also attended. It was a curiosity that it never, it seemed, occurred to anyone to invite any Roman Catholic to any of the functions. Nor, I fancy, to be fair, did it occur to any of the Roman Catholics to ask to be invited, though they did a little later obtain leave to rail off the high altar of the Abbey Church, which none of the Anglicans had thought to do. One might have suspected that, whatever the sincerity of Anglican claims to continuity, the ruined Abbey buildings of Glastonbury were hardly the place at which they could most decently be asserted. It is different from today when there is an ecumenical pilgrimage there every year and the Anglican Bishop of Bath and Wells attends in full pontificals to hear the Apostolic Delegate say Mass.

Yet, so long as we lived in Wells, Catholics did not come in any appreciable way into our lives. At Leeds it was another story though it never occurred to me at that time that it was so. My father was in no way anti-Catholic. He was always ready to rebuke any mis-statements about Catholic beliefs or practices, which were common enough at those times. But it never occurred to him to meet a Catholic. He had no principle in refusal. He would have met one courteously enough had he come his way, but he never did come his way. The two communities lived absolutely separate lives. Leeds is a city with a very considerable Catholic population. There must in the nature of things have been a Catholic priest at Armley, as also at Headingley when we moved there three years later. There must have been a Catholic priest living somewhere not so far from us. But I never heard the least mention of his existence. Leeds is a city also with a very strong Jewish population. I do not remember that we ever met a rabbi or indeed any other Jew. But we were told about the Jews and even on occasions went down into the Jewish quarter to see something of their practices at the celebration of their feasts. I remember going to some exhibition of the varieties of religious customs and the exhibition included a Jewish family celebrating its Passover, but I never heard the least reference to the existence of Catholics. Or rather I only heard one such reference. We were told there was such a person as the Bishop of Leeds. I knew so much of Anglican bishops that it was to me something of a comic eccentricity that there should be bishops other than those of the Anglican episcopacy. Yet such a personage, we were assured, did exist. He even had a house which was pointed out to us. Now at the Grammar School there were a couple of very mischievous boys, twin sons of a neighbouring parson. They had the notion of tying the Bishop's door-scraper, which was outside his front door, to the front door handle, of ringing the bell, then running away and hiding round the corner. They did this. What in point of fact happened I am not quite clear. I cannot see what in the nature of things could have happened except that perhaps the scraper, when the door was opened, would have been pulled back into the hall. However somehow the Headmaster heard of the escapade and properly took a poor view of it. The twins were sent to apologise to the Bishop. No one—that is, no one at the Grammar School—had any notion what he looked like. We awaited with interest their report when they returned from their visit. They reported, much to our surprise, that he was quite a decent fellow though 'one could not understand what he said because of his Irish accent'.

CHAPTER TWO

Shining Morning Face

I

SUMMER FIELDS

I had only been a couple of terms at the Grammar School when one evening, as I was having my bath, my mother came into the bathroom and informed me that next term I was to go away to school—to a preparatory school in Oxford. I burst incontinently into tears. I had not at that time any notion what public schools or preparatory schools might be or what advantage, if any, there was in going to them. Why could I not stay at the Grammar School where I was very happy? Why, if I must go to a public school whither, as I learnt, one went at the age of thirteen, could I, by then nine years old, not stay at the Grammar School for another four years? It was explained to me that, if I was to go to a public school, it was necessary because of my father's narrow means that I should get a scholarship, whatever that might be, and that, though the Grammar School was a very good school, it did not provide the early training in Latin and Greek which was necessary for a public school scholarship. One could only hope to gain such a scholarship if one went first for two or three years to a preparatory school which provided very specially expert coaching for a public school scholarship examination. I was not consoled. I saw no point in all this. When I arrived at Summer Fields I discovered that it was indeed true that the two curricula of education were widely different. I had studied Latin at the Grammar School but the work that was put before me at Summer Fields was at first wholly beyond my capacity. 'I had thought that you would be better at Latin,' said Dr Williams, the Headmaster. But after a few stumbling weeks I soon picked it up and by the end of the term was able to keep pace with the rest.

At the time I was so ashamed of the fact that I was to go away to school that I concealed it from my fellow pupils at the Grammar School and entered into lively conversations with them about what was to happen next term on the pretence that I would be there to share in the adventures. All was in vain and I went to Summer Fields in the September term of 1912. I was told that some generous person—I was not told who—had offered to pay my fees which my father with four children and an income of only some £400 a year could not possibly have afforded. Running a successful preparatory school is, primarily, a money-making business and demands a successful business-man for its organisation. The great public schools have won for themselves over the ages an acknowledged prestige which it would require a succession of incompetent headmasters and assistant masters to undermine. They have a good deal of fat on which to live. But preparatory schools are all the creation of a generation or so—at the most two generations— probably of a particular headmaster. It is not at first sight evident why there should be preparatory schools at all or why any parents should be willing to pay the very large fees which they demand. The public schools for many years got on well enough without them and there were plenty who prophesied that, if times got harder, they would be its first casualties. Indeed in modern times one does sometimes hear tales of wealthy parents who prefer to begin their children at free state schools. It is not easy to think of any reason why they should not, but even up to the present they have not as a fact done so frequently enough to put the competent, efficiently administered private school out of business.

Of Summer Fields it could certainly be said that it provided the article that it professed to provide. Year after year it won more scholarships at the public schools than any of its competitors. It charged for the article which it sold and I have little doubt that the proprietors made a very good thing out of it. It is not for me to complain of its fees, for it was the beneficence of the Headmaster which, I later discovered, paid for my education, nor did he ever, like Orwell's headmaster in *Such, Such Were The Joys*, throw my dependence in my teeth. How far I was unique in this concession I never knew. George Orwell who was with me in College at Eton a few years later has written much of the misery of being a poor boy brought up in the company of those much richer than himself. His complaint seems to me much exaggerated. At Eton I was of course a Colleger. There could have been no question of my father affording for me to be an Oppidan and even among the Collegers I was poorer and more ragged than the rest. But it did not embarrass me. Collegers had in general a reputation for keeping to themselves and not mixing much with Oppidans. I always had more Oppidan friends than the average Colleger and at the end of my career was elected to Pop, although I did not possess the manifold athletic colours that were generally required for such a distinction. I once heard a wise schoolmaster say, 'I'm sure that the largest of all handicaps in life is to be the son of very rich parents.' Short of being born in poverty below the subsistence level, I am sure that this is true. I could never understand why Orwell minded poverty so much.

At Summer Fields the two Headmasters took the two top classes consisting of boys who were considered as scholarship potentialities. I lived in terror of those formidable men, as indeed did most other boys. We sat around them on little stools and stammered out our lessons, whether in geometry, Greek or Latin as the case might be. Usually, to do them justice, nothing worse happened than apprehension, but there was always a sigh of relief when the period was finished without mishap. Occasionally, whether because the boy was particularly dense or the master particularly bad-tempered, there was catastrophe. One hawed and stammered. The Doctor listened for a time with increasing impatience, then suddenly would rasp out 'Take a nought' and a zero would be inscribed against one's name in the mark book. Or perhaps it would be 'Fetch the stick', and the victim would fetch a cane from the desk and hand it to the Doctor. 'Now go on', and either one would somehow stammer on to a dubious and inglorious security or, if the worst came to the worst, it would be 'Hold out your hand' and the cane would fall. There is no autocrat so absolute as a preparatory school headmaster. Autocrats elsewhere, in order to conquer, have to win the support of some grown-ups—of soldiers, policemen or party supporters. But headmasters impose their will only on little boys too frightened to oppose them so long as they themselves show no sign of nervousness, as Dr Williams and Mr Alington certainly never did. The only possible threat to them is from irate parents. If Dr Williams had sentenced one of us to death I doubt if we would have dared to resist the command.

If the school can be criticised it can be criticised for a too great concentration on results. We were unashamedly crammed for our examinations and I am far from certain whether boys in the long run benefit from overcramming. At the other end it can be said that boys who were not of scholarship calibre were perhaps a little neglected. However it is not for me to complain. I was happy enough there and as popular and as successful as I deserved to be. It was a school of strict discipline. Games were of course taken seriously. Everybody had to play cricket in the summer and association football in the winter, and we had matches against neighbouring schools, which it was important to win, or at least not to lose. Horris Hill near Newbury was our most important away game, and they had a very strong team, captained by Douglas Jardine, afterwards to be Captain of England (we also had a future England captain in Gubby Allen). I was in the team, though a very great deal less distinguished than they. Mr Alington had little hope that we would be able to beat Horris Hill. Therefore, when we won the toss he made us bat all day, so we were able to make a draw of it. I was number 9 in the order and held out for an unbeaten hour for 18 in this not very glorious performance.

There were two well-known preparatory schools out from Oxford along the Banbury Road—the Dragons and Summer Fields. Their policies were the direct opposite of one another. The Dragons prided themselves on their free and easy ways. The boys in open shirts and with bare knees were allowed to roam at will over the countryside. At Summer Fields we dressed ourselves in our little Eton collars. We were never allowed out of the school grounds except on a crocodile walk on a Sunday afternoon under a master's supervision. The broad permissiveness accorded to the Dragons boys must at times have caused anxiety to the school's authorities. On the other hand at Summer Fields we lived for years in one of the most interesting and beautiful cities in the world and were never allowed even under supervision to see any of the colleges or buildings. We might as well have been living in Wolverhampton, and that was surely a defect in a school that boasted itself to be a place of education.

Summer Fields was a Church of England school. By that I mean that the two Headmasters and one of the other masters were in holy orders —which was not, I fancy, common even at that time at preparatory schools. We had a chapel of our own—again a rare possession for a preparatory school—and thither we were marched in a crocodile twice on every Sunday and, I think, in the evening on every day of the week.

The boys were presumably of varying religious persuasions, though most of them were at any rate willing enough to profess themselves Church of England and to go to chapel. The Headmaster, the Doctor, was an astute business man and therefore careful not to commit himself to controversial opinions which might be unwelcome to potential paying parents. I would imagine that he was a very strong Conservative and he recited with relish and obvious approval the anecdotes of a parent from Ulster recounting the clever precautions which he had taken to protect himself against the possibility of arrest for his activities in Carson's army. There was one boy with a title in the school, a nephew of Lord Alfred Douglas, of whom we had naturally never heard. He was a good footballer but not clever and was constantly in trouble. In addition to his famous uncle, Alfred, he had also an uncle Lord Archibald Douglas, who was a priest working in a London parish. There was a pious female devotee who lived in quite a different part of London but always went across the town to Lord Archibald's church to make her confessions. Eventually out of curiosity he asked her why she made this unnecessary journey when there were so many other priests so much nearer at hand. She replied, 'Ah, but, Father, it is such an inexpressible comfort to be able to say, "I confess to Almighty God and to you, Lord Archibald Douglas." ' Yet while generally Conservative, the school was favoured by Liberal cabinet ministers. Anthony Asquith, the son of Mr Asquith, was there, and the two sons of Mr Runciman, one of his cabinet ministers. A Buxton, too, and a year or two afterwards the McKenna boys came. The Doctor was careful not to get entangled in party politics. The most distinguished Old Summerfieldeans of earlier years were a Conservative, Harold Macmillan, and its most distinguished master in the post-war years, Cecil Day Lewis.

The Doctor displayed much the same discretion in religious controversies. He was an Anglican cleric and a strong supporter of the Establishment. Any other profession would have been bad for business. When the time came for Dr Williams to retire and he was considering the appointment of John Evans as his successor, the questions of reassurance that he asked before appointing him were, 'I hope that you are a communicant and that you play bridge.' Evans could answer both in the affirmative. The University Congregation was at the time voting on the question whether Nonconformist divines might be admitted to the degree of Doctor of Divinity. It was not in my father's nature to object to such a proposition or indeed to be deeply interested in its controversies. He chanced to visit the school when the voting was on and was at once attacked by Doctor with, 'I hope you've voted the right way.' Doctor was much dismayed when he discovered that my father had not voted at all. But in the niceties of schools of thought within the Anglican communion I do not think that either of the Headmasters was very much interested, or, if he was, he thought it wiser to conceal as much. Dr Williams' son, who came on the staff my last term, was alleged to have Anglo-Catholic propensities, which he revealed by bowing very low at every mention of the name of Jesus, but at the same time he justified his Anglicanism by explaining that all Roman Catholics were liars. Mr Alington was said to have Low Church opinions and to be greatly annoyed when the young Williams genuflected and held up the procession into the chapel, 'Why can't he put up a notice?' he said, sniffing loudly in protest.

If the masters were indifferent to shades of religious opinion, even more so—naturally enough—were the boys. I remember one boy in my dormitory who had inherited strong prejudices against ritualistic practices and expounded them, but I did not understand what he was talking about and was not interested. In general we had little piety but a general feeling that it was wrong to be 'irreverent'. No boy would have expressed any disbelief or indifference to belief. I think that he would have honestly felt that some thunderbolt from on high would have fallen on him had he been guilty of such an impiety. But Christian faith was not a privilege. It was rather a faith that was imposed on us and from which, if imposed, there was no escape. We would have thought it very wicked to speak in any disrespect of the Bible or of any verse in it or to have questioned any of the doctrines of the Church of England. On the other hand one of the boys got hold of H. G. Wells' highly satirical account of the Last Judgement and of the little mortals running up the sleeve of the Almighty. It was handed about from one of us to another and read with high amusement. As for any qualms of conscience about its irreverence, they were wholly and, to our minds, quite satisfactorily set at rest by one boy who explained, 'Of course he's an atheist. So he can say these things.' Atheism was a privilege which some people enjoyed and which, possessed, carried with it perfect freedom.

Religion at Summer Fields was a military affair. Like the pupils at Napoleon's schools, we were marched from religious duty to religious duty. We formed up in lines and went to chapel at a word of command. At bed-time we were commanded to read a few verses from the Bible and to kneel and say our prayers. No instruction was given in what to pray for, nor explanation as to what way we might expect our prayers to be answered. A bell was rung at a certain time, and was the signal to us to pray. Then some ten minutes later the bell was rung again. That was the signal that prayers were over and we might talk again. In between, all talking was strictly forbidden.

It was the Doctor's son who during my last term was in charge of the house at which we lodged. He had been in his day a student at Wells Theological College and I had known him there. I therefore greeted him as an old friend on his arrival at Summer Fields and he reciprocated. For some weeks he treated us with great friendliness. Then one evening, our prayers finished, someone ventured a remark. Others answered it, not, I think, consciously remembering that the talking bell had not yet gone. Suddenly the master appeared in the dormitory and bade the four of us go downstairs to his study. We paraded there and he said, 'I'll take Chris first. The rest of you wait outside.' He then extracted a cane from behind a row of books. 'Now you'll know where I keep it,' he said a little fatuously. He was shaking with excitement. As a general rule the two Headmasters kept the power of corporal punishment in their own hands and we did not know that Doctor's son had the right to beat. However there was nothing to be done about that. 'Bend over that arm of the chair,' he said.

I meditated the rights and wrongs of it in bed. I considered that I had known the rule that forebade talking between the bells and that, though I had not been guilty of any deliberate act of disobedience, I had certainly, without thinking of it, been talking. Therefore I had no grievance. Why there should be such a rule against talking I did not at all consider. I had no sense at all that rules had any duty to make sense, nor that I had any moral obligation to obey them. School life was to me purely a game. The masters had every right to make up any rule that they wished, whether there was any sense in it or not. I had every right to break those rules if I could get away with it. If I was caught I must expect without complaint to pay the penalty, very much in the way that I must go out if I was bowled at cricket.

That was our general attitude. We took for granted the existence of rules and punishment. We disliked being punished but, when punishment came, accepted it without resentment. On the other hand it was the mark of courage and character to break a rule from time to time, hoping to escape detection. In the dining hall we were distributed around at twelve tables. A master presided over each of these tables at lunch. One of the senior boys sat at its head at breakfast and tea when the master was not present. I, while still very junior, was at the table of a mysterious and good-looking young man who was at the top of the school. He appeared under differing names—first with a good old English name, then suddenly transformed into an Italian. I have no idea of the reason for the change. I suppose that it was because of some legal qualification about his parents' nationality. He was very pleasant to me and I was inordinately proud of his company. He was alleged to be of enormous virtue—never to have broken any rule or been in any sort of trouble. After he had left Summer Fields he went to Winchester, and a year or two later rumours began to circulate that he had become very wicked there. We all believed that and discussed, in entire ignorance, what his wickedness might be. I presume that it was of the common sexual type, if indeed the rumours were true at all, but neither I nor, I fancy, any of the other boys ever guessed at its nature.

The only thing in the nature of a religious difficulty that I encountered at Summer Fields was as follows. First thing in the morning before the ordinary lessons began the whole school had to parade in the New Room before the Doctor for Bible Reading. Bible Reading consisted of each boy in turn reading a single verse from a selected portion of the Bible. Doctor then, when the occasion called for it, commented on the verse. On this occasion a boy had to read the verse that tells us that if we had faith, we could say to the mountain 'Be cast into the depth of the sea' and it would happen. Doctor in comment told the story of an old lady who took a room in a hotel and found a mountain just opposite the window blocking her view. In total faith she told the mountain to be moved into the sea and was much disgusted when she woke up in the morning to find that it was still there. The lady—I do not know if she ever existed —was of course duly held up by the Doctor to ridicule. But I was puzzled. I could not quite understand why she was ridiculed. Of course Doctor was quite right to pour ridicule on the old lady—if she did really expect that in response to her prayer the mountain would be removed from outside her bedroom window. I certainly would not have expected such a miracle to happen, and I did not expect Doctor as a man of the world and of common sense to expect it either. Yet, as he laughed the old lady's absurdity away, I could not quite answer a nagging question. 'Of course Christ did not mean that,' said the Doctor. Of course not, since that was obviously not what happened. But, if He did not mean it, why did He say it, and, saying it, give no indication that He did not mean it? Or alternatively if He did not say it, why was it reported in the Bible? If the Bible was wrong about this, might it not be wrong about many other things? What ought one to believe? There was hardly a clearer promise in the Gospels than that of this verse. If it was false, were any of the promises true? When one prayed did one really expect one's prayers to be answered? If not, what was the point of praying? Was it really wicked not to say one's prayers? If so, why? If one did not say them, what happened? If nothing happened, how was the whole business in any way what the modern jargon calls 'relevant'?

The episode did not linger for long in my mind. It was soon expelled by the press of other and, as it seemed to me, more urgent matters of the day, but there still lurked a nagging conundrum. It lurked in my mind but not, as far as I could see, in those of any other boys.

II

ETON

I succeeded in winning my scholarship to Eton—not a very high scholarship—and went there at the age of twelve, the youngest member of a large Election, in September, 1914, coinciding with the outbreak of the World War. I remained there until 1920 and thus the greater part of my school life was overshadowed by war.

During the war discipline had been strict, but as soon as the armistice was signed there was a great reaction to antinomianism and what is today called permissiveness. All rules were defied, all punishments abolished. The war had one curious incidental consequence. Prior to the war the public schools had succeeded in establishing a quite peculiar demand on their pupils' loyalty. It was considered the act of a cad to breathe the slightest syllable of criticism of one's school. One owed to it a degree of loyalty that was demanded of no other institution. The great majority accepted this obligation. The few who rejected it rejected it absolutely, saw no virtue in their school and for their rejection were of course denounced by all right-thinking persons. When after the war the Labour party made its appearance and mildly challenged the establishment in the 1918 election young voters who knew little perhaps, and cared little, about the dangers to our economy of a socialised industry, yet flocked to the polls to vote against Labour candidates under the belief (for which indeed there was not very much foundation) that, if returned, they would abolish the public schools.

I have never been able to take either of these extreme views about the public schools. On the other hand I was a natural schoolboy—one who thoroughly enjoyed being at school and who would have enjoyed being at any school of even moderate decency and quite irrespective of its social status or even of its teaching ability. I enjoyed my time at Eton and wept unashamedly when I came to leave. But that was quite a different matter from approving of it. I do not think that even then I approved of it and I am certain that I do not approve of it now. Eton seemed to me, and seems to me, an absurd but lovable place, 'a zoo' as it was recently called in the *Eton College Chronicle*. I find it difficult to take seriously the loyalty of those exuberant Old Etonians who really think that it is different in kind from all other schools. I remember an ex-schoolfellow who served a term of imprisonment. On his release he was asked how he got on there. 'Splendid,' he replied in a burst of enthusiasm, 'absolutely splendid. It's just like a public school, just like being at Eton,' but then he added in a tone of reflection, 'But of course it's a bit tough on those who haven't been to Eton.' If I were still a Member of Parliament I should not vote for any measure to abolish public schools. If we are going to permit inequalities of income I do not see how it is either possible or desirable to prevent wealthy parents from spending some of it on their children's education. But whether they are wise to do so is another question. I do not see how it can seriously be denied that an educational system by which a very small number of wealthy children are given an education of quite a different sort in a different place from that of the majority, who receive their education free, is a divisive influence in the nation.

When before 1939 we used to sit around and debate whether there would be another war it was generally agreed that, if there were a war, it would be the end of the public schools. They would perish in their present form not because of any Act of Parliament but simply because there would not be sufficient parents able and willing to pay their fees. That confident prophecy has proved false. For a quarter of a century since the war the public schools have had a waiting list longer than they have ever known. There are signs, they tell me, that now some of them are beginning to feel the wind. If so, I cannot regret it. I would rather, if it can be arranged without too gross compulsion, that all children should go to the same sort of school. The state school—whether in a grammar school or in a comprehensive form—would have a better opportunity of achieving excellence if the public schools were no longer able to drain off the abler masters. As long as we still had an empire and were still ruled, for better or worse, by a governing class, there was something to be said for educating at special schools those who were to have quite a different sort of life. I do not know that there is any point in it now.

Yet Eton sets two quite separate questions. First, is the public school system a good system? Second—and quite apart from that general question—granted the public school system in general, is it desirable that one particular school among the public schools should have this extraordinary pre-eminence—should supply so overwhelmingly a large proportion of the country's leading statesmen and the rest? Is there any reason to think that Eton's education is so wholly superior to that available anywhere else as to justify this extraordinary predominance? I cannot really think that there is. It is situated in the dullest and most revolting part of England with Slough as its neighbour—Slough of which John Betjeman so excellently wrote,

Come, friendly bombs, and fall on Slough.

Apart from the river and its splendid chapel there is nothing of great beauty there. Most of the boarding houses are—or were—foul slums that would be condemned by any decent local authority if they were offered for a comprehensive school. It is arguable that its prestige is such that it is able to attract better masters. I think that it got very good masters, and, quite apart from their competence as teachers, they were quite extraordinary in their generous entertainment of the boys. I presume that with servant shortage meals cannot now be offered quite as abundantly as they were fifty years ago, but at that time hospitality was unstinted and it is, on looking back, extraordinary how completely we took what was offered to us for granted. I do not know that athleticism was any more flagrantly worshipped at Eton than anywhere else. We drank the health on St Andrew's Day of J. K. Stephen—*in piam memoriam* J.K.S.—whom we were taught to honour as the greatest of all players at the Wall Game but whom we are now told, without much probability, was really Jack the Ripper. What was unique to Eton and much more debatable was the institution of Pop. Pop, officially the Eton Society, was in name a school debating society, and indeed we did hold debates there from time to time. But it was in fact a self-perpetuating aristocracy. At the end of every half the members met and elected by means of excluding black balls sufficient candidates to fill the vacancies of those who were leaving. The members of Pop enjoyed certain rather ridiculous privileges. They alone could wear braid on their coats, could wear coloured waistcoats, could carry their umbrellas tightly rolled, could walk about arm in arm. They had no precise duties—only privileges. The member of Pop would not necessarily be Captain of his House or of his House's football team. Anyone might be elected, chosen on grounds of sheer favouritism. Like Melbourne's garter, there was no damned nonsense of merit about it. Generally election went to those who had the largest number of athletic colours but it was not necessarily so. I myself was elected, though I was not a gentleman and though I was the possessor of no colour except the completely undistinguished College cricket cap. It was, I think, a bad institution, for it encouraged shameless and degrading toadying by those who wanted to get in towards those who were already in—'vamping your Pop' as it was called. I think that it ought to be abolished.

The Etonian could easily develop an absurd contempt for those who were not at Eton—not merely for those who were at a different sort of school but even for those at other public schools, which were really by any sort of evaluation at least as good as Eton. Eton, they thought, had a pre-eminence in all things—in vice as well as in virtue. The standard of morality was not very high. Even those who deplored this were at the same time a little proud of it. 'There is more immorality here,' I remember a boy once saying to me, 'than at any school except Harrow.' I do not know on what precise evidence he based his accusation against Harrow, though certainly at that date Harrow's general reputation was not very high. But what was amusing about his judgement was that he very evidently knew nothing whatsoever about the great majority of schools in the country. If he had been presented with all the facts and given the opportunity to conduct an exhaustive inquisition into the moral state of all the schools in the nation he would doubtless have found some even worse than Eton or Harrow. But he simply did not count these schools as schools, even in evaluating immorality. It was only schools like Eton and Harrow—schools which played cricket at Lords— that were worth considering. Others could do as they might do. We could not care less about them.

What did the ordinary masters believe? What did Eton suppose religion to be about? They never expressed to the boys any word of scepticism or disbelief. We are told today of the generation gap. For all their friendliness there was a very complete generation gap between masters and boys at Eton. The boys questioned and misbehaved, but it never occurred to us that any of our questions were not utterly original to our generation. I assumed that all the masters believed in religion and in proper conduct, that it had never occurred to them that, for instance, the Resurrection or the Virgin Birth had never happened. I was quite surprised one day when the very strait-laced Master in College confessed to me that in his opinion it was not necessary to believe in the Virgin Birth. During the war Horatio Bottomley one day published in *John Bull* an article entitled 'Do The Bishops Believe?' I remember reading it and thinking it self-evident nonsense. Of course, I thought, all grown-up people believed, even bishops. It had never occurred to them not to. But, believing, what, I now wonder in retrospect, did they think that religion was for? They behaved themselves as decent law-abiding citizens. But did they really think that it was the grace of God which gave them the strength to do so? Would they not have resented it as an insult if it had been suggested to them that they had not within themselves sufficient natural Pelagian virtue to live unaided the life of a good citizen? And indeed what did being a good citizen mean? They lived lives very narrowly bounded by Eton. Most of them had been at school there, had indeed gone for three or four years to Oxford or Cambridge but had then returned to Eton from which except for short holidays they had hardly ever moved since. They showed small signs of belief that the Christian religion imposed upon them any obligation to ask questions about the nature of society—to inquire into the school system or to assert the rights of man. Indeed, was Eton's religion really a Christian religion at all? Or was it rather a religion of patriotism in its peculiar class form? Was an Etonian in chapel really seeking to model his life on that of Christ? Or was he striving to be a good Englishman, suitably dressed in the old school tie? Above all, when he said his prayers, what did he imagine was happening? I suppose that some would think (if they thought about it) and even say that in reciting the formulae of a dedication to a cause, the prayer, after the manner of Coué, was strengthening their will to endure and to achieve. And this was doubtless true. *Possunt quia posse videntur*. But, if that was all that prayer was, then manifestly it was not prayer. Was it any more than that?

There was a very amusing, cynical history master of the name of Tuppy Headlam. One day in a question on his beliefs about a future life, he said, 'Doubtless I shall inherit eternal bliss, but I prefer not to meditate upon so wholly melancholy a prospect.' (I think that he was quoting from someone but I do not know from whom.) The *mot* was passed from mouth to mouth with much laughter at its daring, but in fact of course it very aptly summarises, for all its verbal illogic, the attitude of very many—perhaps of the majority—of people in this country. They cannot bring themselves to believe that their death will mean total extinction. Equally with the averagely respectable life which *'l'homme moyen sensual'* has led, they cannot believe that an Almighty and Merciful God will judge them deserving of the pains of eternal punishment. Yet, even though the prospects of death can thus be demonstrated as unlikely to be so very terrible, death is so gigantic an experience that a surprisingly large number even in old age still shrink from it, postpone it by any and every means as long as they can, and are above all strangely reluctant to talk about it.

The other master who was willing to talk with some freedom on these ultimate matters was a comical science master called Dr Porter. He was an exhibitionist who loved to astonish his pupils. He was a confirmed and enthusiastic spiritualist and did not hesitate to preach spiritualism as the religion of the future to all his pupils. His religion took a peculiar and somewhat exhibitionist form. He brought one day into his division a little bomb. He explained to us that it was the most potent bomb in the world. If it should be dropped it would destroy all Eton. Then he dropped it on the floor and at once bade us fall on our knees and recite the Lord's Prayer. We did this and there was no explosion. 'God has stayed His hand,' he told us and continued with the conduct of his lesson.

I do not know what the masters assembled in chapel or at house prayers imagined to happen in response to their prayers. I cannot imagine that they thought that much happened from the unco-ordinated nature of the prayers that they permitted. When the war was on, once a week we had a special service of intercession in chapel for Allied victory. I never heard of anybody at Eton, except perhaps Aldous Huxley, who came to teach there for a short time, who in any way shared Edward Lyttelton's concern about the world that we were to discover after the war. Most were content without question to accept that the Allied cause was the cause of God and, not infrequently, that the more Germans that were killed in the achievement of their victory the better He would be pleased. All supernatural aids could confidently be called to the pumps to help the Allied victory.

When we first arrived at Eton it was made clear to us by those who were a year our seniors that before long Sixth Form would start beating —'working off', as it was called—any who were guilty of any minor delinquencies; that each among us might reasonably expect to have been beaten before the half was finished; that this was a part of the way of life; and that, if we intended to be respected, we had no alternative but to accept it as such and to make the best of it. I accepted this. I had no notion of a school being run in any other way and, when after three or four weeks the first victim of our election was summoned down to Sixth Form supper and beaten, I joined in the buzz of gossip that hummed on his return from the exciting experience. 'I think one ought to be worked off at least once before long,' I said to a companion and, I think, at the time believed it. Then about three weeks later I muddled or forgot a task of fagging which had been assigned to me—to take some shoes down town to be mended. I returned before lunch from playing fives, all innocent and carefree, and found to my dismay that this was considered a grave omission and that there was a blazing row over it. I and another delinquent presented ourselves before the Sixth Former who had commanded us. I stammered out such quite insufficient excuses as I could invent, but he replied sternly, 'If you are told to do a thing you must learn that you have got to do it,' and dismissed me.

The order of the day was that all executions took place the last thing at night before one went to bed. At nine o'clock we had night-prayers and, if such was our fate, were summoned downstairs afterwards to confront Sixth Form. Throughout the evening I had pretended to companions—I expect most unconvincingly—that I would certainly be worked off but that I did not mind at all. On my knees in night-prayers I resigned myself to terror. Every other expedient having failed, while the Lord's Prayer was being recited aloud, I said to myself, 'God, let me not be beaten. God, let me not be beaten.' Naturally enough my prayer was not attended to, any more than had been that of the old lady who asked that the mountain be removed from before her bedroom window. I had not expected that it would be. I would indeed have thought the less of God if He had upset the order of things thus to suit my convenience.

After prayers Sixth Form assembled for their supper in a tea-room downstairs. One of the fags, who was for some reason unknown called Senior, had to present himself before them and inquire if anybody was 'wanted' and then to fetch down the boy or boys thus nominated. On this occasion I came out of prayers, stood about for a few minutes nervously awaiting my fate when the Senior reappeared to say, 'You're wanted.' I and my companion made our way down together.

'I suppose he'll work us off,' I said with affected gaiety.

'Looks like it,' said the Senior, 'the chair's been put out.'

When we were going down the stairs and out of the other boys' sight, my companion who had shared the offence with me suddenly turned and hissed with real hate.

'Isn't he a beast?'

I was genuinely surprised.

'Oh I don't know,' I said. 'It's only common sense from his point of view.'

Inconvenient as the experiment might be, it never occurred to me that a boy who had attained to the privilege of the Sixth Form would not be glad to take advantage of his privilege. Now that there was no escape I was almost looking forward to it. As I made my way back, not very badly hurt, after it was over, I felt if anything rather exhilarated. Still, as with the lady, what, if it be not an absurdly exaggerated word in such a context, I may call the 'theology' of the incident puzzled me a little. Of course I had not expected God to answer my prayer. But why should He not answer it? Why had He clearly promised that if I should ask I should receive, if such was not at all His plan?

I consulted my tutor on the difficulty. He said that God indeed knew what He was going to do but He wished me to ask for what was good for me. It did not seem to me a very satisfactory answer. What reason was there for thinking that God wanted anything of the sort? The evidence seemed rather to suggest that He was like the gods of the Epicureans living at ease, careless of our fate—that, if the avalanche fell, it was for me to keep out of the way if I wished to survive. If I was out of the way I would be saved. If I was in the way I would be crushed. Doubtless God was reasonable in the sense that He was the Primum Mobile who had set the whole impersonal machine in motion, but there was little reason to think that He interfered in the particular direction and accident of it. Then my tutor said that petitionary prayer was a very low and doubtful form of prayer—that the only true prayer was that of Our Lord in Gethsemane, that 'not My Will but Thine be done'. This seemed edifying and sensible, but it did not seem to me what the Gospel said. The theologian and the metaphysician might condemn petitionary prayer, but the Lord's Prayer, while it indeed contained a prayer of the nature of Christ's words in Gethsemane, 'Hallowed be Thy Name. Thy Will be done on earth as it is in Heaven,' also asked, 'Give us this day our daily bread.' Surely that was petitionary. It is true that it was not a self-seeking petition. It was not I alone but we who were to receive the daily bread. There was no suggestion that one person—that I alone—should get bread at the expense of others. The request to God was to send abundance to all. But there were other verses in the Bible of which the plain sense was that all petitions would be granted—knock and it should be opened to you—and that the believer would be protected against physical evils and the snake bite. These promises were manifestly not fulfilled. It was idle to say that they were not fulfilled because those who made them had not faith. Doubtless the great majority of those who prayed had not faith in the sense that they were not so foolish as to imagine that such prayers would be fulfilled. If that was what a lack of faith meant, it was a somewhat circular argument. We were told that our prayers were not answered because we had not got faith. But we had not got faith because we had discovered that our prayers were not answered. But there were a few strange, simple souls who had total faith in God—who asked, not doubting that their prayers would be answered, and there did not seem any particular evidence that their prayers were in fact answered any more frequently than those of other people. 'God,' said my tutor, 'does not intend prayers to be answered in that sense.' How did he know? And if God did not mean what He said, why did He say it? And, if He did not say it, what reason had we to believe that any of the record was true?

In the nature of things a number of the boys at Eton must have been the products of broken marriages and the like. Today it is taken for granted that such boys are one of the inevitable problems of any school. I never remember in my own school days any boy confessing that his parents were divorced or receiving any rumour to that effect from any other boy. When I had been a year or two at Eton Alec Waugh's *The Loom of Youth* appeared and was passed from hand to hand. Masters and preachers commented on it—rejected as not only disgusting but also as incredible the language of the boys as there quoted and some of the incidents described. 'We never remember this sort of thing happening when we were at school,' they used to say to us. The incidents and the language were so wholly familiar to our lives that we had no alternative but to conclude either that our elders were liars, or that the world had wholly changed, or that they remembered nothing, or that they thought it safer to live in a world of fantasy on to which reality was not allowed to impinge. The last was most nearly the truth.

The very strain of the war years made natural a strong reaction once the war was over—or, to be precise, two separate reactions. To the authorities the normal and desirable reaction was as far as possible to restore everything to what it had been before the war—to recreate the life that they had loved.

To us who had never known these festivals and done well enough without them for four years that was far less important. We wanted a new life in a very crude and childish fashion. We did not want a recreation of the old world. We wanted a relaxation of discipline. In a quite incoherent fashion, we started to criticise the propriety of Eton's claim to be a unique school—to advocate some more nearly egalitarian system, by which boys of a wider social variety of origin should be allowed to come to the school. We certainly had no coherent notion how that should be done. I do not think that we really wanted it to be done, and with the savagely reactionary Parliament that was returned at the election of 1918 there was certainly little prospect that any legislation to introduce any such scheme would be put upon the Statute Book. The reforms of which we spoke were not something to be done. They were rather something to be advocated. Talking about projects was an end in itself. Whatever abridgement of privilege there might be, it never, I think, occurred to any of us that our own privileges would be abridged —that we ourselves should have less education or a narrower choice of jobs when we went out afterwards into the world. Ever since the Second World War various plans have been in the air—the Fleming Plan and others—both at Eton and elsewhere to give a public school education to the sons of poor boys. One such experiment is now being tried out at Eton. The trouble about such plans is that they offer the public school education to deserving poor boys—to good boys—and thus their best pupils are taken away from the struggling grammar schools. What is desirable is that an Eton education should indeed be offered to a dozen poor boys, but the essential qualification for such reward should be that they should be bad boys. The boy from the approved school would be much more like the average Etonian than those especially selected from the inordinately virtuous, and much more likely to benefit from the Eton discipline, which was so much more rigid than any to which the boy would be subject at a secondary modern school.

We challenged the whole system of discipline—the authority anu power of privilege which the bigger boys had over their juniors—and op the whole the challenge was, I think, beneficial. When big boys stopped punishing little boys the absurdity of the system was at once made manifest by its mere abolition. Practice, or rather the abeyance of practice, made it evident how very little contribution to good order the whole system of elaborate rules had ever made and to how large an extent they were a mere satisfaction of sadism. The young so often tell us how they are wholly original in revolting against their elders, and their elders themselves, whether to reprove or to sympathise, very often agree with them. It is of course great nonsense. There was at Eton and, I fancy, at most other schools, a far more persistent demand for the permissive society immediately after the First World War than there was after the Second. Indeed in the first years after the Second War it was rather remarkable that, though the troops all voted Labour at the election before they were demobilised, they showed little of the revolt against established order that everyone had expected of them. It was not until some years later that permissiveness became fashionable and, as far as one can see, is now going out of fashion again. The pendulum swings. The difficulty about schemes of self-government for schoolboys such as are in the air at the moment is that the big boys want to exercise their power at the expense of the small, while the ambition of the small is to be free from the big. There is no general will.

It was natural enough that, questioning all else, we should also question religion. I dare say that we would have done so in any event. It is probably natural enough—indeed almost inevitable—that young people in their late teens—more particularly if the more articulate of them are herded together into one another's company as we were in College at Eton—should go through a phase of loss of faith and agnosticism. The young need to shed the religion in which they were raised in order to think out for themselves what is going to be the religion of their own discovery. In any event this phase, through which most of us would probably have passed in any event, was certainly invited by the rebellion through which we were passing. As I have said, I had assumed that the Christian religion was true, without being specially interesting. I had not objected in any way to attending its services, whether at home or at school, or to what it taught. I remember very well the first blow which I received to this very tenuous and petty faith. In College at Eton the great majority of the boys lived in one of two long passages known as Upper Passage and Lower Passage. From the end of Upper Passage there ran a little by-way to the right which was known as the Muke, or Corner, and which contained two little rooms of its own—Big Muke and Little Muke. My room was the Little Muke and the Big Muke next door was occupied by an older, abler, bigger boy who was at the top of our election order. We were discussing one day some problem arising out of Sunday Questions, a paper of essay questions, the answers to which we all had to write every weekend. The matter at issue was something out of the first chapter of St Luke where the Virgin Birth of Christ is described.

'But do you really believe that?' asked my companion.

Oddly enough it had never until that moment occurred to me to question it, nor indeed, I suppose, even to think about it.

'I suppose so,' I said. 'After all it's what we're taught.'

'It doesn't seem very probable,' he said, and he explained how in the nature of things the evidence for it could only be that of one person, and one person advancing a highly improbable story which could not in the nature of things be cross-questioned. He told me of Hume's principle that, confronted with the obviously unusual, we should consider that it was much more probable that witnesses were lying or deceived than that the miraculous happened.

'How do you think He was born then?' I asked.

He was not quite prepared to say bluntly that he thought that Jesus was probably illegitimate, though I dare say that that was what he thought. He preferred to dodge the direct question.

'How can it be certain that Mary ever made such a claim?' he asked. 'Paul does not seem to have heard of it. There is no reason to think that he even knew the name of Christ's Mother. At any rate he does not seem to have thought the question of His birth of any importance.'

He had read a bit of Frazer's *Golden Bough* and was able to tell me of the numerous instances of Oriental religions which claimed a Virgin Birth for their founders or heroes. It was, he said, surely much more probable that the claim was never made during Christ's lifetime and invented at a later day by His disciples who would not allow their founder to be outdone by any of His rivals.

'After all even Mark and John do not seem to have known or at any rate to have cared about it,' he said. 'Surely it is very strange if they knew about it that they did not mention it. It shows at any rate that the story had not then any of the central importance we are now told to attach to it.'

I went away pondering and the more that I pondered the more cogent his reasoning seemed. Was it common sense to accept all these miraculous stories on the assertion of two men, writing on we knew not what evidence or at what date? And of course up to a point I was certainly right. One cannot logically base Christian faith on the Virgin Birth. One must accept the Christian faith, if one accepts it, for other reasons and then the whole gamut of probabilities changed. If He was Almighty God there was no reason why He should not be born of a Virgin, or walk upon the water, or raise Lazarus from the dead. It was at least as probable as not. But such beliefs must be the consequence of Christian faith. It was absurd to base Christian faith upon them.

So I—and most of the rest of us—came in these last years to a position of agnosticism. I do not pretend that our conclusions were particularly important or particularly original. In fact we were merely going through a phase through which probably the greater number of young men pass at that age. It is hard for me to say exactly what we believed. The challenge as we saw it was to the claims of Christ to divinity.

'What do you mean by saying that He was God?' I said. 'Do you mean that He created the universe? How could He do that and then be born into it?'

I was challenged by the definitions of the creed and was contentious.

'Begotten and not made?' I said. 'What can it mean? It is not a question whether one believes it. It is a contradiction without meaning. How can one believe what has no meaning? If there was a beginning there must have been a time before the beginning. What was God the Creator doing before He created? Why should a Being, by definition self-sufficient, wish to create at all?'

For a time I would have said that there must be a God because everything was made by something and therefore there must be a first cause of everything. Then one day, as I stood waiting for a shower bath, there occurred to me in my naïveté, 'If everything must be made by somebody, who made God?' It was true that the notion that things had just been going on—whatever their original form—since the beginning of time was a notion so wholly beyond our imagination that it hardly had any meaning. But was not the notion of a creating, absolute God beyond our imagination also? Either way round, the first origins were quite incomprehensible. Was it not therefore more sensible merely to say that things were incomprehensible, to leave them at that? Was any purpose served by producing an explanation which did not really explain anything?

I almost shouted with exultation at my own cleverness as I turned on the hot water tap. I hastened to inform others and to boast of my originality, to demand applause for its brilliance, and I was considerably annoyed in the next few days to discover that there was a large number of people, from St Thomas Aquinas down to the most twopenny-halfpenny agnostic journalist of our own time, to whom these not very sophisticated reflections had already occurred—to learn that in reply to Bonaventuer Aquinas had said that we cannot prove that the universe has a beginning.

In general, in spite of having difficulties I think that both I and the rest of us probably would have said that on the whole we believed in God, though what sort of a God and what sort of belief we had in Him it was not easy to say. He certainly was not a God who acted in the world. But, whatever account we gave of obligation, wherever we derived it, whatever we may have thought happened if we did not fulfil it, we accepted a code of conduct which over the larger field did not so greatly differ from a code that might superficially pass as Christian. We would have argued that it was wrong to lie or murder or bully or cheat. We accepted an obligation to help the poor and bereaved, even if we did not very often do much about it. The one place where the Christian code did not appear to prove its case was over sex. We had our natural desires and curiosity. Was it wrong to satisfy them? What harm did we do if we did satisfy them?

So we sat around for endless hours debating that question. Was it really wrong, or was it just a senseless taboo, invented by religion and one which we would be the wiser and the more fully men if we defied? The broad question had some sense to it, but the manner in which we debated it was extravagantly infantile. Sexual immorality was not unknown at Eton. Eton was divided into twenty-six houses. All boys were locked up in their houses at night and opportunities for immorality between members of different houses were therefore limited and their occurrence rare. The tone of each house was very much dependent on its housemaster and there were always among the twenty-six one or two houses which were thoroughly bad and where misconduct reigned almost unconfined until eventually some incident came somehow to authority's notice. Drastic action was then taken. There was a general investigation. Numbers of boys were sacked, and probably the housemaster also at the end of the half or the end of the year was relieved of his post. The boys in other houses than these were not with few exceptions especially saintly. Language was quite grotesquely crude. There was debate about the validity of moral rules. There were sentimental friendships between big boys and pretty little boys which were perhaps unhealthy and ridiculous but from which no great harm came. The attitude of the housemaster was that his prime duty was to prevent immorality. If any case of it was discovered the punishment was instant expulsion. It was the sin of sins—the sin crying to heaven for vengeance. We were reminded of Dr Keate's famous sermon. 'Blessed are the pure in heart,' the Doctor proclaimed! 'All boys will be pure in heart. If any of you aren't pure in heart I'll flog you.' But the peculiarity of the system at Eton and, I fancy, at almost all other schools at that time was that women played no part at all in the life of the schoolboy. From the beginning of term, or half, to the end the boy for all intents and purposes never set eyes on any woman except the matron and perhaps the housemaster's wife. Immorality, such as it was, was exclusively homosexual. I remember hearing of a boy in an Oppidan house who, as was said, was caught in bed with some woman up in Windsor. He was indeed expelled, but the general reaction was that he had been caught doing something quite extraordinary and almost unnatural.

It is the general fashion to think that all conduct among the young is much laxer than it was a generation ago. The friends of the permissive society applaud this laxity, traditionalists deplore it. I am far from certain that it is true. Naturally no statistics are available. But George Lyttelton, who knew Eton for sixty years first as a boy and then as a very shrewd and experienced master, gave it to me as his opinion that the consequence of the absurd rigidity with which all contact with the female sex was in the first years of the century prevented was that immorality was more

common than it is today. Nowadays a certain mixing, through joint
dances with girls' schools and the like, is possible and it makes, I am sure,
for a more healthy atmosphere. Homosexual affections of no very deep
seriousness were common enough among Etonians and, I suspect,
among all other boys at boarding schools. Serious homosexual love
affairs are wretched things, if for no other reason than that, inevitably,
one partner is going to demand a reciprocity of affection that the other is
neither capable of giving nor willing to give. Therefore all ends in tears.
Yet the ordinary casual homosexual affairs do not survive into later
life.

III

GOD BE WITH YOU, BALLIOL MEN

In October, 1920, I went up to Balliol. Whatever incidental gestures of
revolt we had demonstrated at Eton, whether in dialectic or in active life,
that was certainly a life under control. The authorities thought it their
duty, whether they always fulfilled it completely or not, to keep us under
control. We lived thus and punishments might always be invoked if
anarchy became unendurable. Oxford was by contrast a permissive
society—though I do not think that the actual phrase was then in fashion.
The names of the new psychologists had just seeped across from Vienna
to Oxford. They were a popular talking point.

> Joy was it in that dawn to be a Freud
> But to be Jung was very heaven.

One of the great undergraduate triumphs was a few years later gained by
George Edinger, who had a room next to mine in Staircase 7 in Balliol.
He was of a German Jewish origin and master of the German language.
He had the notion of impersonating a fictitious Austrian psychologist,
whom he named Emil Busch, and giving a bogus lecture under his
name in the City Town Hall guying and parodying the psychologists.
His effort was a complete success, and none of the Dons who heard
it spotted the fraud. Most of us—and I certainly among them—could
not claim to know in any detail what the psychologists said. But we
had a vague and not very accurate idea that, whereas authority had
always inculcated the duty of self-control, Freud condemned such a

practice as a dangerous and harmful repression. He taught, we were told, that sex had a pervasive influence on all our life and was not merely seen, as we had been taught, in the crude physical sexual act. This seemed to me true from my own experience. I approved of it and I wondered how preceptors and parents and other elders and betters could have thought that it was otherwise. Yet the Dons were in general very hostile to the new psychology. Throughout past ages the clergy, whether of the Catholic or of the Anglican communion, had, I had read, always fought bitterly for any secular privileges and never surrendered any title until they were compelled to do so. I now discovered that this determination to hold on to privilege was not a peculiarity of clergymen but to be found in every establishment. The psychologists were repudiated in the name of the divine right of Dons. For myself I was, and still am, a strong believer in freedom of discussion. Truth can only emerge from a permission for everybody to have his say and from seeing what comes out of the rubbing together of opinion against opinion. It is true, of course, that, when applied to undergraduates, this means that a good deal of nonsense will be talked and that there will be much absurd airing of opinions about books that he who airs has never read. It is reasonable that older Dons should find such experiences tedious, but after all they are what universities are for. A few years ago when the Lady Chatterley case was on, a solicitor wrote to me to ask if I would give evidence in it. I replied that my view was that it was without exception the silliest book ever written but that I thought it entirely absurd that it should be banned. Most happily it was decided that such evidence could be helpful to neither party, so I was not called. Nonsense should be tolerated even when it cannot be liked or admired.

On their merits the psychologists, in so far as they taught us to know ourselves a little better, were to be approved, and certainly as one considers some of the beliefs that were tolerated in the name of discipline, whether from parents or from schoolmasters or from big boys against little boys in Victorian England, one cannot but be amazed how those in authority can have been so wholly blind to the real motives which were impelling them in their actions. But there is another side to it. The Victorians, seeing sex only in the actual sexual act, sometimes tolerated gross sadistic cruelty. But it also meant that they performed innocent acts of kindness, friendship and sentimentality, of which the modern psychologist would tell us—perhaps truly—that the basic motives were sexual, but of which in their simplicity they never thought to inquire the origins. See what the modern critics make of Lewis Carroll and his little girls. This constant introspection is by no means an unmixed good. His colleagues at Christ Church found before the end of his life the company of Lord Cherwell quite embarrassing, since every time that one of them passed the potatoes or rose to close a door, he would raise his eyebrows with a knowing look, as if plainly to indicate, 'We all know what that means.' My eldest son in his late thirties chanced to have a psychiatrist as his next-door neighbour. His neighbour was quite shocked to discover that my son wrote a letter to his mother every week. He thought that such a dangerous and unusual complex required urgently full psychological investigation in order to discover and to prescribe a remedy.

Then, as now, the psychiatrists ministered often enough to a mind diseased and by doing so rendered great services to humanity. But the mind should be diseased before it betakes itself to them. Sometimes —particularly in America—it is thought fashionable for perfectly healthy people to go to the psychiatrist. 'All these girls have been psychoed,' said the President of an American middle-aged women's club to Lady Lavery, much shocked that she had never availed herself of these fashionable amenities. Who can read today such a poem as Browning's 'Porphyria's Lover' or study the character of Dennis in Dickens' *Barnaby Rudge* without being conscious of depths of obscure sexuality in Victorian England? But is it wholly an advantage to be always so fully aware of all these implications?

Oxford of the 1920's was, as I say, a permissive society—in many ways more permissive than the Oxford of today. By that I do not by any means imply that every undergraduate lived a life of total abandon. I merely mean that in contrast to our schoolmasters who thought themselves responsible for our conduct, the Dons disclaimed responsibility and made no attempt to find out what we were doing unless we forced our actions on their attention. From time to time I read in modern newspapers some protest of Angry Undergraduates that morals are the students' 'own business' and that the University authorities have no call to interfere with them. I do not very well understand what such protests mean. Certainly fifty years ago the Dons made no attempt to pry into or to control undergraduates' private lives unless they were forced to by a delinquent who out of bravado compelled attention to his conduct. There were, it is true, certain rules but there was no pretence that they had a moral content. One had to be back in one's college by twelve o'clock at night, but there were ways of climbing into every College for those who were beyond the hours and the penalty for any who were unable to negotiate these difficulties or who were caught was merely a fine. One was supposed to wear a gown if out in the streets at night, but no one did. (For some reason this rule was more strictly enforced at Cambridge than at Oxford.) Whereas at Eton it was of course a serious offence to be caught in a pub, at Oxford, though pubs were forbidden, there was no attempt to control drinking or even drunkenness. Indeed on a convivial occasion such as a bump supper, many of the Dons were as likely to be drunk as the undergraduates. All that the University authorities cared about was the destruction of property. If in your cups you destroyed some property you had to make restitution. Otherwise you could get drunk as often as you liked, and since drink was then much cheaper drunkenness was a great deal more common than it is among the undergraduates of today. Servants also were more plentiful than they are today and it was possible for undergraduates to get their scouts to serve luncheons in their rooms. On the other hand drugs were unknown. That was the great difference between the undergraduate of those days and the undergraduate of the present day. I only remember one undergraduate who took drugs.

There was one other great contrast between school life and University life and between the University life of those days and that of today. Of course the undergraduate population of today comes from a greater variety of social origins than did that of fifty years ago when the proportion of them from public schools was much greater. This is doubtless in itself a good thing but it means that the undergraduate of today is more earnestly concerned with his examination results than he was fifty years ago. A young man's career is, or is thought to be, much more directly dependent on his class in schools, and the menace of the final examination reduces life to a misery for many. Suicide is, I believe, more common among undergraduates than in any other class of society. In my time, the penalties of academic failure were less. We had not yet fully invented the miseries of a meritocracy and there was no pretence that *la carrière* was *ouverte aux talents*. It was success which was oppressive. I can only recollect one undergraduate who committed suicide in my day and he had but recently been elected a Fellow of All Souls. But the consequence of this great weight of responsibilities which the young of today feel they carry on their shoulders is that, oddly enough, they are for ever clamouring to be allowed to have their say in the management of the University. It is said that they mature younger—I cannot think on what evidence. What this student demand for student representation may mean and why it should be favoured is indeed hard to understand.

In all the world there is surely no duller task than that of the administration of an educational body and that anyone should demand as a right and a privilege to sit on these committees is unbelievable and surely in itself proof of an adolescent lack of maturity. We should rather threaten them with membership of committees as a punishment. Fifty years ago things were just the opposite of what they are today. Fifty years ago it was possible at schools to get the boys with some relish to perform the duties of prefects and monitors, but at the University it was impossible to get them to undertake such responsibilities. Few would be found willing to serve on J.C.R. committees.

Dons in the 1920's counted for less than they had done before the war. Between them and the undergraduates there was a gap not so much of the generations as of the war. The memories of the Dons—or at least of the older Dons who had not themselves been fighting in the war—were of the world before 1914. To them, as to the Masters at Eton, the world before 1914 was the golden age and their one ambition was to get back to it as quickly as possible. The undergraduates differed from the Etonian schoolboys in that a large number of them had themselves been fighting in the war. To them, returning from the trenches, rules which required them to be in their Colleges before midnight seemed absurd. The new generation of post-war Dons, of whom Maurice Bowra was the first and the leader, had not yet appeared. We younger undergraduates who came straight from school certainly were, I think, very insensitive about the feelings of those who had known the life before 1914. Ronald Knox whom later in life, when he was to live in my village of Mells, I was to come to know most intimately was at that time teaching at St Edmund's College, Ware. He sometimes came over to Balliol and I think that the first occasion on which I ever spoke to him was when he found me reading a notice announcing a forthcoming Union debate. The motion was to be 'That in the opinion of this House the French and the Russian Governments shared with the German and the Austrian in the responsibility for the late war.' To me the motion was amusing in its confident assumption that the only question for debate should be the degrees of responsibility for the world's calamity to be shared out between various foreigners. I murmured something about it never having occurred to them apparently that the British might have any share of the responsibility. But to Ronald Knox with his memory of so many dear friends lost the reaction was quite different. He saw in it no joke, only sadness. 'One might have known that they would be talking about something like that,' he murmured.

My own Oxford career was totally undistinguished. I was a scholar in the technical sense of having gained an award at a scholarship examination and having the right to wear a scholar's gown. But I had, and have, none of the gifts of scholarship. I am incapable of accuracy and of organising my work. I did a good deal of reading—more perhaps than I was generally credited with—and had hoped that the results in the end might have been better. There was, I was given to understand, a certain difference of opinion among my examiners where to place me. 'He's intelligent but he does not know enough,' commented one to a companion. But in the end I was awarded a Third—doubtless justly. Yet, disappointing as that was, I did not feel that my time at Oxford was wasted. I made very many friends and, though few among them gained academic distinctions, many like Evelyn Waugh—who was perhaps my closest companion—were in later life a great deal more distinguished than those who had won their place in the First Class. I played a part in two ephemeral Oxford papers, the *Cherwell* and the *Oxford Outlook*. But the only place where I gained any sort of public distinction was at the Union. During the war all of the normal activities of University life had come to an end—far more completely than they did in the Second War, when conscripts were allowed by the authorities a short time at the University before they were taken into the forces. The Union had in any real sense come to an end, but immediately after the war it started up again with great vigour. Many of those who had come back from the war were burning with political opinions and political ambitions. Politics had then a prestige which it has now very largely lost and the Union was then a much more important place than it is today. The speakers of the Union looked on it as a training ground for their subsequent public political careers. There was no notion of using it as a sounding ground for local Oxford grievances.

The path for a Union career was especially well smoothed for a young undergraduate at Balliol, for the Union was then dominated by Balliol. All its three officers when I went up were from that College. Beverley Nichols was the President, Alec Beechman was the Junior Librarian, and Maxwell Fyfe, afterwards to be Lord Kilmuir and Lord Chancellor, was the Junior Treasurer. The Union was still entirely in the hands of those who had returned to it from the war. Those who had come up straight from school were despised as immature infants.

Beverley Nichols was famous because he had written a book, an account of his life at Marlborough. He had not yet told Oxford and the world how he had attempted to murder his father. He was a Liberal of a sort but not a defiantly party figure. If he at that time entertained political ambitions he never in later life made any attempt to realise them. The great political figure of Oxford in those days was Alec Beechman, then the Union's Librarian and at the end of my first term elected its President. Beechman was the great ward boss for whom the highest of political honours were quite confidently prophesied. It was considered the first step to success to be invited by Beechman to have dinner with him at the Gridiron. He was the son of a wealthy Hampstead Jew who looked with undisguised delight on his steps towards the higher fame. Dining alone at home on his solitary chop, the old father would boast of his son, 'Last night he dine mit Askitt.'

The Union had inherited from the past—from Asquith, Simon and Birkenhead—a tradition of being the nursery of statesmen and only the most distinguished of politicians were in those days thought acceptable as its guest, and they only on very rare occasions. The debates were predominantly debates of undergraduates against undergraduates. It was only once or twice in a term that a distinguished visitor from London was invited down as the Society's guest. Now, for all the boasts of the generation gap and of age's incapacity to understand the young, undergraduates seem strangely incapable of doing anything for themselves and neither at the Union or at any other society does any meeting ever take place without a middle-aged visitor from London being decanted down to address it. Sometimes the Union has as many as four guests to a single debate—a confession of intellectual poverty that would have been quite unthinkable in our time. There was then a Union manner— a certain talent for paradox and verbal dexterity. Ronald Knox and Philip Guedalla were usually held up as its chief masters, and G. K. Chesterton, though he was not an Oxford or a Union man, yet had a great influence over the Union not perhaps for the more important content of his thought so much as for his verbal paradoxes as he stood truth on its head and produced it in unexpected form. Douglas Woodruff was by far the best of Union speakers of my time, the coiner of endless sets of verbal conceits. I think that I say that I possessed this Union manner sufficiently to bring me after a certain struggle to the Presidential chair. Perhaps I possessed it too much. Years afterwards when I was in Parliament, William Barkley, an admirable Parliamentary reporter on the *Daily Express*, a man full of kindliness and friendship, most anxious to do any friend a service, complained to me that I set him and the other reporters a hard task because, he said, 'I was a permanent undergraduate.' And it is probably true that I had picked up from the Union experience a liking for putting my points in an unexpected way which was an advantage at the Oxford Union but a disadvantage in the House of Commons where simple-minded members prefer a speaker who calls a spade a spade in obedience to the party line.

The Union was in those days a very political but a very unrealistically political place. The Asquithian Liberals had gone down to disastrous defeat in the national election of 1918 and the event was to prove that they were not capable of resurrection. Yet the Union politicians had no suspicion of that, and the great majority of the aspirants for office at the Union were Liberals, as I was myself. It did not greatly matter to me what was my political creed as I did not look forward to a political career, and indeed in my last year after my presidency I largely dropped both my attendance at the Union and my political interests. My opinions —such as I had then—were those of a follower of Hilaire Belloc and G. K. Chesterton, of the denunciation of the Servile State and the advocacy of a wide distribution of property. I took it on myself to denounce impartially all established political parties and indeed the whole system and to proclaim myself independent. It was not very helpful nor particularly intended to be so.

Apart from the Union I got pleasure from visiting the home of Philip and Lady Ottoline Morrell at Garsington. How I got my first entrée into that circle I cannot remember. One met there an almost bewilderingly exuberant company of the most distinguished young writers of the day. Philip Morrell was not usually so much regarded as his wife. 'I love the lower classes; I married into them myself,' Lady Ottoline said at an election meeting, speaking on behalf of her husband. But he was in fact an old Etonian, a member of the most respectable brewing family. I got on very well with him and in token of my good relations he sometimes invited me to stay on for supper on a Sunday after the mob of the tea party had departed. A little improbably he used to go to the village to read the lesson and then return to the Manor for a quiet and relaxed supper. He had been a Liberal member of Parliament for Burnley but had been a pacifist during the war and when the 1918 election came had been firmly dropped by his party. As a consequence he held a considerable bitterness for the party, a bitterness from which alone Mr Asquith was excluded. Asquith used to enjoy driving over from Sutton Courtenay in order to observe Ottoline Morrell's literary young celebrities—what he called 'your animals in the zoo'. Such figures as Aldous Huxley, D. H. Lawrence, Siegfried Sassoon and of course Bertrand Russell paraded about the lawn which they shared with a number of peacocks at Sunday tea-time. Ottoline Morrell was extraordinarily generous in the hospitality which she dispersed to casual undergraduates. How she could have borne with so many guests I could never understand, any more than I could understand how Dr Alington at Eton survived so much hospitality or later Hazel Lavery with her constant lunch-parties. I only once remember Ottoline Morrell jibbing at a guest. For some reason she had taken a dislike to Basil Murray, Gilbert Murray's son, and drew the line at him. He was forbidden the house, I do not know why. Her general line was, 'Of course we are very glad to see your friends but frankly most of the people who come here are creative artists.' Her clothes were peculiar. Grotesquely overpowdered and over-painted, she wore yellow stockings, cross-gartered like Malvolio. Immensely tall, she looked somewhat like a horse and sucked and crushed continually between her enormous teeth large quantities of bull's-eye peppermints.

The generation of returned soldiers soon vanished from Oxford, as was inevitable, and the University passed into the hands of those who had come straight from school. Among them there were those who worked hard at their books. There were the athletes who won their blues. There were worthless idlers. But apart from all these there were those who won no distinction in the schools or on the playing fields but who nevertheless established themselves as outstanding personalities. Evelyn Waugh came up to Hertford a couple of terms after me. We first heard that a brother of Alec Waugh had come up to Hertford, but soon I met him in his own personality—I forget how or where in the first instance. We went about together, lunching along with other friends in his rooms at Hertford on bread, cheese and beer in a company that we knew as Offal to distinguish ourselves from the upper-class members of the College. Superficial judgement would have written our whole company off as total enemies of all the laws of God and Man and up to a point they would have been right enough. His recent Diaries may have seemed to some a confirmation of this interpretation. They do indeed give a picture of one facet but only of one facet of our lives. But they were not written for publication, and tell us nothing of his great generosity. Evelyn, who remained devoted to his old friends until his death to a degree that is almost uniquely rare, certainly had a strangely intense capacity for hatred of those who encountered his disfavour. As his autobiographical book, *A Little Learning*, shows, he turned this attack of hatred most unsparingly on to his tutor, Cruttwell, afterwards the Principal of the College, a man who never, I fancy, did him any particular harm, and also on certain undergraduates who met with his contempt. His attacks on them were at times beyond pardon. Yet he had been brought up by a pious Anglo-Catholic father, Arthur Waugh, Chairman of Chapman and Hall, the publishers. He had many clergymen in his family tree. He had himself been through a period of calf-piety of *bons dieuseries* at Lancing and, though he would not at the time of our first friendship have suspected as much any more than I would, he had always a natural hankering for talking about topics in religious terms, even if only to ridicule them. He showed this even in his earlier wholly inconoclastic novels. Take the Catholicism of Philbrick in *Decline and Fall* or the character of Father Rothschild and the absurd antics of Mrs Ape and her angels in *Vile Bodies*. These all gave hints that his subsequent development was not to those who knew him best as surprising as either he or most other people had expected. After his early life of Rossetti which he wrote immediately after going down he toyed with the idea of writing a life of Charles Wesley.

The most colourful member of our set was Harold Acton who, as a flamboyant extrovert, astonished the world when, dressed without embarrassment in flaming colours, he read his poems from his sitting-room window to the surrounding multitude through a megaphone. He and Peter Quennell, then a great admirer of Rupert Brooke, were the two leading Oxford poets of the day who had both published their books of verse. Alec Douglas Home—Lord Dunglass as he then was—was an orthodox Conservative undergraduate at Christ Church, a college which he shared with Harold Acton. He by no means approved of such antics. He greatly disapproved of Harold Acton and wondered whether I disapproved equally of Peter Quennell who was at my college of Balliol. 'What sort of a fellow is Quennell?' he asked. 'Is he quite decent or something like Harold Acton?'

The age of the 1920's differed from the present only in three respects. First, women were then still comparative newcomers to Oxford. The women and the undergraduates did not mix together whether in personal relations or in any other way nearly as much as they do today. Most undergraduates hardly ever met an undergraduette. Secondly, as I have said, the undergraduate population in those first years of the 1920's still consisted largely of men who had returned from four years of fighting in the war. They brought a sophistication into Oxford life far greater than that of the undergraduates straight from school who form the clientèle of any normal period. Later when national service was imposed with the Second World War and a proportion of the undergraduates were older men who had returned from doing that service, it was possible to find this leavening of sophistication among the undergraduates. With the abolition of national service there has been a notable decline in the maturity of the students.

Thirdly, birth-control devices were not nearly as familiar or as easily available then as now. Fifty years ago contraceptives indeed existed, as they have existed in one form or another throughout all history. But most young men did not very well know how to get hold of them. Girls who had any wish to retain a reputation for respectability were not willing to take risks with them. The young were not sure how reliable they were and many who were by no means strait-laced yet felt the use of them as vaguely shameful and repulsive. Dr Marie Stopes came down to Oxford. The Vice-Chancellor, Dr Farnell, would not allow her to speak in any regular College Hall. But Ruskin College was not technically under the authority of the University and they let her speak there. Gerald Gardiner, subsequently to be Lord Gardiner and Lord Chancellor in Mr Wilson's Labour Government, was her great protagonist among the undergraduates. We all gave her a dinner at the Mitre and afterwards went to her meeting. I forget what impression her speech made on me but for a few days afterwards I had a vague feeling of unease that the College might take some action against me for my association with such a meeting. Sligger Urquhart, who was the Dean of the College, was also a Catholic and took the line which almost all Catholics would have taken at such a date, that the whole business was 'disgusting' and 'a disgrace'.

It was the time of the libel actions between Dr Halliday Sutherland and Dr Marie Stopes, and Monsignor Barnes, the Catholic chaplain, had Dr Sutherland down to the Newman Society where he debated against Gerald Gardiner. The whole controversy was alive in the air, as I suppose that it would not have been a few years before. Those of us who prided ourselves on being progressive and permissive were vaguely in favour of birth control but really of course knew very little about the subject. To the Victorians shortly before, contraceptive devices were under any circumstances abominable. In our day the issue had been for the first time raised in polite society and many respectable people, like Dean Inge, argued in favour of it—of course only within marriage. They took it for granted that what was called pre-marital intercourse was to be condemned. But to the young the contraceptive raised a wholly new issue. 'Up till now it had been right,' it was argued, 'to abstain from such intercourse because of the risk of children. If children could be prevented was there any reason for continence?' There were obviously two answers. The statistics of illegitimacy proved, and still prove, that contraception was not, and is not yet, as foolproof as had been pretended. Experience showed what had been less suspected, so long as the main objection had been the simple objection to a consequence, that sex without love and merely for the sake of physical experience was crude and unsatisfying. For as yet marriage was hardly a reality to us. We knew naturally that people got married and had children. We had heard about the problems that marriage brought with it. We were prepared to go to debates and argue about divorce. But marriage was hardly more of a reality to us than death. The practical problem with which we were concerned was whether it was right or wrong, a good thing or a bad, to have sexual experience here and now; and still, as at school, we thought even of that problem in a strangely immature fashion.

We talked about whether sexual experience was good. We thought of sexual experience as something to be accepted or rejected in itself. It did not occur to us that it made much difference whether sex was an expression of love or whether it was merely a physical experience by itself. There was a strange, eccentric old man with a red beard who used to give public lectures to the empty street in the middle of the Giler. His theme was 'industrial bondage for which Herodotus was primarily responsible'. His reasoning we never discovered. We had no idea what was his real name but always called him Ahenobarbus. One day he was heard explaining at the top of his voice to the embarrassed librarian in the silence room at the Bodleian how he used to be in holy orders, but then he said, 'I was unfrocked. I was unfrocked for immorality,' (he pronounced 'immorality' with a long 'a') 'I was unfrocked for immorality. It was not what you or I would call immorality. I was only living with a black woman.' Our general reaction was that this conduct was comical but not unreasonable. A year or two later when I was planning to be received into the Roman Catholic Church, Monsignor Barnes was instructing me. Explaining to me the teachings of the Church, he said that if a man committed fornication he committed sin. That I did not doubt. But then he added if in his fornication he used a contraceptive device then he committed a second sin. Since in the mood in which I then was I had no intention of fornicating at all, I dismissed it as an academic point of no importance whether, doing so, I would commit two sins or one. But afterwards the precise enumeration of sins did seem to me a strange legalism and as divorced from reality as the theorisings of undergraduate permissiveness. Surely one either does right or one does wrong. If one does wrong, if one's actions are turned away from right, who is to say and what purpose is there in saying exactly how many wrong actions one does?

The fallacy of permissive theories in any extreme form is surely this. Let us leave aside for the moment any consideration of religion or dogmatic revealed truth. Hedonistic pleasure or happiness is then the one reasonable end of man and to attain happiness man should satisfy as many as he can of the desires of nature. One obeys the motto of Rabelais' Abbey of Thelême '*Fais que voudras.*' Well enough. Let us for the moment rest on that and seek for no higher ground. But what does a man want? Of course he has his desires and he wants to satisfy them. But he equally wants to be free of them. As Shakespeare put it, desire which is 'past reason hunted' is also 'past reason hated'. So a very little experience teaches one that the problem is not simple—that one cannot attain to happiness by mere unbridled indulgence—that one must live according to a pattern—that even in order to enjoy sex one must keep it under control and not let it become an obsessive master. The fact that there must be a pattern does not in itself prove that the Christian pattern is exactly the right one. That is a matter for further argument, but it does at least prove that there must be a pattern.

So I, having left school and come up to Oxford, came up, like most others, full of brash and confident agnosticism. I cannot quite understand what people mean when they talk about the decline of religion. Obviously if we compare this century with the last century there has been a very great decline of at any rate formal religion. A hundred years ago it was possible to organise society on an assumption that religion was true. Public opinion was willing to allow large privileges to the officers of religion or to accept a general obligation of more or less universal church-going. Whether such a strength of official religion was on balance to the advantage of true religion, whether we truly purified Mammon by the service of God or whether we rather adjusted the service of God to the convenience of Mammon is a very open question. But at any rate such was the situation—a situation very different from that of today, when every tradition of Christian morality and belief can be challenged in utter freedom. The world of today is a very different place from the world of 1870. But whether the world—at any rate the University world—of the 1920's was a very different place from the world of 1974 is not to my mind certain. Certainly in 1920 it was general to leave school an agnostic. One met few undergraduates who were true believers at Oxford. Such as they were, were generally Roman Catholics. The great majority of the rest simply took the falsehood of the Christian claims for granted without especially bothering about them.

I am far from convinced that there has been any further decline as between 1920 and 1974. I should be rather inclined to think the reverse. The decline of the strength of imposed orthodoxy has, I think, been the cause of more genuine religious search and thinking than previously. Religious topics are much more discussed in the secular press now than then.

As I have said, I came up to Balliol, like the majority of public school boys, an unbeliever. Nor was there much in the Balliol of that day to tempt me to change my position. Half a century before, Oxford life and English life had been organised on an assumption that the Christian religion in the Anglican form was true. The headmasters of schools and the heads of University Colleges were always in Holy Orders. As Jowett, Master of Balliol, said, 'In every society the most powerful people have always been the priests of the dominant religion and they have always disbelieved in it.' Such privileges were by the 1920's rapidly perishing and at Balliol had already gone. Among the Dons, Urquhart, the Dean, was a Roman Catholic. Kenneth Bell, the Junior Dean, a strange roistering character, was to end up his life as an Anglican vicar in a parish near Coventry, 'praying away,' as he explained to me, 'like hell.' But no one would at that time have foreseen for him such a destination. There was a College chaplain, but he was an inconsiderable man, not much regarded by anyone. Balliol chapel is the most revoltingly ugly of buildings and attendance at it was no longer compulsory, and not much practised. Few of the undergraduates, except a handful of Catholics, believed in any form of religion. Even among the Catholic flock some lapsed. Monsignor Barnes accepted the inevitability of that with much complacency. He had been chaplain at Cambridge before he was chaplain at Oxford. He had thus spent almost the whole of his adult working life in University Catholic chaplaincies and from this double cure of souls he had derived the conclusion, 'All the young men give up religion at eighteen but they all return to it at twenty-three.' Coming from one who had spent his whole life ministering to the young of those ages it might seem a cynical complacency.

I was in those days a great disciple and hero-worshipper of Hilaire Belloc, who was a frequent visitor to his old College, Balliol. His highest years of glory had been in the first decade of the century when young men like Alan Herbert or Wade Geary, quite innocent of Catholic interests, had hailed him as the greatest of living writers of English prose. Conservative property-owners, terrified by the threats of the 1906 election, saw in his oratory the threat of the tumbrils which awaited them. 'Belloc is in' went the message round the rich houses of Mayfair when the election results came through. They feared the worse. But in fact he did not take kindly to the House of Commons. 'A brilliant man doomed to sterility who found consolation in the art of letters,' said of him, a little fatuously, Birkenhead, who had been his great rival at the Union at Oxford. He tried and failed to get an academic post at the University. All Souls to his great embitterment would not have him and Balliol which he loved—'God be with you, Balliol men'—had, as he felt, insulted him by refusing him but electing Sligger Urquhart, another Catholic, in his place. His writings by the 1920's had lost the supreme high spirits which had filled them before the war. He was to some extent an embittered man and there was always a tinge of bitterness about the jokes that particularly amused him. He went about much with a rich Australian friend, Jim Allison, who had a farm down in Sussex near to Belloc's own home and that of Leonard and Virginia Woolf. One day one of Allison's cows got loose and strayed on to Woolf's front lawn. Leonard Woolf protested. 'Imagine my feelings,' he said, 'as I was sitting writing my article for the *New Statesman* and I looked out of the window and saw your cow standing on my lawn.' 'And imagine my cow's feelings,' replied Allison, 'as it was standing on your lawn and looked in at the window and saw you writing an article for the *New Statesman.*' Belloc abounded in controversy and quarrel. His spirits were often low. Yet, as Chesterton said, 'Belloc's low spirits were higher than any other man's high.' To young companions—myself among them—he always was full of generosity, encouragement and kindness. I came to owe much to this remarkable man.

Meeting him on one occasion in Sligger Urquhart's room, I told him of Monsignor Barnes' saying as if I considered it a pleasantry. Belloc rebuked me.

'No,' he said, 'he's quite right. The Faith is never truly held unless it is held in challenge. The young man must get rid of what he has been merely taught and then rediscover it for himself. If he doesn't do that it isn't really his. It's not worth having.'

And he himself developed the plausibility of the sceptical case.

'You're asked to believe that an obscure Syrian peasant was the Creator of the Universe,' he said. 'Well, if you aren't surprised at that you must be a cretin.' He pronounced the word cretin with a characteristically rolled 'r'.

Encouraged by his apparent scepticism, I proceeded to air my difficulties. 'Was it not more probable that the story was untrue than that it was true?' I asked. Then he turned on me.

'Of course you must take the evidence just as you would for anything else. Take it as a detective story. What happened on Easter Sunday morning? Both the Jews and the Romans had every motive to expose the story. If the body was still in the Tomb, why did they not take people to see it and show it and they could have blown the whole story sky high.'

Clutton Brock, the critic, was present and they fell into an argument about the authenticity and the authorship of the Gospels.

'Well, who do you think did write the Gospels?' asked Clutton Brock.

'I think they were written by four gentlemen called Matthew, Mark, Luke and John,' said Belloc.

'Why will you always try to be clever?' said Clutton Brock and stamped out of the room in disgust.

Belloc continued in high dogmatic fettle. From the Gospels he soon got on to the French Revolution. He maintained that the Revolution deprived no one of anything that they had a right to possess. In the corner of the room sat a meek little man. Nobody quite knew who he was or why he was there.

'Heads?' he asked in a quiet, soft voice. Belloc continued his oration. He returned to his exposition of the Catholic faith.

'Of course, it's difficult to believe,' he said, 'but it's even more difficult not to believe. Have you ever read *Bishop Blougram's Apology*? I don't read much but I have read that.'

As a matter of fact I had read it. At Eton they had an arrangement of what was known as Sunday Private, by which all boys went on a Sunday morning to their tutors and read with them some stimulating and improving work. My tutor's selection was some of the works of Browning —among them *Bishop Blougram's Apology*.

'Very good,' said Belloc, 'rasping good stuff. Only I wonder how many Catholic bishops have ever read Euripides. They say Blougram was Wiseman. I'm sure Wiseman hadn't.'

I turned back to Blougram again and, having re-read him, I felt, as did Pasternak, like 'an atheist who has lost his faith'.

I cannot very easily define exactly what was my attitude towards these problems in the middle years of my Oxford career. I remember one day in the Presidential office at the Union, falling into an argument with

Ronald Matthews, a young man, afterwards a distinguished journalist but who was then, I think, the Junior Librarian. He straightly challenged why I believed in God. (He himself later became a Catholic, but he was by no means a Catholic then.) In reply to my contentions he produced Immanuel Kant's refutation of the traditional proofs of the existence of God. 'If everything must be made by someone then who made God?' It was the conundrum which I myself imagined that I had discovered for myself some years before at Eton. Anyway round, things go out into a mystery and one cannot extract from the argument any proof of the existence of God. I remember an argument with an atheistic friend in the rooms of L. P. Hartley by Folly Bridge. He was arguing against the existence of any moral law. There could not possibly, he said, be such a thing as obligation. The only possible code of conduct was the hedonist. One must so act as to give oneself the greatest possible pleasure. If one was civilised, one required for one's pleasure to behave in a reasonable social fashion and to be agreeable to one's friends in order to retain their friendship. But that was quite a different thing from obligation. Yet I could not but feel, for all his arguments, that we had such a thing as obligation. After all we can hardly frame an English sentence without using the word 'ought' and 'ought' means 'owe'. If we owe a debt, we must owe it to someone. If there was an obligation, to whom was it owed? he asked. I mentioned God. The notion that anyone could possibly believe in God was clearly quite strange to him, but he conceded the logic of the appeal at once. 'Oh, of course, if you believe in God, it's quite logical,' he said, and I fancy that that was the position on the whole which I came to hold. I did not think that I would behave well because God commanded me to do so. Rather did I believe in God because I felt within me the obligation to behave well, and in taking up that position I was of course in very considerable company—Kant, Wordsworth, Newman—though I am not quite sure how fully aware of my company I was at the time.

Yet I must confess that I was still in some confusion. I would certainly have attacked in argument the Deist position, have asserted the possibility of miracles and of God's intervention in the affairs of Man. But I can hardly deny that in everyday affairs of life it would have been quite beyond my imagination that what Meredith called 'the army of unalterable law' was not entirely triumphant. If a motor car had broken down, not only would I have believed that it had broken down for a reason. It would have been quite beyond the capacity of my thought that it did not break down for a reason and in accordance to law. I might not know the law—might not be able to diagnose the defect. That was neither here nor there. That there was a reason—some intermediate reason—that the breakdown was not a mere lawless act of God was to me a necessity of thought. Indeed, even today, when they tell me, as they sometimes do, that in the last analysis there is no reason why one atom splits and another does not I cannot very well understand what they are saying. I have always liked going to church and felt that a life from which church-going and worship were wholly absent was an empty, unfulfilled and untidy life. Even if I did not believe I would still feel that a life in which I never went to church was an uncompleted life. The complacency of those who think that they are freed of an incubus by not going to church has always annoyed me. Shortly after the war I included in an article that I was writing the sentence, 'We can see something degrading in the faces of those who never go to church.' I wrote it admittedly to annoy. I was so accustomed to the gibes of those who imagined that, so far as they could do without religion, they were the superiors of believers that I did not see why they should not be paid back in their own coin, and after all what does stamp a face more clearly than a total lack of curiosity about ultimate things? And a curiosity about ultimate things that does not express itself in a social act, in the company of his neighbours, is positively dangerous. As Tawney truly says, 'the man who believes in a purely private God inevitably comes to see himself as God and is worse and more dangerous than the atheist'. Yet, as I say, I wrote the sentence—perhaps unwisely—mainly to annoy and I was surprised how much umbrage it gave. The printers who had to set it protested in demonstration against the insult. Harold Nicolson—to move to another level—complained of it as an example of bigotry, as if I had advocated that free citizens should be marched compulsorily to their nearby church. Yet one might say that a man's face was unpoetic or his voice unmusical without being considered to be doing more than making a judgement on facts. I should think that on the whole my judgement was true. The importance of going to church seemed to me at that time much more evident than the importance of what happened when one got there. Arguments about the validity of the Sacraments had then little meaning for me.

I am not concerned at the moment to write an apologia—to give what are necessarily good reasons for my position. I am only concerned to give, as far as I can, an account of my reasons. If they were insufficient I cannot help it. To a large extent I agree that they were insufficient. The critic may very reasonably say, 'I can see why boyhood beliefs induced you to return to the practices of religion. But why did you not return to your boyhood's religion? Why did they induce you to go to a new religion?' It is a fair question. I could give the answers of the text-book apologetics, but I am trying to say not what should have been my answers—not what were the answers of the professional apologists— but in all honesty what were my real answers. I do not find it altogether easy and indeed do not pretend that the answers were always very good answers. Long before I came up to the point of reception into the Catholic Church I had of course equipped myself with the formal answers. Christ, I had learnt, had patently founded only one church— not a variety or federation of churches. The task of the Christian was to find what was the church which Christ founded and to join it. I had been introduced to Wiseman and the *Dublin Review*, St Augustine and the Donatists, '*Securus iudicat orbis terrarum*'. It was manifest that the Church of Rome had a claim to speak for the general mind of the church which neither the Church of England nor any other body could challenge. What were the claims of the Church of England? I was told that they claimed indeed that their bishops had the Apostolic Succession and that her sacraments were therefore valid sacraments, but I was told also that this claim was very doubtful and that the Anglican Orders had been condemned by Pope Leo XIII. Indeed the claim was only tenable if total continuity was preserved and even if, for the sake of argument, we allow that the Anglican continuity was preserved through the time of Elizabeth and of Archbishop Laud, how could anyone seriously pretend that the men whom the Duke of Newcastle made bishops in the eighteenth century possessed, in face of their protests against any such pretensions, the Apostolic Succession? The Church of England did not pretend that it was the whole Catholic Church. It claimed no more than to be one of the branches which, together, made up the Catholic Church. And of these three branches which by definition together made up the infallible Catholic Church, it gave an account quite different from what each branch gave of itself. It told the Roman Catholic Church that it was no more than a branch of the Church. Rome denied it. It told the Church of England that it was Catholic and not Protestant. The greater number of professing Anglicans repudiated such a description. It told the Greek Church that Anglican orders were valid and the Greeks denied it.

So I was well enough furnished with these and similar arguments. They had their force, but as in so many of such arguments the conclusion that comes out of the computer depends on the information that has been fed into it. The average Anglican was not particularly concerned whether his bishops had or had not the Apostolic Succession. The whole controversy was to him unimportant and meaningless, and indeed, though I was full now of such controversies and the rights and wrongs of them, I should have reflected, had I ever stopped to reflect on it, that in my own boyhood I had never so much as heard the Apostolic Succession mentioned and would not have had the faintest idea what it was.

My father, who throughout all this controversy which I maintained in such an aggressive and inconsiderate way behaved with an almost unbelievable charity and restraint, once raised the point with all gentleness and without pressing it, as he might have been entitled to do. 'The Church of England,' he argued, 'offered me the freedom of all these religious practices. I could go to confession if I wanted to. I could abstain from meat on Fridays if I wanted to. It offered me the Body and Blood of Christ in the Real Presence as opposed to the Roman Church which only offered me the Body.' Why had I made so little use of what the Church of England offered, and indeed almost found it ridiculous, and then welcomed it as admirable when offered by the Church of Rome in a compulsory form? It was a fair question and certainly, whatever might be the general truth about the contention that Catholics took their religion seriously and that Anglicans had lost all reality of faith, I could not honestly claim that it applied in my case. My father clearly had a depth and sincerity of religion which I could not pretend to rival.

It was of course undoubtedly true that English culture was a strangely insular culture. A generation or two earlier I would doubtless have been subject to crudely partisan reasons of history and told that the English way of life was in every way the superior of that of lesser breeds without the law, that England was the one true home of freedom and for its virtue especially pleasing to God.

> The nations not so blessed as we
> Must in their turn to tyrants fall.

The England to which I would have been invited would have been the Land of Hope and Glory of Cecil Rhodes, convinced that, if there was a God, He must wish the British Empire to extend from the Cape to Cairo. Things had changed since my boyhood from the habits of the Victorians and the world of Charles Kingsley. The Liberal support of Irish Home Rule, bitterly opposed as it was, had yet made a great difference in the habits of language—the more so because of the remarkable fact, not sufficiently emphasised as remarkable, that the English Non-conformist bodies, being Liberal, gave their support to the cause of Home Rule for the Catholic Irish and opposed the Presbyterian Unionists of Ulster. History was by then at least discussed in courtesy by the Universities.

The influence of Belloc on me was at that time considerable. Yet, though I would not have admitted as much and though I was all too free in quoting him, I could not in truth, and cannot now, quite understand his position. To him the Church was the imperial projection of the Roman Empire. 'The faith is Europe and Europe is the faith.' It was an authoritarian and military institution. For the modernist speculations of the time he had nothing but contempt. Maud Petre was a leading English modernist of the day. She was a cousin of my friend, Billy Clonmore, and I met her a few times in her old age. She seemed to me a pleasant and kindly old lady, but Belloc dismissed her with a parody of Our Lord's words to St Peter, accusing her of thinking that Our Lord said in His inauguration of the Church: 'Thou art Maud Petre and on this rock will I build my Church.' Yet, clamant as he was for the authority of the Church, he did not bother greatly about the Church's rules of fasting and abstinence. He imposed upon himself the voluntary mortification of giving up strong drink during Lent but did not scruple to eat ham on a Friday if there were no non-Catholics present. A young lady of my acquaintance had fallen strongly in love with a man who was divorced. Belloc was very insistent that she should not go through any form of marriage with him. 'What should I do?' she asked. 'Live in sin,' he replied, 'live in sin.' I could not quite understand his point of view. The Church to him was an institution to be honoured rather than to be obeyed.

My father was doubtless right in saying that there was a streak of sheer perversity in my character and that I partly turned to Rome simply out of a desire to be different. I had, as I have said, always a liking for turning things upside down, which I had learnt from Bishop Blougram, and Bishop Blougram was after all a Catholic bishop. But up to a point I only differed from many of my contemporaries in desiring to push things to a practical conclusion. Oxford society was, as I have said, entirely and complacently secular. The falsity of the official Anglicanism with which they had been presented at school was taken utterly for granted and in consequence of that was to cause a certain reaction towards Catholicism. It was common enough to hear people say, 'Of course it's all a load of rubbish. But if I were to become anything I would become a Roman Catholic.' If any of it was true, they felt, it was logical to accept it all as true.

What did becoming a Catholic mean in the Oxford of fifty years ago? One knew of course that there were people who accepted their religion as a total denial—became monks or nuns—shut themselves entirely off from the world—devoted themselves wholly to asceticism and prayer. Without knowing much about them we were prepared to honour such people but we never considered any serious possibility of imitating them. Even the priests that we met were by no means priests of such a sort. We did not force our way into Carthusian monasteries and the priests that we saw we contrasted to their advantage with Anglican clergymen as easy and agreeable social companions. Father Martindale was the dominant Catholic priest in Oxford and he was a man who could of course more than hold his own in any social company. We were greatly in error in thinking that all Catholic priests shared his social and intellectual gifts. In general the Catholicism that we felt ourselves called upon to accept —the Catholicism of *l'homme moyen sensuel*—was an agreeable enough regimen. I felt a moral duty to belong and wanted to be a member of a society which gave recognition to that duty of membership. The Catholic Church, in the form in which I accepted it, seemed to me a very convenient society to which to belong. Of the Catholic poor in the great towns, of the Catholics among the prison population I knew nothing. The only Catholics at Oxford at that time were well-appointed young men from the expensive Catholic public schools. Their academic records were perhaps below the average, but they were very well behaved. They rarely went to prison nor indeed were they often in conflict with the authorities except perhaps for failing in their examinations. Douglas Woodruff, who was my closest Catholic friend, spoke of his religion in a different way from that in which he would speak of it today or even a few years later. He contrasted his Catholicism with that of some other more implacably rigid fellow undergraduates. Catholicism was, he said to me one night over dinner at the Golden Cross, in his opinion 'a hint'. The Catholic solution of social problems which we most frequently heard preached were those of the distributism of Belloc and Chesterton. It suited me very well since Catholic apologetics, though they recommended the Pope's social teaching, did not greatly insist on them. It was a good thing to study social problems and our obligations to the poor but it was not an absolute obligation. To neglect them was not a mortal sin—not of the order of eating meat on Friday. I had of course no foggiest notion of how the principles which I was enunciating should be put into practice or indeed of doing anything about them. Making a speech at the Union which had about it a veneer of originality was at that time an end in itself.

In many ways the Catholics seemed in those days to stand for greater freedom than the generality of society. There was more drinking in the Oxford of the 1920's than there is today, and the influence of Belloc and Chesterton was potent in giving an appearance of consecration to Catholic alcoholic consumption—Cathalcoholism as Douglas Woodruff called it in a Union speech. Years later I got into some trouble because of what I had thought of as a very casual comment on the freedom of language of Catholics. I had intended it as a compliment but I found myself rebuked by a number of co-religionists for having insulted them. Yet there is no doubt that for better or worse Catholics were and are freer both with drink and with the passing 'bloody' or 'damn' than other people. We told one another that, far from being guilty of sin, we were performing a Christian duty in downing the Puritans and Nonconformists and in drinking as much as we were capable of—not infrequently more. There was a certain justification for our absurd conduct, for at that time the United States had just embarked on prohibition and did not as yet show any signs of abandoning it. In England the Liberal party and the Nonconformists often spoke of total abstinence as the ideal and, as an immediate programme, fought for local option, or a system by which each locality should decide by its own vote whether or not it would have licensed premises. It could be argued in a way in which it could hardly be argued today that the temperance movement threatened freedom and that all lovers of freedom should unite to fight it. We read Chesterton's *Flying Inn* and united to bawl together the songs of *Wine, Water and Song*.

There were other ways in which the Catholic ethos was different from the Protestant ethos which surrounded us. I had been brought up to look on all forms of betting and gambling as evil. I think that most Anglican clergymen would have taken this view. I found that in the Catholic world it was taken for granted as entirely respectable. As a matter of fact I am totally devoid of all gambling instinct. There is nothing that bores me so completely. I have on a few occasions for politeness' sake taken a ticket if I found myself sitting where some raffle or sweepstake was taking place. But I have never placed a bet in my life and, while not perhaps quite demanding that the Church should denounce all betting as a mortal sin, have always been shocked at priests' readiness to raise their parochial funds by countenancing unlimited indulgence in the idiotic game of bingo. What is more absurd than that, whenever there is a postal dispute, the first concern of the authorities must be to give assurance that the football pools will be punctually delivered?

As I have said, I had come out from Eton self-confident in my scepticism. I would have said without hesitation that the Christian religion— and probably the Catholic Church in particular—imposed superstition and asceticism. They bound on their disciples a burden too grievous to be borne and theirs were extravagancies from which I was very happy to be free. Further experience showed me that both these contentions were far from being true. There may be a case to be made in mere logic for sheer scepticism. 'We cannot know and we are better if we frankly confess that we cannot know.' But experience taught me and has increasingly taught me that, whether or not it ought to rest there, the mind cannot rest in mere scepticism. 'All things go out into mystery', and man is not able to refrain from inquiry and wonder about the mystery of things. He inevitably makes his guesses and, if his guesses have not the support of reason, they are made without reason. 'A man who does not believe in God will believe in anything,' truly said Chesterton. One of the strangest discoveries of my life has been the strength of superstition in entirely irreligious people. The Pope may tell us not to believe in St Christopher, but that does not prevent agnostic motorists from fixing St Christopher medals on their motor cars and thinking that in some way they will be a protection to them. During the war when I was in the R.A.F. I had occasion to fly to Malta. It so chanced that my journey was booked for Friday, the 13th of, I think, October. It never occurred to me to think twice of the matter, but a hard-boiled secular civil servant begged me almost with tears to change the date. I was summoned to a business luncheon one day when a railway strike was threatened. My host's secretary rang up to ask if I would be able to attend. I replied that from my inquiries it seemed probable that there would be a train. If so, I would be on it but that in the uncertain times I could not be sure. Would it not be all right, I asked, if I left it open— turned up if I could and, if I couldn't make it, why, then I couldn't. 'Oh,' said the secretary, 'but if you don't come, that will make it thirteen and Mr X. particularly does not like sitting down thirteen to the table.' To my amazement this was apparently an insurmountable difficulty and, if I was not coming, they were prepared to sally out into the street and collect any casual passer-by in order to prevent the mystic number. Yet, when in spite of obstacles I eventually made the journey, I heard my host explaining that of course he did not believe in God or a future life or the Divinity of Christ. He was nevertheless leading an entirely Christian life, exactly as Christ would have approved of it. He was in fact shuffling his shares so as to give himself a slight increase of income. One has only to look at the sort of superstition with which the lives of sportsmen and actors are bedevilled—superstitions, half believed, half disbelieved but always rigorously obeyed. 'I'm mildly superstitious,' I read that Jill Bennett says, 'I've so many things to bring me luck you wouldn't believe it. I have an ivory god, a green boot, a collection of all sorts of pigs, and a teddy bear. It's pathetic really, but I get very nervous if they are not there.' Actors and actresses always think that to play in *Macbeth* brings bad luck.

Later when I used to go to the Council of Europe at Strasbourg I made great friends with a young German, the sceptical son of a most distinguished German savant of European reputation. He said to me one day at luncheon, indicating the wife of his colleague across the table, 'That woman is a witch.' She seemed to me a very ordinary woman and his reasons for his belief about her to be quite unconvincing but I found that he had no doubt at all that the slowness of Europe's progress towards unity was entirely caused by the malevolent necromantic powers which she was able to exercise. Boenhoffer, that very noble victim of Hitler's persecutions, has told us that 'Man has come of age,' and that, important as is obedience to the moral law, we can in the mature twentieth century no longer believe in a God who interferes in the affairs of this world. It is a strange judgement—particularly from a man who believed passionately that in its own day the Resurrection really happened. I should have thought that the twentieth century was quite exceptionally immature and that there was never a time when people believed more and for less reason, that belief in preternatural intervention in the affairs of this world—usually of a very childish and ridiculous sort—was almost universal. I have been told that the most widely read pages in the Sunday papers studied by 80 per cent of its readers are those of astrological prediction, and a recent opinion poll showed that there are more believers today in astrology than in Christianity.

In many secondary ways, then, the Catholic seemed to me to live a freer and more careless life than other people and the Church did not appear to have any objection to his doing so. We who became Catholics drank a good deal and we told ourselves that not only did the Church raise no objection to drinking but that, though indeed there was such a sin as drunkenness, it was a sin that was very difficult to commit and

about which we had no need to bother ourselves. We told one another—
I have never checked up upon what authority—that one only committed the mortal sin of drunkenness if one set out in cold sobriety with
the deliberate intention of getting drunk and fulfilled that intention.
That we never did, nor can I imagine many people deliberately doing
such a thing. We quoted to one another the saying of Maurice Baring as
he arose from his study of a manual of moral theology, 'As far as I can
see it takes a very able man to be in mortal sin.' Today I find the company of middle-aged alcoholics quite peculiarly boring and unattractive
and run far to avoid their company. How far they are in sin it is not for
me to say. As an undergraduate I considered drinking as an exercise in
high spirits. I did not at all understand that there were some—of whom
I was lucky enough to be one—who had no taint of alcoholism at all
and could take a drink or abstain without any difficulty, and others
who had the disease of alcoholism in their system and to whom drink
was a veritable curse. I know nothing nor have ever known anything
about the higher culture of wine and the whole matter does not bother
me at all. Catholics vary from one another in their habits, but on the
whole, I think, they drink too much—as indeed do probably the majority of educated people in England.

But if more liberal in other ways the Catholics of course differed from
others around them in being a great deal stricter about sex. Premarital
sex was forbidden and indeed many moralists, not content with forbidding the sexual act, also laid down somewhat absurdly detailed regulations about what kind of kisses and embraces were permitted. Marriage
was not yet a present possibility to us. Therefore a ban on premarital sex
meant in effect that sex of any sort had to be rejected as an evil. With the
details of incidental regulations—what was allowed and what was forbidden—I am happy to say that Monsignor Barnes was wise enough not
to bother me. So I never knew about them. His moral teaching was
straightforward and not in the least hysterical. To commit fornication
was a sin but he never suggested that, contrary to all biblical teaching, it
was a unique sin or a sin of sins.

I had up till then confidently believed that Man was naturally free and
that Christianity had wantonly imposed on us its unnatural taboos, forbidding us from doing 'what comes naturally,' thus unnecessarily
depriving us of happiness. A very little learning was sufficient to teach
me the absurdity of belief in the free, noble savage. His life was bound in
with taboos at least as strict and unnatural as those of Christianity. It
was Catullus who taught me that the life of pre-Christian pagans was by

no means a life of carefree innocent indulgence—that it was in nature and not through any teachings of a dogmatic religion that indulgence which was past reason hunted was also past reason hated. The priests of Attis, Catullus tells us, in revulsion against the tyranny of sex which excessive indulgence had imposed on them, castrated themselves as the only possible means of freedom.

Indeed if we look at the old world or indeed at the present world around us we can see that Christianity, far from inventing asceticism, controls it and is careful to impose a regimen which keeps it reasonable and in bounds.

I think that I was right in seeing the English culture as an excessively insular affair. I think that I was right in recognising the Catholic Church as the great cultural institution which, far more than any other, made civilisation. It was a great achievement. But what does that prove? It does not present itself to its disciples as the great disseminator of culture. Such achievements, if they are true, are quite secondary and irrelevant to its purposes. Christ presented Himself to His disciples as the Lord of Life, the promiser of Eternal Salvation. There is no evidence that he was even interested in 'objets d'art' or great literature. If he was a poet he was so merely in incident and careless throwaway. Obviously logic of a reasonable apologetic requires one first to demonstrate the existence of God, then to demonstrate the Divinity of Christ. Only then does it become relevant even to consider the claims of the Church. If Christ was not God, how does it matter whether He founded a Church or whether the existing Roman Catholic Church is the Church which He founded?

Yet I must on self-examination confess that my own approach was an illogical one. To me it was the Church that came first. I felt the need to live according to a pattern and the magnificence of the Church as it stretched through the ages impressed me as it had impressed Macaulay in his famous essay, but Macaulay, very logically, while admiring the Church, did not find that a reason for joining it. On the other hand I, less logically, accepted the Church. Of course, accepting it, I accepted it as an authority and was ready without questioning to accept what it taught. I obediently accepted the claims of Christ because the Church told me to do so. I accepted the existence of God because the Church told me that it could be proved. But, as I have shown from my account of my argument with Ronald Matthews, when challenged on my reasons for believing in the existence of God, I did not give a very convincing answer and similarly, if a devil's advocate had challenged me as to why I accepted the Divinity of Christ, I do not know that I would have done much better.

Accepting the authority of the Church, I accepted it fully. I accepted the existence of God because the Church told me. I accepted the Divinity of Christ because the Church told me. Indeed I accepted almost everything that those in authority told me was in accordance with the mind of the Church, which involved me in accepting a number of propositions that I had no need to accept and of which today I would be far from certain.

Whatever the complex of reasons that led me to take this religious step most certainly the fear of death—whether the fear of Hell or the desire for survival—was not one of them. Accepting the Church's authority, I accepted what it had to say about death. I accepted the general teaching about survival and rewards and punishments, but it did not bulk large in my mind. For at the age of twenty-one or twenty-two I did not much consider death. Naturally I knew that I would die one day, but my imagination did not embrace the possibility of it. In any speculation about the future I always took it for granted that I would be there to see the scene. It is, I fancy, natural enough for healthy people up till their forties to think of themselves as immortal. It is only after that that one is continually thinking of death, and after sixty it becomes increasingly difficult to be seriously concerned about the affairs of this life. Instead one continually reflects of any coming event that one will not be there to see how things develop. If we consider how narrowly I had escaped the war, it was perhaps odd that I should have had so little of a sense of death. After all, many who had been only slightly senior to me had gone out and got killed. Had the war continued for another two years I would have had to go myself and there was no reason why I should not have been killed. But somehow, contrary to every probability, it never occurred to me that I should be involved in the war.

I have no doubt that there must have been many among my friends and acquaintances who thought that the step that I had taken in joining the Catholic Church was feeble and foolish. The Church of Rome might be properly defended in debate but it was common to say that it was the refuge of those who had not the courage to face reality. But, if I chose to take that step, they did not consider it any business of theirs. The only friend from whom I can remember to have received vigorous protests, was, oddly enough, Evelyn Waugh, who was himself of course to take the same step a few years later. At Balliol, Gilbert Simon, the son of Sir John Simon (as he then was), had been a friend of mine and Sir John had shown me great kindness and had entertained me at his house at Fritwell near Banbury. I was surprised to learn that he had expressed strong disapproval of my step. I could not see, and indeed still cannot see, why he

minded one way or the other. He was himself the son of a Congregation-
alist minister who had transferred his allegiance to the Church of England. But I cannot think that he had any fixed or serious denominational
beliefs. He was at that time engaged on a vigorous campaign against the
rule of the Black and Tans in Ireland from which one might have deduced that he had certain Catholic sympathies, but the deduction would,
I think, have been unjustifiable. He threw himself into the Irish campaign
partly because he felt that the Liberals needed a popular cause with
which to re-establish themselves and partly because of the influence of his
second wife whom he had recently married, a nurse, a vigorous Irish
nationalist, for all intents and purposes a Sinn Feiner, but also a strong
Protestant. I fancy that the explanation of Simon's disapproval was his
intense belief that it was the duty of a man to win for himself competitive
success. I am thankful to say that I never had any great appetite for
success and indeed, when considering the step that I was to take, I can
honestly say that it simply never occurred to me to wonder whether it
was to the advantage of my career. Plainly it was to the disadvantage of a
career as Simon reckoned a career, but since in any case I had no wish to
have a career in that sense the matter did not bother me. I think that
Simon did not so much directly disapprove of the tenets of the Church of
Rome—though doubtless his Nonconformist upbringing at a time when
political differences owing to the education controversy were very largely
denominational differences did give him a certain anti-Catholic bias—but
he felt vaguely uncomfortable in the presence of a young man who was
not much concerned with success or failure in his own career. It seemed
to him unnatural. But it is only fair to say that at the end of his life when
he had travelled far from being a Liberal of the type whom Asquith
nicknamed the Impeccable we used to meet again and I received from
him much courtesy.

The enthusiasms of Simon's wife were less disciplined by reason or
coherence. It used to be our pleasure to take enjoyment in her manifold
malapropisms. When they were in India he took her one evening to
see the Taj Mahal. On her return she expressed her enthusiastic appreciation. 'I think that the most beautiful thing that I ever saw in my life,' she
said, 'was the sight of the Aga Khan by moonlight.'

But of course these matters were of very secondary importance. All
that really mattered were my relations within my own family. My father
was then the Principal of Wells Theological College and a Canon of the
cathedral. I could not shut my eyes to the fact that I was by my conduct
putting him into a position of considerable embarrassment. There were

those who would have expected him, if not to bar me from the house, at least to treat me with some coldness. I remember when I was at Eton a conversation in which a general opinion, from which I alone dissented, was expressed that Bishop Knox had done very wrong in paying out of his salary for a meal of which Ronald Knox, after his conversion to Rome, had been permitted to partake. The point of view seemed to me even then very ridiculous and my father, whatever the embarrassment and sorrow that I may have caused him, uttered no word of reproach. His example most certainly made it for ever afterwards inevitable that I should refute suggestions when I heard them, as I sometimes did, from Catholic tongues, that sincere Christian belief or practice was never found among Anglicans or that the Anglican faith was a fraud or a mummery. I knew that true charity and faith were to be found there.

CHAPTER THREE

Sighing Like Furnace

I

AMERICA

Bates College, a small college at Augusta in Maine, had for many years specialised in debating, which was not highly regarded at most of the American universities, where it was thought of as 'a minor sport'. But at Bates, almost alone, they took it seriously, planning to gain prestige out of their success. With this in mind in 1922 they issued a challenge to the Oxford Union to be allowed to debate against the Union speakers. The challenge was accepted and the debate took place. It was not a great success because the English and the American habits of debating were quite different and not sufficient trouble had been taken beforehand to compare notes and to make sure that the two sides were trying to do the same thing. In England a debate, as we know, is, as it were, a parody of Parliament. The speakers all get up in turn and express their opinions. No especial attempt is made to integrate the opinions of one speaker with those of another. According to the English, or at any rate the Oxford custom, jokes and serious points are intermixed, serious arguments are put in a whimsical or comical fashion. At the end the audience votes not on the merits of the speakers but on the merits of the topic debated.

To the Americans on the other hand the debate is rather a parody of the Law Courts. A team is debating. The points of one speaker are carefully coordinated with another. Jokes, if admitted at all, are admitted as anecdotes quite irrelevant to the argument. Americans have little sense of making a serious point in a comical way. The mere attempt to do so, as Adlai Stevenson discovered, is considered somewhat indecent. Either you are making a serious point or you are telling a funny anecdote. You cannot make a serious point in jest. The speakers did not say 'I think' but 'Bates says'. The verdict at the end of an American debate is an award of a prize by three judges on which side has debated the better. When the verdict went against Bates and for the Oxford Union, their debate-coach refused to allow the Bates team to attend a supper-party afterwards. 'A defeated team,' he said, 'does not accept hospitality.' Few of the English audience knew that they had been defeated.

To Americans, jokes are jokes and serious matters are serious matters. If it is worth while competing at all, it is worth while winning. They told me at the English Benedictine school which the Ampleforth monks have built at St Louis how a film of the school life was made. Then the question arose who should present this film in public. It was suggested that it should be presented by the English Headmaster. A prominent Trustee objected: 'No doubt Father Timothy would do it very well, but—' he lowered his voice to a tone of reverence—'he might make some jokes, and after all it is about money.'

A consequence of Bates' visit to Oxford was that in the subsequent Michaelmas, or Fall, as the Americans call it, the Oxford Union was invited to send three debaters back to debate for a few weeks on the American east coast. I was selected to go on that team along with Edward Marjoribanks, the half-brother of the present Lord Hailsham, who had been my Captain of the School at Eton, and Kenneth Lindsay, afterwards a Labour Member of Parliament and the Union's first Labour President. We spent three very pleasant and interesting weeks visiting most of the Ivy League coast Universities. That was the first of my many visits to America which have extended over fifty years, and during which I have seen many changes in that country. America, when I first saw it, was the most conformist of countries. It is only in very recent years that demos at Universities have made their appearance there. I remember being asked some five or six years ago in Pennsylvania whether such demonstrations then taking place in America were known in other countries. I replied that undergraduates had behaved thus in every other country of the world since the beginning of time. It was only in America that such antics had been unknown. Certainly any such demonstrations, though natural enough at Oxford, where at that time we all demonstrated in favour of a municipal bus strike, or on the Continent, would have been in the early 1920's quite inconceivable at an American University. In the 1920's the first ambition of every American student was to discover what was 'our American point of view' and to repeat it. It was thought unpatriotic to have opinions of one's own. America in the 1920's had been politically independent for a hundred and fifty years, but she still was, as Matthew Arnold says, 'intellectually a colony'. Students were educated on books that had been written in foreign countries—principally in Britain. An English book could in those days take it for granted that it would find an American publisher. Things are very different today. The Second World War was intellectually the American War of Independence. In spite of the reaction towards isolation, the main news in the papers in the 1920's was still news from foreign countries. The correspondents in American papers were the superior of such correspondents in English or any other foreign papers. Today there is little news or interest in American papers on what is happening outside America other than what Americans are doing, as in Vietnam—and particularly little news on what is happening in Britain which has become in American eyes a very insignificant country.

Two years later I made a second visit to America on a more extended trip which took us right across country. I was then in the company of Douglas Woodruff and Malcolm Macdonald. We made our way gradually right across the country, debating with University after University, some fifty in all, until we eventually reached the West coast and sailed from San Francisco to Hawaii, Fiji, New Zealand and Australia.

I thus saw a good deal of American trains of the period. The trains were slow by English or Continental standards. It was natural enough that they should be so considering the many thousands of miles of track to be maintained, but I found that many Americans greatly resented the suggestion that British trains ran faster. It was a matter of pride to them that everything in America was faster than everything anywhere else in the world. Of course the truth is that a lot of things, for better or worse, are much faster in America than in this country. The telephone system for instance is much quicker. One picks up the telephone and is connected with a number in any part of the country in a few seconds, and I would not deny that in general Americans do live in a greater hustle than we. But they do a number of things much more slowly than we do. They write longer novels. They use longer words such as 'elevator' where we say 'lift,' or 'automobile' for 'car'. Most notably it takes much longer to get a meal served in America than in England or indeed in any country of the world except, I suppose, Russia which I have never visited. There is reason behind this slow-motion. The management very rightly thinks that it does not make much money on the food. Its profits almost entirely come out of the drinks, and the slower its service of the food, the more will its customers drink while they are waiting for it. Unlike the diners of all other countries Americans drink like fishes while they are waiting for their food, and with their food have nothing more appetising nor more expensive than iced water.

Buying a ticket for a journey is also a strangely slow business in

America. In the old days of trains the booking-clerk would write out in pen an interminable series of tickets covering every stage of one's journey. Today with aeroplanes, if you want to change any detail of an itinerary, it can only be done after endless telephoning back to the office of the original booking and a delay of a week or so over what in most other countries could be done by the clerk with a stroke of the pen. But this slowness of travel was not without its advantages. One could at least see the scenery. The world contains within itself a marvellous variety of prospects but air terminals are not among them. They are exactly like one another in every corner of the world. Air travel has greatly narrowed the mind. I remember a tourist in Tunis. He was making a booking of a ticket. 'Did you say Bucharest or Budapest?' said the clerk. 'Hell, what can it matter? I want to go places,' the tourist answered.

It is no great distinction to have been to America today. Most people go there sooner or later in their lives. Fifty years ago things were very different. Up until the war the Americans were proud of their isolation. A few wealthy, cultured Americans made their European trips and were proud of them. But the average American never crossed nor ever wanted to cross the Atlantic. In particular the immigrants, glad to have escaped from an ungrateful homeland, were very confident that they had come to a better country and had no wish to return to their original home. The war of course made a difference and brought to Europe as soldiers many Americans who would never otherwise have dreamed of going there as tourists. For the most part they formed no very high opinion of it. Whereas before the war they had not visited Europe but had been content to recognise it as the home of their culture, now, seeing it, they did not think very much of it. They despised the poor standards of living that they found in the old world—its deficiencies in plumbing and bathrooms, by which they meant shower baths. Few of them ever guessed that Englishmen despised them because they preferred a shower to a bath in which one could lie down. They enjoyed noise and thought it a sign of progress. It is true that in this they have in recent years greatly changed, and, though the country is still as noisy as it ever was, at least they have become most deeply pollution-conscious and think it desirable to take steps to prevent the universal desecration of the countryside by the decibel. On the whole, while the majority of Englishmen have to live in towns in order to make their living but prefer the countryside and retire out of the town as soon as they are able to do so, Americans prefer the town and live in it from choice. They have little liking for privacy. Things are perhaps better now, but when I first went to America it was common enough in specially provided university guest rooms to find that guests were expected to doss down two to a bed without any thought that such an arrangement was a disamenity. Life there is more public than with us. Whereas the English like to keep things private, and many secrets about the private lives of public men are common knowledge yet never appear in any newspaper, the Americans tend to think that all news should be public property. I have seen American Catholics queuing up in a church outside the confessional, their ears a-cock and obviously straining to hear what the penitent in front of them is saying. During the war I had occasion to ring up Mr Herbert Agar at the American Embassy. I got through to their switchboard and asked for Mr Agar. They put me through on a wrong line to a gentleman who was reporting on the experiences of Mrs Roosevelt who had recently paid a visit to Britain. In Scotland, he said, she had been very well received by everybody except for one prominent peer whom he named, 'who was a perfect swine'. I reported the failure of security but no one in the Embassy seemed much concerned. 'Your good luck,' they said.

The strangest misconception about America—a misconception frequent both in America and on this side of the Atlantic—is that American society is matriarchal. In no country have women played a smaller part in political life. Because women congregate more frequently in clubs in America than in other countries it is thought that they are more important. In fact there is no country except perhaps Ireland and Mahommedan countries where they are more carefully excluded from male society. At dinner parties when I was later teaching at Notre Dame I always found, and my wife complained, that after the meal male and female were rigidly herded into separate rooms until it was time to go home. Later when I was in Parliament I was much attacked—I do not quite know why—by feminists as an opponent of women's rights. I was not so much their opponent as I did not think them very important. Women seemed to demand votes at the very moment that men were beginning to think that it was not worth having them. What does the vote matter? The condition of civilisation is that men and women should mix easily on social terms and nowhere does this happen less than in the United States.

The American view in 1920 was that Europe had been proved to be a continent of incurable warmongers. In the nineteenth century they had been careful to keep out of Europe's troubles. In 1917 they had much against their wills been involved. Wilsonian ideals had deduced from the fact of American involvement a lesson that America must play her part in remaking the world. The average American, as post-war elections very soon showed, drew rather the lesson that Europeans were incorrigible, that their blunders were beyond remedy and America must at all costs see to it that never again should she become involved in their quarrels.

Thus even after the war the number of English visitors to America, if slightly more than before 1914, was not yet large. It was quite a distinction then for a young man to have been there and certainly it was an important opportunity to him to see a little of this great country which had become suddenly a country of such moment and of which he himself knew so little. American policy was to the uninformed undergraduate, as indeed to every other Englishman a great deal better informed, 'puzzling, puzzling,' as Birkenhead put it in a speech at the Oxford Union before Mr Beck, the American Attorney General, at that time. As we understood it, America had come into the war reluctantly and, as we thought, discreditably late. Coming in, she had assumed for herself the direction of Allied policies. She had told us that we were fighting for democracy, which most Englishmen had not hitherto suspected, and that after the war we must establish an international organisation, a League of Nations, to make sure that there was never another war. These purposes were included in Wilson's Fourteen Points and we had accepted them. We had in particular accepted the League of Nations, an idea to which we were not opposed but about which we had considerable suspicions. But it was essentially an American idea, which America offered to—not to say pressed on—the rest of the world. Then to our great surprise the Americans, having forced this idea on us, themselves repudiated it.

Of course to those who understood a little more about American party politics, about the relations between Woodrow Wilson and the Republicans, about the constitutional authority of the Senate in treaty-making, the strength of minorities, Irish, German and others, these developments were not so wholly inexplicable, but few of us—certainly not I—knew much of such things. By 1922, at the time of my first visit to America, Wilson and the League of Nations had already been repudiated by the American electorate. Harding, of whom we knew little and certainly none of the scandals which have since become public knowledge, was President. Wilson was still alive but a total invalid. When we were in Washington, Edward Marjoribanks was offered the alternative of visiting George Washington's home or of visiting Woodrow Wilson. He chose Wilson; Wilson was told of his choice. 'Well, at least I am alive,' he said wrily.

Regret for American refusal to enter the League of Nations was one of our subjects for debate in this first little tour of the Colleges on the East coast. We obediently took the side of deploring American abstention. It seemed the reasonable side, but, though I argued the case with sincerity, I did not argue it with passion, for never at that time or for some years afterwards did it occur to me as a possibility that there would in my lifetime be another World War. It was a pity, I felt, that America had stayed out of the League of Nations, but it did not really matter.

At Harvard we debated against and were entertained by the man who is now Senator Cabot Lodge and who was then an undergraduate. His grandfather was the Senator who was the leader of the campaign against American entry and indeed against all policies submitted by Wilson. One always thinks of other countries as predominantly interested in foreign affairs and is surprised to find them more concerned, as they usually are, with domestic party politics. Other countries' party politics invariably seem slightly ridiculous, and we in England who had formed coalitions during the war were puzzled and slightly contemptuous of the American refusal to rise above party, and of the totally party elections which they fought, to enthrone a Republican Congress and to thwart a Democratic President just as what seemed to us the most important war in history was coming to an end. Cabot Lodge was a most cultured and courteous host but we were a little surprised at the seriousness with which he took American politics and at the frequency of his laudatory appeals to the authority of his grandfather, who, in so far as we had heard of him at all, we had not generally heard very favourably spoken of in the English press, which naturally enough did not give much praise to American isolationists. Eventually, Edward Marjoribanks was tired of this constant appeal to grandpapa and said, half in earnest, but perhaps not altogether happily, 'It is rather American to agree with one's grandfather.' Marjoribanks' mother was of an old Southern family from Tennessee and he had come up to our debates after visiting with them and was full of Southern enthusiasm against the 'Damn-Yankees', which I was not at the moment sophisticated enough either to appreciate or to share. I think that I would hardly have known that there was a Civil War and would certainly have known little about it.

Whatever the mixture of motives that had brought it out we were certainly surprised during that short visit at the vigour of isolationist opinion even on the East coast. We were assured—and I have no doubt rightly—that we would have found prejudice far stronger if we had penetrated into the Middle West.

Our other debates were mainly on Trade Union policy—the closed shop and the open shop. There again there were lessons to be learnt. In England by the end of the First War the Victorian battle of the Trade Unions was on the whole won. There were plenty of people in England who disliked Trade Unions—who thought that they prevented honest work—that they were tyrannical—that they kept wages too high and so on. There were pockets of labour into which Trade Unions had not yet made their way and employers who, with varying success, still contrived to fight against any Union membership in their factories. But in general Trade Unions, like it or not, had succeeded in establishing themselves in the great industries and capital had no alternative but to deal with them. The great showdown in 1926 was still in the future and as yet not much foreseen. We had been brought up in a vague belief that America was a more progressive country than England and in particular less class-ridden, and it was a surprise to discover how very much less developed and accepted was the Trade Union movement there than it was with us. It was the general habit at business-men's luncheons such as those of the Rotarians or the Lions for prosperous manufacturers to proclaim without hesitation that nothing would induce them to have Union agitators in their shops and to receive general agreement from fellow Babbits for such pronouncements. At Yale we debated against a pleasant, well-mannered, well-dressed young undergraduate. In the debate he spoke violently against Unions and when we talked to him afterwards at supper he explained that his father was the owner of a factory in the neighbourhood and reported a horrible tale of Union violence against his father—attempts to blow up the plant, attempts to murder his father and members of his family. It was, he explained, all due to foreigners from Eastern Europe. I have quite forgotten his name. I never saw him again and have no notion what happened to him. Naturally I have no means of knowing whether what he told me was accurate or whether, if accurate in fact, the fault was all on the one side. But the lesson that he taught me was very certainly true—one which I had up till then not at all appreciated but which has throughout all the years been most regularly confirmed—the lesson of the extraordinary prevalence of violence in action in American life, which at that date at any rate went hand in hand with an equally extraordinary conformity of opinion. My Yale friend attributed this violence to the immigrants—to foreigners who had recently come into the land. In that ascription he was of course repeating a very common prejudice of the day. The Americans who throughout the nineteenth century had always prided themselves on offering a ready home and refuge to the foreigners of every land had after the war suddenly turned most violently against their own tradition and imposed very strict quotas against immigration. They justified themselves by holding the foreigners responsible for all the lawlessness and violence in the country and my Yale friend in retailing the accusation was merely following fashion. How far the fashion was justified is a matter for debate. Certainly it must be confessed that when the battles of prohibition became overt, immigrants—and particularly Italian immigrants—were responsible for a large proportion of the murders and acts of violence. As certainly there was nowhere where violence was more rife than with the Ku-Klux-Klan in the Southern States, where the white population was almost entirely Anglo-Saxon and where immigration was smaller than anywhere else in the country. The frontier had left the American a tradition of violence which owed nothing to recent immigrants.

It was a different America to which I returned on my second trip, this time in the company of Douglas Woodruff and Malcolm Macdonald, in 1924. By then Harding was dead, the full catalogue of his crimes as yet hardly known. 'Washington—Lincoln—Harding' ran an absurd fulsome eulogy on him displayed in Congress. Coolidge was summoned to the Presidency. It is a common complaint against the American constitution that, so long as the elected President survives, the vice-Presidency amounts to so very little that only quite inconsiderable persons are willing to accept it—men who, if a vacancy occurs, are found wholly incapable of filling it. There have been many instances in American history where that has proved true. But between the two, Coolidge was a better man than Harding. Coolidge was by no means one of the great statesmen of the world, but America was certainly the gainer by his substitution for Harding. At least he was against sin, which was more than could be said for his predecessor.

It was the year of the presidential election, but the Republican party was still the predominant party, the country was prosperous and few doubted that Coolidge would be re-elected, as indeed he was. The Democrats had their difficulties in finding a candidate to oppose him. At the party convention there had been an interminable conflict, stretching out over ballot after ballot, between McAdoo, Woodrow Wilson's son-in-law, and New York's Governor and favourite son, Al Smith. Eventually the party pitched on a compromise candidate, John W. Davis, a Wall Street lawyer who had been Ambassador at St James'. We were taken to a big meeting in Madison Square Garden to hear Davis speak.

He made a reasonable enough speech—'less of the bunk about it than one would expect from a candidate,' a Republican host who had taken us pronounced. But it did not set the world on fire. The main interest to us and, I fancy, to many others was in Al Smith. After the Democratic Convention McAdoo, defeated, had gone off in a sulk to Europe and, doing so, destroyed his political career. Al Smith had on the other hand buckled to and campaigned for Davis, thus paving the way for his own candidacy four years later after Davis had been defeated. He spoke at this meeting. A Catholic and 'wet', he was a man of very localised experience. He had at that time never been out of America, though later he paid a visit to Rome and was received by the Pope. He had indeed hardly been outside the State of New York. He made no pretence to culture, but there was a vigour and personality and cheery wit about his oratory which made him in some ways to a foreign visitor seem more like a European than the average American politician, reading out his dreary oration from a carefully prepared typescript.

Douglas Woodruff and I went out to America a month before the debating started and put ourselves at the disposal of the English Speaking Union who had then—and perhaps have still—a plan for arranging hospitality for English student visitors. We asked to be accommodated with hosts in the Southern States since none of our debates were to take place in that part of the country. We went down first to the University of Virginia to recapture the spirit of Thomas Jefferson and then to most charming and courteous hosts in Savannah and Louisville. The charm of our hosts led us perhaps into a blunder. I too easily fell into thinking that the culture of my hosts was a culture which was possessed by all the inhabitants of the Southern States and thought of them as a land inhabited by generous aristocrats. They told me how happy the negroes were under the arrangement of society as it then existed. My host at Savannah told me that his confidence in his negro chauffeur was total and that he would have no hesitation in entrusting to him the key of his whiskey cupboard, knowing that the chauffeur would never abuse such a trust. As I had happened to see the chauffeur the day before helping himself from the cupboard I was a little sceptical. Nevertheless I do not greatly blame myself for having believed that the Southern whites had succeeded in solving the negro problem and in establishing a relationship which was satisfactory to both sides and likely to survive.

I do not suppose that black and other coloured people, whether in America or in the British Empire, ever particularly liked white men, whatever the whites may have persuaded themselves. 'I'se no use for a black man what will eat with a white man what will let him,' was the comment of an Alabama negro on Booker Washington's visit to Theodore Roosevelt for lunch at the White House. But ever since, I suppose, the defeat of the Indian Mutiny, the whites had a prestige of victory. If there was any conflict between white and coloured, the victory of the white appeared inevitable, and therefore the coloured thought that revolt was futile and that they had no alternative but to make what terms they could with their masters. The cinema probably dealt the first blow to that prestige. On the screen, the coloureds for the first time were given a picture of the utter futility of their masters' lives. The work that the cinemas had begun was completed by Singapore. Singapore and the Japanese overrunning of south-east Asia taught them that the white man was not even inevitably victorious. King Alfonso of Spain visited the United States shortly before his abdication. Wherever he went he asked the people, 'What are you going to do about your colour problem?' but he was, he said, quite unable to discover anyone who thought that there was a colour problem. The white man's dominance had always been to a large extent a dominance of bluff, or prestige. He had not the strength to rule the non-European majority by force. He could only dominate so long as his dominance was accepted. After Singapore it was inevitable in the British Empire and in the United States alike and everywhere else for the white man to make terms with racialism, and it was equally inevitable that the black man should no longer be content to accept as his standards the standards of the white man. Before Singapore he had no ambition but to ape the white man. I remember after the war visiting in Kenya a Kikuyu school. The boys were all engaged in writing an essay. The subject was, I was told, the radio. Out of curiosity I looked at what the boy in the desk in the front row was writing. He had written, 'And he, like a white man, did twist the knob solely for refreshment.' Unselective listening was to him a contemptible activity in which only a white man would indulge. The writer had risen above it.

The America of 1924 was, as I say, a different place from the America of 1922. By 1924 the battle against internationalism had been won. The Republicans had once again re-established themselves as the dominant party and the master of the country. They held all the important posts and Republicanism meant a final repudiation of all projects for international involvement, a firm restriction on immigration, high tariffs, opposition to the Trade Unions, and prohibition—especially prohibition. To English opinion—and indeed to the opinion of European men in general—the notion of compulsory national teetotalism was so strange that one could not believe that it was generally popular. Drink played so integral a part in the European literature and the European way of life that we could not imagine a civilisation that had wholly banished it, and therefore it was natural to most people in England to argue from a few stories which they heard about bootleggers and illegal drinking that the experiment was generally repudiated and was indeed something of a farce. It had got passed, we were told, in a moment of national war-time hysteria but it could not work. In 1922 the experiment was still too novel to be much debated. By 1924 it was the nation's main point of argument and it was one of the topics for our debates. We debated it right across the country from college to college and we were left in no doubt from the votes that were taken at the close of the debates that at that time prohibition was supported by the great majority of American opinion. It was a more actual problem to us than the League of Nations because in England the Liberal party was still the party of what was called Temperance, advocating Local Option as its drink policy and with a little encouragement quite prepared to come out in favour of prohibition—'that great moral experiment', as it was the fashion of Liberal oratory to call it. It did not seem impossible that the cause of prohibition might be destined to become the fashion of the century across the world. The size of the votes at the colleges in favour of prohibition may of course to some extent have been caused by our own insufficiencies and the irresponsibility of our debating manners—to some extent by a possible ambition to support 'our own boys'. But there was no doubt of public support for the experiment. Some greeted it as an unqualified success and attributed entirely to prohibition the nation's great material prosperity. We were told of the number of ice-boxes, washing machines and motor cars which the American people were able to produce as the result of saving money that might otherwise have been spent on liquor and were assured that 'these are the things that count'. Others admitted the difficulties that enforcement had brought with it. The wars of the bootleggers had not yet assumed the appalling dimensions that they were to attain later in the decade but they were already sufficient to give re-sponsible citizens serious concern. But the general feeling was that, though a problem and evil, these difficulties would prove to be no more than a passing evil. The evil could and would be conquered in time. It might be difficult to break the old of their drinking habits, but a new and cleaner generation would grow up which had never used liquor and which would never want to use it. Any attempt at praising drink as a good thing even in moderation was dismissed as an absurd joke and it was taken for granted that the maker of it could not be serious. That drink might be succeeded by drugs was never suspected.

Now a Republican America was also a W.A.S.P.—that is to say, an Anglo-Saxon Protestant America—though I do not think that the phrase W.A.S.P. had at that time been invented. The Anglo-Saxon Protestants thought of themselves as the original, native inhabitants of the country. The immigrants were their inferiors and the W.A.S.P.s must defend their culture against the menace of the immigrants. Such a city as Boston, originally the home of indubitably Protestant Pilgrim Fathers, had been overrun by Catholic Irish. The American way of life was in danger. At the time of Independence the Catholic population of the United States was small—a few parishes down in Maryland. With the Louisiana Purchase a few Frenchmen from New Orleans were added. The nation was built up upon a proclamation of religious freedom. Catholics along with others were allowed the vote and every post in the land was nominally open to them. But, as the career of Al Smith showed, as late as the 1920's it was in practice not possible for a Catholic to be elected President. With the American need for labour—particularly on the railroads—and with troubles in their home countries, immigrants poured in during the nineteenth century—the Irish first and, after them, Germans, Poles, Hungarians, Italians. They got jobs but naturally only the worst jobs. Catholicism was the religion of the poor and the un-educated.

These immigrants were on the whole anti-British and had opposed the American intervention in the war. Why should they not be anti-British? They were either Irish or they were immigrants from Continental countries which had for the most part fought against the British in the war but which in any event had bequeathed to them no tradition of the English way of life or of the British Constitution. Of all Europeans the French contribution in America's population was the smallest. The Anglo-Saxon Protestants were on the whole pro- British but did not like to have their British sympathies taken for granted. They were our generous hosts.

'We are Americans first,' a young man sensibly said to me, but then he added, 'If we have to look to any foreigners we much prefer you to any others.'

'Do the Catholics think like that?' I asked.

'Oh! the Catholics,' he said, as he might say 'the animals', 'they're different.' 'Of course we like England,' he continued, 'we have inherited traditions from England. But that does not mean that we like the British

Empire. We revolted against British Imperialism and we can't see why the Canadians and Australians don't revolt against it now. We would think it right if they claimed their own freedom.' I found that he thought that the British really owned and governed Canada and Australia.

At the time of my first visit to America in 1922 I was not yet a Catholic and had not much interest in ecclesiastical developments. I do not think that I attended any church during my visit—my only involvement of such a sort was of a very different nature. One day in the previous summer term at Balliol, Jim Collis, my fellow collegian, had come to me and to a number of others to tell us that in his rooms that evening he would present to such as would attend a very remarkable man. This man had changed innumerable lives and would be likely to change many more in the future. Jim Collis was proposing to launch him on Oxford. We were invited.

We were, most of us, ribald agnostics and in that mood accepted the invitations, promising ourselves a good laugh. We were not altogether disappointed. This mysterious prophet, Frank Buchman—for so he was —was an india-rubber-faced little man. A score or so of hearers were gathered to meet him, sprawled around on sofas or on the floor in Oxford fashion, déshabille in dress and spilling our cigarette ash all over Jim Collis' carpet. Buchman gave us his message. He told us how he was in contact with God—how every morning he lay down on the floor and received the Divine instructions on how he could best serve Him during the day. He wrote down these messages on a piece of paper. What did he do then? we asked. Did he just obey blindly or did he exercise his own judgement on whether the advice was wise or unwise— on whether, as he put it, the messages really came from God or from another source? He tested them before acting. In what way then were these so-called Divine messages different from any other random ideas that might come into any secular head? He had, to our minds, no very clear answer. He did not give us the impression of being a great thinker —certainly not in any academic sense in which we at Balliol were perhaps excessively apt to evaluate intellectual excellence. Yet he seemed a decent and friendly enough man, doubtless sincere and, through what- ever intellectual processes, probably on the whole acting for good. Some of our questions were cheeky and silly. 'What is God's handwriting like?' we asked. He answered with good-humoured frankness, 'A big round writing.' We liked him, but what I did not in the least feel either then or at any subsequent time was any sense of a mysterious, mesmeric, charismatic influence in him. However we left on friendly terms and a few months afterwards when I was in New York I received from him a telegram which announced, 'Silas K. Jerome, prominent financier and cousin of Winston Churchill, invites you to dine at the Yale Club on the night of' etc. I went along. There was a large company in a private room, half guests and half hosts. We had an excellent dinner, of course with no wine. For the Buchmanites, quite apart from prohibition laws, were always strict teetotallers. I sat next to Mr Jerome. He talked pleasantly of experiences in Europe and wished that he were coming back with me to England in a few days' time. Then when dinner was finished he led me aside and said to me, 'Who was the greatest salesman who ever lived?' I could not guess what he was talking about. But the answer was of course, 'Jesus Christ, because He delivered the goods.' 'What goods?' I asked in, I think, justified bewilderment.

I never became a Buchmanite and have never visited Caux. A good deal of their vocabulary was to me unattractive and vulgar. I sympathised with Alan Herbert's campaign some years later against what seemed to me their impudence in claiming for themselves the name of the Oxford Group. Frank Buchman came in his day to say a number of very silly things about Hitler—but he was not the only man who did that. They had no theology and no philosophy. They never attempted to analyse what they meant by God. 'Who made you?' asked a catechist of a young American boy who had fallen under their influence.'Why, Gawd of course,' he answered. 'Do they teach you to answer like that in America?' he was asked. 'No,' he replied, 'we just take it for granted.' And there was a naïve simplicity in their advocacy of the three 'absolutes'. Absolute love was perhaps a lesson to be preached. The practice of it was not so simple. Truthfulness was doubtless in general a virtue but was absolute truthfulness? Was it really right to tell the truth and the whole truth absolutely and in all circumstances? Malcolm Muggeridge's son, a Plymouth Brother, was working on the western side of the Iron Curtain in Berlin. Some refugees who had escaped from the east and across the Wall came under his notice. He discovered that in order to outwit the East German guards they had told them some untruths. He said that they ought to go back and confess their deception. Was this common sense? And was it Christianity?

Evelyn Waugh's first marriage was not a success. After very great difficulties he succeeded in obtaining both a secular divorce and an ecclesiastical annulment. He was just about to set out on his second and very happy, much-desired marriage when the gentleman who had decamped with his first wife ran into Dr Buchman and was changed.

Evelyn received from him a postcard saying, 'Dear Evelyn, I have done you a great wrong,' and he was terrified that at this highly inconvenient moment the first wife would be decanted again on his doorstep.

I did not much care for Frank Buchman's fondness for dropping the names of famous acquaintances, for the comfortable living of many of the Groupers and for a habit of which hosts had often reason to complain of: their failure to keep commitments with the casual excuse that it was the Lord's will that they should not do so. Nevertheless with all their faults I am sure that on balance they did more good than harm, as Professor McTaggart said of God—a qualification which, as Dean Inge tartly commented, would hardly, except under post-war conditions, obtain engagement for an under-housemaid.

As I say, at my first visit to America in 1922 I had no special Catholic interests. At my second visit in 1924 I was fresh from my reception and of course intensely interested in observing the state of American Catholicism. My hosts, I must say, gave me no great facilities for obtaining it. Though two out of the three of us—Douglas Woodruff and myself— were Catholics, the Carnegie Foundation who arranged our itinerary sent us to some fifty Colleges but not to a single Catholic one. This was doubtless not out of conscious prejudice or hostility. They doubtless did not know that two of us would be Catholics, but, if they had reflected on the matter, would have taken it for granted that it would not be so. If they had been challenged why they did not send us to Catholic Colleges, they would have replied that there was no Catholic College of sufficient standing. And indeed it was true that at the time Catholic education was certainly the inferior of that at other places. The reason was simple enough. The Catholic body consisting almost entirely of immigrants was still very much below the average of the nation in wealth and education. The increase in their numbers merely strengthened the determination of the leading Protestants—of the W.A.S.P.s—to keep power in their own hands and to keep the ethos of the nation Protestant. The attempt of Governor Smith to obtain the nomination for the Democratic candidacy in the 1924 election had shown the belief that the nation was not willing at any price to have a Catholic President, and his overwhelming defeat when he did run as a candidate in 1928 showed that the belief was as yet correct. He could not even hold a number of the believedly solid Democratic states in the South, and in the South the Ku-Klux-Klan, which was still powerful, had largely turned from baiting negroes to baiting Catholics—and Jews—and had apparently increased its popularity by doing so. Alarmed at the influx of immigrants, the

Americans, in spite of their tradition of offering hospitality to all who came as refugees to their shores, reversed their policy and introduced strict controls on immigration which were very deliberately designed to be especially deterrent to Catholic immigrants.

I had up till then never at all come across Catholicism except in its English attire. I had at that time only spent a couple of days in Ireland. I did not at all take in how uniquely untypical of Catholicism English Catholicism was, and it was an education to see the totally different American Catholicism. I have spoken of the constitution of the American Catholic body and of the confident conviction of the Protestant Establishment that Catholics should indeed be tolerated but should unhesitatingly be treated as inferior and second-class citizens. The Archbishop of Cincinatti city told me how he had once patted a little negro child on the head and had then asked him, making conversation, 'Are you a Catholic, my son?'

'No,' the boy had answered, 'I'se a nigger and a bastard. That's bad enough.'

Now the Americans were, and indeed are, much greater church-goers than the English. The common complaint about empty churches is often raised in England with an assumption that it is a world-wide disease. It is by no means so. It is an English and possibly a Scandinavian disease. The Americans went to church. They also were naturally conformist to what to an Englishman was a strange extent. Like the debaters from Bates, they did not say 'I think', but 'Our American point of view is', and their ambition seemed to be to discover what was the American point of view and to repeat it. A much greater proportion of the American youth in America than of English youth in England, then as today, went to College, as it is called, and this meant that, while a few of the American Universities were excellent, the general standard of many of them seemed hardly more than that of an English school. Those who wanted to get a serious education had to take post-graduate courses. Many of the students lived in hostels known as fraternities with names curiously derived from Greek initials such as Phi Beta Kappa—the more curious since Greek was hardly studied among them. These fraternities have now fallen into some disfavour and have in most Colleges been abolished.

The students wished not to be caught out in eccentricity and their ambition of conformity was as evident in American religion as in secular matters. It was evident alike among the Protestants as among the Catholics. It was as evident among the riot of fancy religions in California where there was an abundance of different names of various sects who all in fact professed the same ethical codes. Among the Protestants, as was to be revealed a year or two later in the anti-evolution trials at Dayton in Tennessee, fundamentalism was still strong and the Bible belt still broad. The various Protestant churches resorted frequently to trials for heresy. The Catholics too had had an Irish rigidity. They were obedient. They went to Mass on Sunday. They ate fish on Friday and— what was more remarkable—they rigidly obeyed the Index and thought themselves in sin if they read any book that the Index had forbidden. I had never in England come across any priest who seriously expected obedience to the Index.

Now, church-going as the nation at large was, there was of course a vigorous minority among the intellectuals, or those who called themselves intellectuals, who vigorously denounced church-going and repudiated religion. These secularists had been opposed both to the Protestants and to the Catholics, but in the early years of the century had tended to think the Catholics the worse because more bigoted and more enslaved to authority than the Protestants. Now the secularists, opposed to merely fashionable opinion, were of course also opposed to prohibition. Prohibition was roundly denounced week after week in such a paper as Mencken's *American Mercury*, and its champions guyed as the Booboiserie. But of course among the religious, Protestant opinion was overwhelmingly in favour of prohibition. It was to them a crusading cause. The Catholics, recent immigrants from wine-drinking countries, were opposed to it. A result of the prohibition controversy was then to make the secularists think a little more kindly of the Catholics. For instance in Chicago we made the friendship of Clarence Darrow, a man whose name at that time was famous, though I dare say that he is hardly remembered today, at least among English readers. Clarence Darrow was one of the leading American criminal lawyers of the day. He had just made himself famous by the defence of two young undergraduates of millionaire families, Loeb and Leopold, who had perpetrated a peculiarly hateful murder for purely sadistic reasons of a school-fellow called Bobby Frank. Darrow defended them by the plea that they were not responsible for their actions and succeeded in saving them from the electric chair and obtaining for them a sentence of life imprisonment. 'They killed him,' said Darrow, 'as they might have killed a spider or a fly, for the experience.' He expressed the hope and belief that psychiatric treatment might turn them into good citizens. In the event Loeb was in a few years murdered by his fellow prisoners but treatment appeared to be successful with Leopold. A year or two later Darrow was again in the headlines for his defence of a young school-master of the name of Scopes who was prosecuted in Dayton, for teaching in the public schools the evolutionary theories of Charles Darwin. Darrow was a kind and generous man, untidy in dress and a friend of bounteous living. He was a strong enemy of all forms of religion, taking it for granted that religion was a reactionary force. A pleasant young atheist from the University of Chicago took us to see him and afterwards we went together to hear him give a lecture in a Jewish synagogue. Our friend pointed with glee to an inscription which proclaimed the glory of God, taking it for granted that we would join him in ribald laughter. He asked Darrow about his view on Catholics and Protestants. 'Well it was the Protestants who hit at me the most,' said Darrow. Darrow's own views on religion were strangely ill-informed. Nothing could dissuade him from the belief that the most important of beliefs to all religious people was their belief in the literal truth of the first chapters of Genesis and of all the Old Testament miracles. He went on asking William Jennings Bryan, his opponent in the Dayton trial, whether he believed in the story of Jonah and thought that Bryan's beliefs were sufficiently exploded when he stated dogmatic-ally and quite untruly that 'all educated people' rejected them. He struck me as an intelligent man who had never met very many other intelligent men. He denounced as cruelty all theories which taught that a man was in any way responsible for his actions. This crusading determinism landed him obviously in great difficulties. If man was not responsible for his actions, then clearly men who believed in God were not responsible for their belief in God, and it was foolish of him and unjust to abuse them for their faith. We came across an example of this dilemma in him during the excellent dinner which he gave us. He asked us what part of the country we had liked best. We replied, in accordance with the prejudices, probably mistaken, which I have already described, the South. As a progessive he was surprised at such an answer, as indeed he might well be. At a time when such opinions were not as common as they are today he was alive to the evils of racialism, but, alive to them with one part of his mind, the determinist side of him told him that they were inevitable. 'Of course I dislike their policy to the blacks,' he said. 'But then they can't help that. It's the way they're made.' His general view of the human race was, 'Think of them as animals and they ain't so bad.'

Sweeping generalisations about the life of a whole continent are obviously unsatisfactory, but I do not think that it would be unfair to say that American Catholicism was, like Irish Catholicism, lacking in poetry and the feeling of mystery. It was too much a matter of propositions. They used to tell me in those days that the American character did not take naturally to the contemplative life. They did not become Carthusians and preferred Jesuits to Benedictines. This charge, largely true in the 1920's, was refuted in the next decade when, with Thomas Merton as its best-known figure, the house of Gethsemane in Kentucky began to flourish. The very hustle of American life perhaps tempted some to resort to contemplation in reaction from it. But, I am told, after a brief period of fashion, like other religious houses it has now its difficulty of numbers.

Tolerance always brings its own problems. 'There are few ways,' said Doctor Johnson, 'in which a man can be more innocently employed than in getting money.' But Charles Wesley more wisely saw that, if his disciples lived ascetic and hard-working lives, the inevitable result would be that they would become rich and then the whole business of making them Christians would have to be done all over again. So, when all the grievances of the Church are satisfied, vocations always dwindle. It is today, I am told, only in Hungary and Poland that vocations are abundant. Savage persecution is doubtless more than weak human nature can take. But a moderate, steady discrimination against it seems to be almost necessary for the Church's health. We should always welcome mildly anti-Catholic governments so long as they are mild. How much better the Church did in Italy under the Masonic regime of the years before Mussolini than it has done since the war under the Christian Democrats! Rome is today a missionary city, and its priests have to be imported from North Italy, which suffered under the Piedmontese anti-clerical laws. Nevertheless the Catholics in America, isolated as they might be from the general life around them, had been in some ways infected by the ambient air. The Gospel of Work, the belief that a man is only in grace if he is constantly active, makes some sense in a simple society which requires for its survival the energies of every able-bodied person. Few are they who do not rot in idleness if they have not some activity to occupy them, and perhaps fewer among Americans than among other people. Yet the Gospel if we seek for it a theological origin is rather Calvinist than Catholic. Still the Catholics had inherited a bit of it. A sophisticated society easily transforms the Gospel of Work into the Gospel of Wealth. Great wealth is, in the eyes of those who accept this Gospel, the mark of God's blessing, and this in its theology is clearly Jewish rather than Catholic or Christian. The early American Catholics were fortunate in not being rich. In the course of time a few had raised themselves to great affluence and they accepted this dangerous gift without trembling or without any great awareness of its challenge to the Gospel.

As for my own religion at that time it was enthusiastic but in retrospect strangely insufficient. I do not complain of that. I remember Maurice Baring once saying, 'The Catholic Church can only be understood from within.' I fancy that every convert always joins it for reasons that are to some extent insufficient—one in one way and one in another. My own insufficiency was that I saw the Church far too much as an authority. I obeyed its regulations. I would not have dreamed of missing Mass on Sunday or of eating meat on a Friday. I was careful to obtain rulings from priests, and to obey them, against in any way taking part in non-Catholic worship or prayers and would cheerfully risk discourtesy sooner than disobey a rule. I defended without qualification the rules against birth control or for the preference of the child before the mother in difficult cases of child-bearing. In my celibate state these rulings were of course purely academic, but, perhaps for that reason, I defended them unquestioningly. But the Church was to me very much an organisation and I looked to it much too much as an author of regulations. Unlike most enthusiastic converts, in that respect more reasonable and sensible than I, I did not at once eagerly seize the full privilege of its sacramental life. I went to Mass because the Church told me to go to Mass but from the first it was my habit to go to a late mid-morning Mass and not to communion. There was no compulsion about going to communion except perhaps at Easter. The Church only advocated it and I was concerned only to obey ordered rules. I went to confession from time to time. I disliked confessing my sins but was in no doubt that it did me good to do so. But I thought of the confession as an exercise, as I might have thought of confession to a psychiatrist, valuable for its medicinal effect, much more than I thought of the grace of absolution.

II

AUSTRALIA

Australia I found a more interesting country than New Zealand and more interesting again today than it was at my first visit. In 1925 there was no great movement in Australian art except Norman Lindsay's not very exciting vitalism. At the end of the 1920's there came the great outburst of Australian painting, particularly in Melbourne, which makes it today such a fascinating country. In the earlier years of the century the only non-English-speaking immigrants, apart from a few Chinese, in the very early years had been the Germans who came to work in the vineyards, mostly in South Australia, in the middle of the nineteenth century. In Australia as in the United States there was a sundering cleavage between Protestant and Catholics. The Catholics were overwhelmingly Irish—more so even than in the United States. The foundation of the Catholic population had been Irish convicts, filled therefore with a hatred of British rule even more violent than that of the Irish at home. Some years later I visited the convict museum at Fort Arthur outside Hobart in Tasmania and saw the record of offences for which prisoners had been transported. It was a terrifying and shaming experience. The great majority were young men, most often in their teens, who had been transported for the most trivial offences of petty theft, often the theft of some small article of food by boys who were probably starving. The bitterness of these men against British rule was not surprising. Thus, if for a slightly different reason, the Catholics in Australia, as in the United States, were for the most part poor and poorly educated. Since the time of which I am speaking and after the Second World War there has been a large influx of immigrants—many of them Catholics—from the countries of the European Continent—Dutch, Hungarian, Italian and Jugoslav—who have in many ways greatly enriched the country's culture. Unlike the Catholics in America, the Catholics of Australia, though poor and on the whole ill-educated and a minority, were able from the first establishment of the Commonwealth to obtain for themselves a reasonable share of the nation's political posts. More important, the immigrants were able to teach their fellow countrymen to drink wine and to some extent to wean them from the habit of the consumption of unending cups of tea. They have built up an excellent production of Australian wine, even if they have not yet learnt how to, or do not wholly bother to, bottle it so that it can travel successfully overseas. There is a healthy rivalry between the different vineyards. One of my first experiences in Australia was to be earnestly adjured by a waiter in a Sydney restaurant always to buy my wine from the Italians in the Hunter Valley rather than from the Germans in the Barosa Valley of South Australia.

The Catholic population in the early 1920's was as I say overwhelmingly Irish. This had the curious consequence that, though Ireland and Australia were the two countries in the world geographically most distant from one another, Australian politics were to a large extent fought out on Irish issues. John and Willy Redmond both took their wives from Australia. The Irish troubles and the Black and Tans were but a few years behind us and a number of Australian Catholics had relatives in Ireland who had played a part in the troubles. We were given much kindness by a young, as he was then, journalist in Sydney of the name of Barry, a cousin of Kevin Barry, whose execution had aroused such bitter feelings during the so-called 'cross times'. The Catholics, since they were of the working class, almost all belonged to the Labour party. There was, I think, only one well-to-do Catholic family in New South Wales—the Hughes—but, though all the Catholics were Labour, it by no means followed that all Labour men were Catholics. The result of the conscription controversy was that a number of Labour's non-Catholic members had supported conscription and left the party with Hughes, the war-time non-Catholic erstwhile Labour Prime Minister. The Irish were unanimously opposed to conscription and remained in the party. Hughes had to leave and form a National party in coalition with the Liberals. The Catholic proportion of the Labour party which before the war had been about a quarter of the party jumped up after it to almost a half. But the predominant machinery of the Labour party remained in secularist hands and was anti-Catholic. As early as the 1920's, many Catholics predicted to us that before long there would inevitably be a breach between the Catholics and the anti-religious elements in the Labour party, as of course happened in our own day, when Mr Santa Maria and the Democratic Labour party broke with the regular machine, and were strong enough, by withholding their votes, to put the Liberal party into power.

Mr Santa Maria is a remarkable man who, himself refusing to enter Parliament or to hold any office, has played an outstanding part in organising the opposition to the regular Labour party and by splitting the vote has been very largely responsible for its defeat. A mild and cultured lawyer who has never visited Europe, he issues his instructions on how his supporters should vote in a manner that is a little reminiscent of Parnell, if not of more sinister masters. His strength is that he barred the road to power of a near-Communist party. The figure cut by Dr Evatt over the Petrov case can leave no one in any doubt of the reality of the danger. His weakness is that he can only rule by merely holding a balance of power and has no hope of serious representation, still less of a majority for himself and his party. Democratic Labour candidates cannot be elected themselves. All that their members can do is to transfer their votes to Liberal candidates and thus procure their election in seats that

might otherwise go to official Labour. It may be very proper on a particular occasion for a group to defeat a party by withdrawing its support
from it; but that surely should not be a general and continuing policy.
In general, power should be wielded by majorities, not by holders of a
balance, and in general those who manage a party should be members of
the legislator and not workers behind the scenes.

The leading figure in Australian Catholic life in the 1920's was, as he
was to continue to be for another forty years, the most remarkable
Archbishop Mannix. I was to call on him at his country house at Portsea
down the coast from Melbourne in 1964, a day before his ninety-ninth
birthday. My host took me down to luncheon in the hotel across the
road. There were, as we went in, four men wearing open shirts, smoking
cigars, drinking whisky and watching a horse race on the television.
They greeted my host. 'How are yer, Bob?' He responded and introduced me. We went on together into the dining room. I asked who these
men might be. I had imagined from their demeanour and habits that they
were perhaps some bodyguard whose duty it was to protect a Democratic Labour politician. 'Oh, just four priests,' he said.

The Archbishop was seated on a garden chair reading without
spectacles. He was undoubtedly one of the leading figures in the Catholic
Church during his lifetime, even if owing to his contempt for curial
politics he never played the direct part in Roman affairs that one would
have expected. He had two careers about equal to one another in length.
Up till the age of forty-five he worked in Ireland where he was Rector of
Maynooth and, as I have always heard tell, caused George Moore to
leave the Catholic Church by receiving Edward VII at Maynooth. Then
shortly before the First World War he was sent out as auxiliary bishop
to Melbourne, arriving there convinced that he had only a year or two
to live. He lived for over fifty more years and survived the auxiliary
appointed to relieve him. Soon after his arrival he had made himself into
one of the most prominent figures in Australian life through his intervention in the conscription controversy. It is the teaching alike of
common sense and of the Catholic Church that conscription is of itself
a great evil. The great Benedict XV had denounced it as such when it
was adopted by all the countries of the European Continent. It was,
argued the Pope, only justified in the extreme case that a country's existence was in danger and a conscript army was the only way by which it
could be defended. It would be hard to imagine any circumstances to
which that test was less valid than that of Australia in the First World
War, 'a great trade war', as Mannix called it. In that war, it will be

remembered, the Japanese were on our side. There was no conceivable threat of any kind to Australia. Indeed so little at that time was Australia conscious of a yellow peril that in 1912 the South Australian Government had invited the Japanese Government to populate the Northern Territories for which South Australia was then responsible. The Japanese Prime Minister had replied that Japan had enough problems without taking on this further commitment. If Australians out of nostalgic feelings or out of personal affiliations voluntarily chose to go and fight in a British war there was no reason why they should not do so. But to compel men to fight in such a war was surely a very wicked project. Therefore it was most reasonable for Australians to oppose Billy Hughes' plan to impose conscription on the country and Mannix won enormous support (and enormous hostility) for the dominant part which he played in the controversy. He received adulation far beyond the boundaries of his own communion. I remember a tough old digger who drank with us as we sailed up from Brisbane to Christmas Island, who used to say, 'I've no use for God, but if that man were to cross the road I'd kneel down and kiss the ground he trod on.' He was victorious in his controversy. His brilliant oratory saved the country from conscription and drove Mr Hughes from office. His standpoint was on its own merits most defensible. Whether it was wise for a cleric, and in particular a cleric who was then but a recent arrival in the country, to take so prominent a part in a political controversy was more doubtful. The Archbishop was always most careful, whenever he spoke on an anti-conscription platform, to explain that he spoke as a citizen and not as an ecclesiastical authority, but nevertheless his very success undoubtedly confirmed the belief of many Australian Protestants that the Catholic Church would exercise political domination if ever it was given the chance to do so.

The Second World War was alike to Mannix and to all Australians a very different affair. Then, as the Japanese swarmed over Malaysia and Indonesia, Australia was very directly menaced. No one could be certain that, having conquered Indonesia, they would not go on to invade Queensland, and indeed it is not to this day quite clear why they did not do so, any more than it is quite clear why Hitler did not invade England after Dunkirk. Nor is it at all clear how the Australians would have confronted them had they done so. Mannix was in favour of World War Two.

Almost immediately after the First War the Sinn Fein troubles broke out and Mannix from his Australian distance threw himself vigorously into that battle, denouncing the Black and Tans and the English refusal to grant the right of self-determination to Ireland. He became a figure of the first prominence in the press of every country of the Empire, the more so when the British Government refused to allow him to land in Ireland to visit his mother and in a scene which Mannix turned to brilliant ridicule had him taken off the boat by a destroyer at Cobh, or Queenstown as it was then called. Mannix had a great gift for comedy which he turned good-humouredly and unsparingly on all who crossed his path, whether they were Government officials or fellow ecclesiastics. 'One of the greatest victories of the British Navy,' he said of his arrest, 'and won without a single life lost.' He was never personally unfriendly to English people for all his controversies with the British Government. 'Charming people,' I remember him saying as he cut the beef at his table. 'I differ from them politically, but charming people.' He always got a good deal of fun out of mimicking and teasing his fellow Archbishop of his early days, Archbishop Kelly of Sydney, and indeed he was never on very good terms with the world of Sydney. With Cardinal Gilroy, the Archbishop of recent years, his relations were not very good. Archbishop Mannix vigorously supported in Victoria the anti-Communist Democratic Labour party which had broken with the regular party for its alleged Communist sympathies. In New South Wales Cardinal Gilroy opposed the Democratic Labour party and threw his influence behind the regular Labour party. It was said that Rome was so nervous of Archbishop Mannix' political activities that the Australian Cardinalate was given to Cardinal Gilroy rather than to him. Cardinal Gilroy was the most charming of men but was not as colourful a character as his brother of Melbourne nor as intellectually vigorous—a natural Conservative, so conservative as to support the Labour party. I was in Australia at the time that the Vatican Council was meeting. The Queen and the Duke of Edinburgh were also visiting Australia at that time. Cardinal Gilroy told me with delight how the Queen asked him whether as a result of the Council there might not be great changes in the liturgy of the Church. When he said that there might be, the Duke interrupted with, 'Don't you change anything. Don't let them change anything. You stick to what you've got.' Both Mannix and Gilroy were teetotallers—a rare achievement among Australian Catholics. In Brisbane the Archbishop was then the nonagenarian and knighted Archbishop Duhig, the oldest consecrated bishop in the Church, who prided himself on his Greek scholarship—an achievement even rarer among Australian Catholics.

Mannix was at bitter odds with the Italian Apostolic delegate, Archbishop Pannico. Up till recently it had been the general custom to fill Archiepiscopal ecclesiastical posts by importees from Ireland. At last it was found possible to appoint a native Australian to the Archbishopric of Adelaide. A celebration luncheon was held at his consecration and at that luncheon the Apostolic Delegate spoke and with an obvious sideswipe at Archbishop Mannix said how joyful a day it was when it was at last possible to appoint a native Australian to an Australian see rather than an importee. Archbishop Mannix, when it came to his turn to reply, agreed that it was indeed a joyful day when Australia could at last supply her own archbishops, but that he hoped that one day they might see the even more joyful day when Australia could supply her own Apostolic Delegates. A new Anglican Archbishop had recently arrived in Melbourne and there had been correspondence between their two chancelleries as to which of the two Archbishops should pay the first courtesy call on the other. Eventually the Anglican wrote to Mannix a letter of apology, saying that he had not understood that Mannix was ninety-nine years old and a Jesuit and therefore prevented from paying visits. Of course he would call on the Catholic Archbishop. 'Wherein,' said Mannix, in recounting the story, 'he was guilty of two errors—first in imagining that I was a Jesuit, and second in imagining that if I had been a Jesuit I would not have gone out to dinner.' The attitude of Australian Catholics towards bishops was ambivalent. The bishops—more particularly those of the older generation who had come from Ireland—tended to claim an Irish obedience to their authority. But Australians do not accept easily authoritarian claims. They are natural anarchists. The bishops had never had sufficient authority for outspoken rebellion against them to be necessary. But they were regarded by the faithful as something in the nature of figures of fun, to be gently laughed at. I remember some years later in answering questions after a public meeting, saying about the doctrine of hell that there was after all only one man of whom the Church gave us any sort of authority to say that he was in hell, and he was a bishop. The journalists all sharpened their pencils in eager attention. 'Who could that be?' they asked. 'Was it the Bishop of Ballarat?' They were most disappointed when I confessed to them that it was only Judas Iscariot whom I had in mind—a much less probable and exciting candidate to their way of thinking.

During my first visit, one or two friends suggested that I ought to settle down in Australia. Neither I nor they took the suggestion seriously and I therefore never got around to discovering what sort of job might have been available for me there. I am too old to uproot myself now, but I am not quite sure that I would not have been wise to have accepted the invitation half a century ago. It is only fair to confess that both on this and on my second visit I was lucky enough to be entertained by exceptionally pleasant and cultured hosts. I might easily have fallen—I am well aware—into cruder company. Yet it always seems to me extraordinary that everybody does not emigrate to Australia. Life there seems to me very much happier than elsewhere—certainly happier than it is at the moment in England. Its only serious defect is in its public drinking habits. The Australian pub, called a hotel, is the most sordid in the world. Happily they have by now changed the old rule by which it used to be closed at six o'clock, and men on their return from work would rush in and make it their business to drink themselves drunk in as few minutes as possible. There is more liberty now than there was forty years ago, and Sunday in Australia, though not a day of great joy, is at any rate not as dreary as Sunday in New Zealand. Yet the hotels are still fairly sordid.

It is a common enough comment that Australia is a country where population is distributed in the most extraordinary fashion, the greater part of it all concentrated in five capital cities, four of them huddled into the south-east corner of the Continent. People often compare Australians to Americans, but to my mind there is a great difference between the two countries. Australian life is a great deal more easy-going. The Australians are very careless about their future. Their life on an enormous and sparsely inhabited Continent, with Asia and its teeming millions so close at hand and admittance of Asiatics restricted, is a constant challenge. I found Australians strangely ready to admit that the country could not last, but also strangely ready to say that it did not much matter whether it lasted or not. An adventist group, announcing that 'millions now living will never die', took the Sydney cricket ground for the advertised day of the world's end. They easily sold it out, but when the day came had to announce that the 'Last Judgement' had been 'unavoidably postponed'. There were considerable demands from spectators who had thus inconveniently and, as it turned out, unnecessarily put themselves into a state of grace, that they should get their money back. Australians do not have ulcers—also they do not have poverty. Though the circumstances are somewhat different, one could not say that the Australians have treated their aborigines any better than the Americans have treated their negroes. Yet, however that may be so, the aborigines are few and there must be a smaller proportion of the population living in poverty than in any country in the world except New Zealand. Australia of course has no history—no records of unhappy wars fought out within her territory. The different states have their jealously guarded local rights and the Commonwealth is indeed only of this century's creation. It was only with considerable difficulty that it was brought about. But there is no great difference between the constitutions and the habits of life of state and state. People move from one to the other without any difficulty. The Americans, when they want to protest against something, protest in physical violence. There is little tradition among them of free speech, just as indeed there is little tradition of the interchange of conversation. It is a country of competing monologues. The Australians on the other hand have imposed the cockney tradition of heckling and their electoral interchanges are a great deal more lively. I had the great privilege of being booed by the Hill on Sydney cricket ground. Sir Robert Menzies was to give a cocktail party at lunch-time during an England v. Australia test match. It chanced that half an hour before lunch it rained, so, since there was no cricket to be seen, he thought that he would advance the hour of the party. He got someone to announce over the tannoy, 'Will Mr Christopher Hollis please go to the President's room?' The spectators on the Hill who had been looking for some news about the restarting of play were disgusted at this irrelevant piece of absurdity and very properly burst out into large booing.

In 1964 I went to the outbacks, to Bathurst, Dubbo and Orange. At Dubbo kindly hosts asked me what I would like to do one afternoon. I replied, as is my general habit, that I would enjoy some sight-seeing. So they drove me in a car to the waterworks and then to the abattoir. Then they said, 'I'm afraid there is nothing more to see after that for the next thousand miles.' As a matter of fact there was twenty miles away a wood where kangaroos ran wild. I was intensely interested to see them but to the inhabitants this seemed a matter of strangely small interest. They knew that there were kangaroos in their neighbourhood but I do not think that they had ever bothered to go and look at them. In Australia there is an amazing variety of quite unique animal-life—kangaroos, wombats, bandycoots. The marsupial is unique to Australia. Yet the Australian country-dweller as a rule takes very little interest in those animals unless to make money out of them.

The only Australians who have shown any capacity to build an established countryside are the German Lutherans in the wine country in South Australia. Australians are in general irretrievably metropolitan. They cannot bear not being in a capital city and are almost childishly amazed at the complexities of city life in contrast to the simplicities to which they are accustomed in the outbacks. For a nation of such great and enthusiastic cricketers it is amazing how little there is of village cricket. The notion of a village raising a local team is almost unknown. Boys from the country prefer, like Bradman from Bowral, to traipse in every Saturday to the capital to play in one of the League teams there. 'God, it's bloody marvellous—different sorts of cheese,' said a gay young Queenslander confronted with the fare spread out at a city restaurant. Early Australian architecture was often very good—thanks largely to Greenway, a deported convict who had been so misguided as to forge a cheque in Bristol but who Governor Macquarie sensibly saw would be better employed in building houses than in breaking stones. He was responsible for a number of excellent Georgian houses in and near Sydney and also in Tasmania, where to this day country life has more of a reality than anywhere on the mainland. Domestic architecture became deplorable in the 1840's in Australia as in England and elsewhere. It has improved more recently, but, though they have less ridiculous houses to live in, Australians are still reluctant to reconcile themselves to country life as the most natural form of existence.

John Betjeman had preceded me the year before my second visit and was, as he always is, deeply popular. There had recently been a railway station at Orange but the line had been closed down and the station demolished. He insisted on visiting the derelict station and was loud in his praise of the corrugated iron of the former waiting room which lay there scattered on the ground. 'The curve of that iron,' he said. 'Did you ever see anything so beautiful?'

A reservation must be made. Though Australians like to live in great cities and in affectionate nickname call farmers 'hatters' after Lewis Carroll's Mad Hatter, yet they like also to conserve a pretended zest for the 'natural' life in the outbacks—the life of Ned Kelly or that of Nolan, or of Drysdale or of Arthur Boyd's pictures. Australia is a new country but it has a peculiar difficulty among new countries. It is the inheritor of a culture whose images and scenery of the year are exactly the opposite of its own, and where birds abound but do not sing. How difficult it must be to grow up in a country where Christmas comes at midsummer and still to feel that one had inherited the traditional Christian culture. (Perhaps it is because they live upside down that Australians and New Zealanders—Phil May, Dyson, Low—have been so overwhelmingly predominant among English satirical caricaturists.)

The standard of appreciation of painting is in general higher than that in England. Poetry is in general obedient to traditional forms. White is their outstanding novelist. Of course Australia has, like other countries, perpetrated its eccentricities but they have generally been met with some ridicule. In South Australia a patron of modern poetry started to produce a magazine of *art nouveau* which he called *Angry Penguins*. James McAuley, now perhaps the best of living Australian poets and a man of most admirable bonhomie, had the whim to concoct a work of gibberish, cut it up into arbitrary lines, call it the *Doubting Ecliptic*, and pretend that it was the autobiographical confession of a Melbourne tram-driver called Ern Malley. He sent it to the editor of *Angry Penguins* who fell for it with enthusiasm and published it with a laudatory commentary. The paper did not survive the exposure of the hoax.

On my second visit to Australia in 1963 I was sent round the country visiting all the universities on behalf of the British Council.

The position of the Catholic body was, as I have indicated, in some ways similar to that in America. The Catholic proportion was somewhat higher, but the total numbers were of course substantially smaller than in the United States, and this meant that the Catholics were not numerous enough or wealthy enough to maintain their own universities. The system was that at each of the universities the students were distributed out among the colleges of each of the denominations—an Anglican college, a Methodist, a Presbyterian and a Catholic college. This had the incidental consequence that, while the Government with its non-denominational politics would give no financial assistance to denominational schools, Catholic or otherwise, the Catholic students at the universities received support. The colleges were of course formally of equal status, but, much as with the Carnegie Foundation in the United States, we found when we arrived at Sydney that, though two out of the three of us were Catholics, we had automatically and without question been distributed among the three Protestant colleges and the Catholic, St John's, had been left out. It had been merely assumed that no one would stay at a Catholic college if he could possibly stay anywhere else. It is only fair to say that when we went on from Sydney to Melbourne we were entertained at the newly founded Newman College by the most admirable and learned Father Murphy, a Jesuit recently arrived from Ireland, who was to remain out there till the time of the next war, and win for the Catholic community at Melbourne University a most full and unchallenged position of prestige. At the time of my first visit to Australia in 1925, although there was no legal discrimination against Catholics in a university or elsewhere, their social ostracism from the life around them approached almost total segregation.

When I returned again to Australia forty years later I found a wholly different picture in this as in other respects. The Vatican Council was then sitting. Archbishop Mannix had shown himself a firm friend of ecumenism, and under his auspices an able Jesuit, Father Stormon, had preached in Melbourne's Anglican Cathedral. Whether it was because of the influence of Pope John or of Archbishop Mannix or of such priests as Father Murphy the whole picture was entirely changed. The colleges still remained denominational but social relation between the Catholic and the non-Catholic clergy were now easy and frequent. Catholic and non-Catholic clergymen, who forty years ago hardly spoke to one another, now were on the easiest social terms. Of course there were exceptions. Before the troubles of 1969 and 1970, when Terence O'Neill was still the Prime Minister, I would have said from my own experience that relations between Catholic and Protestant in Northern Ireland were slowly but steadily improving. Events have proved the lack of substance behind that opinion. So in Australia, though social relations seemed over forty years to be so dramatically improved, no doubt there are still remnants that could be uncovered of anti-Catholic bitterness. Indeed the visit of Pope Paul to Sydney, while it was in general successful, was not able to pass wholly without protest. The Anglican diocese of Sydney is particularly Low Church and hard to tame and the Anglican Archbishop did not feel himself able to join in any welcome to the Pope. Things are easier in Melbourne.

At Melbourne the chair at our debate was taken by a rising young barrister, slightly older than ourselves, of the name of Mr Menzies. He had not then begun his political career but for some strange reason this not very important event in his life remained in his mind. He very kindly entertained us at the time and he kept always a friendly feeling for us. I saw him a number of times in England and called on him at Canberra in the closing months of his premiership. His countrymen complained of him, as Americans complained of John Kennedy, that he was more easily at home in England or Scotland than in his own country and that in Australia he could not bear life unless he was in a capital city. He despised too much the small towns. Whether or not the complaints were wholly justified he was certainly more of a European than the average Australian politician. When I was in Melbourne in 1963 my good friend Mr Wright told me that he now lived in the house in which Mr Menzies lived in the 1920's, and he was kind enough to entertain me there where I had been entertained nearly forty years before.

Australians are not, any more than Americans, Englishmen living abroad and he is guilty of a great folly who expects them to be such. It is rather surprising that in two great wars they should have been so ready to cross the world to fight for England's cause. They differ in most ways from Englishmen but they are still ready to be strangely dependent on England for their educational influences. This did not greatly surprise me on my first visit in 1925. It was more surprising to discover that it was still so in 1964—that great schools like Geelong and St Peter's, Adelaide still imported their schoolmasters from England and were conducted, so far as I could judge, on lines strangely similar to those of an English public school. I was going one day to the Adelaide Oval to see Sobers bat and, arriving a little early, I turned in at the beautiful Anglican cathedral which stands up splendidly over the ground. A girl's school was conducting a service and I heard the clergyman at the altar pronounce, 'Let us pray for Wantage.' It seemed that the school had been founded from the convent at Wantage and the schoolchildren still piously prayed for their distant founder. But, though they import their schoolmasters from England, schoolmasters are not in general highly thought of in Australia and, though Australian life is free and easy, censorship of literature is very widespread.

III

STONYHURST

When I returned from debating round the world I went to teach at Stonyhurst. On the whole most people are happier in the profession which has been generally followed in their family, and the strongest of all arguments against the celibacy of the clergy is that England and other Protestant countries have been so largely built by clergymen's sons. Whatever the advantage in other ways—which are many—it may not do harm to clergymen that they should not have wives, but it does great harm to a nation that they should not have children. I was the son of a clergyman. My mother was the daughter of a clergyman and ours was in general a heavily clerical family. It may well be that if I had remained an Anglican I would have become an Anglican clergyman, for, though I have no great liking for the company of high ecclesiastics with their names in the papers, the life of an Anglican vicar would have been very agreeable and very congruent with me, and I have always, even as it is, greatly enjoyed the company of the Anglican clergy and found them better company and more intelligent than the average of the laity by whom they are surrounded—particularly than their critics. It has always been a standing mystery to me why sincere and believing Protestants remain laymen. Life in orders seem to me so obviously more agreeable and more valuable than most lay occupations. But as it was, of course, that road was closed to me. Next to being a clergyman my father had given a great part of his life to teaching and I had always had a natural bent towards that profession. I had never seriously thought of being anything but a schoolmaster and, when I became a Catholic, I naturally thought it reasonable that I should go to a Catholic school. I applied to Sligger Urquhart and he arranged for me to go to Stonyhurst, which I agreed to do as soon as I returned from my debating tour.

It was a curiosity that although, as in my Eton days, I was in theory opposed to public schools and would argue that it was wrong that a boy's education should be dependent on his parents' income and that the town day school was on the whole better than the boarding school, yet it never occurred to me or, I fancy, to any other boys that, whatever re-forms might be introduced to make it possible for poorer boys to get into Eton, it could quite possibly mean that I myself would be excluded. So now when I wanted to go to a Catholic school, while I would have been quite ready, for what little I knew of them, to defend in theory the big town Catholic day school, it never occurred to me that I should not myself take a place at a public school. The Protestant public schools on anything like their modern scale were the creation of the nineteenth-century capitalists who were anxious to give their sons an education which would distinguish them from the sons of their workmen. The Catholics in the penal years when Catholic schools had to be overseas had no alternative but to make their schools largely class schools, since the working-class Catholic could not have afforded to send his son overseas for his education. In the nineteenth century when the schools were allowed to establish themselves in England they still predominantly preserved their class character. It is a pity that under modern conditions they have not made themselves more egalitarian.

Stonyhurst, the leading and senior Jesuit school in England, lies on the borders of Lancashire and Yorkshire. In what county the modern reforms of Lord Redcliffe Maud have permitted it to be I am not quite sure. It is some twelve miles out of Preston on the harsh and rather bleak

Pennine Fells. It has a past of enormous distinction. The Jesuits first played their part in English history with the mission of Parsons and Campion in the reign of Elizabeth I. The notion of the foundation of these Catholic schools in exile came to Cardinal Allen. Cardinal Allen was born at Rossall. I once heard a preacher on the morrow of the cricket match between Rossall and Stonyhurst, talking to the Stonyhurst boys, say, 'And only yesterday you were playing at cricket on the very spot where that great man was born, and it was no wonder that you won.' It was, it seemed, a tricky spot in the pitch with which it was not to be expected that Protestant batsmen would be able to cope.

There can be few, if any, schools in England so magnificently situated as Stonyhurst. One approaches it down a splendid drive which leads from the Lady Statue at the corner on the road from the not very attractive little village of Hurst Green, between two lakes, to the twin towers of the College, with their surmounting eagles. It has many treasures, largely from the donations of James II, who, when he was driven into exile, gave to the College at St Omers the Catholic possessions of the royal family. There is St Cuthbert's Gospel (eighth century), the Book of Hours used by Mary, Queen of Scots on the scaffold, Campion's rope and Thomas More's bed-cap. In what is known as the Stuart Parlour are portraits by Nattier, Lely and others of all the leading members of the Stuart royal family. It is, as an inspector once said half in complaint, 'more a museum than a school'. They had a very sensible custom by which one class-period a week, known as Peripatetics, was devoted to a guided tour to the boys of the treasures of the College. Under Parsons the English Jesuit school was established at St Omers and remained there until the suppression of the Society in 1773. Then, expelled from St Omers, it found refuge under the protection of the Jesuit-loving Bishop of Liège in that city. It was expelled in its turn from there when the French Revolutionary forces overran the Low Countries. Great Britain was by that time at war with France and, on the principle that they must make friends with the enemies of their enemies, the British were less hostile to the Catholic émigrés than they had previously been towards Catholics. The pupils and their masters, expelled from Liège, were allowed to cross to England. They landed at Hull, not knowing where they would find a resting place, but among their pupils at Liège had been Mr Thomas Weld of Lulworth in Dorset, the friend of George III and one of the largest landowners in England. Stonyhurst in Lancashire was one of his second houses. It was unoccupied and he offered it to the Jesuits, his old preceptors. It was thus that the Jesuits established themselves at Stonyhurst, a Jacobean mansion, in which Cromwell had slept at the time of the battle of Preston. At first they thought that it was no more to them than a passing home in which they would remain as a place of exile until with the return of peace they could go back to their normal home in France. But of course the war went on with only the small intermission of the Peace of Amiens for nearly another twenty years. When eventually it finished, a slightly more tolerant England was prepared to allow the Fathers to remain at Stonyhurst. Since this was an English school there seemed no reason why they should not remain in England, if they were permitted to do so, and they have stayed there to this day. The Gordon Riots were not so far away and it would have been imprudent to have established a Catholic school in a large town. The Jesuits at Stonyhurst, like the Benedictines at Ampleforth and Downside, established themselves in a most deserted countryside—in this case a Lancashire countryside where there was a considerable native Catholic population. There, even though local Protestants sometimes turned out to stone outdoor processions of the Blessed Sacrament, they in general felt themselves secure.

At first Stonyhurst was without question the leading Catholic school in England. But the Jesuits had always their critics and before long complaints began to be raised that their ways were too Continental. Their discipline, it was said, was too strict. They did not allow the boys the freedom which was natural and healthy to an English boy. They encouraged the boys to spy upon one another. They would never take their word. Cardinal Newman thought that if the Catholic Church was to win English converts it was necessary to provide for the converts an education that was more in accord with English public-school traditions. He founded the Oratory School at Birmingham. Newman had never himself been to a public school and his ideas on what one was like were not very well founded. Whatever the harshness of the régime at Stonyhurst it was certainly nothing to compare with the brutality of Keats' Eton or of other Protestant schools at that period. Nor indeed was the Oratory, when it was founded, notably a milder place than Stonyhurst. Its life was full of controversies and there were soon accusations of the excesses of discipline there. However that may be, the Oratory School still survives, though it has now moved from Birmingham, and no one wishes to speak other than well of it. But its academic achievements have not been such as to enable it to supplant Stonyhurst. Later in the century the great Benedictine schools at Ampleforth in Yorkshire and Downside in Somerset rose in popularity and by the time that I went to

Stonyhurst in 1925 the school was indeed still comfortably flourishing, but it no longer had the social supremacy which it had enjoyed fifty years before. The greater number of the Catholic aristocracy now went either to Ampleforth or to Downside. There was no great loss to Stonyhurst in that. A Catholic aristocrat is a curiously hybrid being. Belloc always used to say, and surely rightly, that it was not possible to be both a Catholic and a gentleman.

The only time that I heard of Stonyhurst during my Eton days was when Father Cortie, who had been in charge of the astronomical observatory, came down to give a lecture to the Eton Lower boys. Father Cortie was an excellent and racy populariser, a great *bon vivant* and witty raconteur. His lecture was a very great success and the Lower Boys, under the impulse of Mr Ramsay, the Lower Master, afterwards wrote to him a Latin letter of thanks to which he sent a Latin reply. How far the Lower Boys really composed their letter themselves, or how far indeed Father Cortie composed his reply, I cannot say. All that I remember hearing about him at the time was that he was a Jesuit Father who came from a 'big place in the North of England'. Soon afterwards he died, with on his lips the final words, 'Chaps, I'm going to peg out.'

The greater number of the boys at Stonyhurst were the sons of Lancashire Catholic parents. There was of course a London contingent. There were a good many foreigners—French, Spanish and Italian. I welcomed these boys who seemed to add to the variety of life and to have a natural and proper place in a Catholic school. I was a little shocked soon after my arrival to hear Father Weld, the very Old English Catholic Rector, express concern at them and announce that it was his policy to restrict their numbers.

One day a great friend of mine, a young Mexican—a pleasant high-spirited youth but, as I imagined, quite without guile—came to me in great distress. His parents had received a letter from the Rector, requesting them to withdraw him at the end of the term. The Rector gave no reason. I went to him. I was prepared to be told that the boy had been guilty of some crime that needed to be kept confidential and would have accepted such an assurance. But to my surprise I found the Rector ready to admit that he had no charge against the boy but claimed that he was not prepared to discuss the character of a boy with any master. 'I would answer just the same way if any of ours had come to me,' he said. I was dismissed not quite with a rebuke but with a clear indication that my complaint would receive no discussion. I did not doubt that a Jesuit would have been treated just as cavalierly as I. That however was not my point. My point was that the boy was being treated unjustly. The boy had shown me a letter from his non-Catholic parent telling him the news and asserting that the Rector's treatment was most un-English. I had not shown that letter to the Rector, but subsequently he got to hear of it, or to see it, and then at once collapsed. The boy was allowed to stay on at the school. The Rector was not willing to face a public row but very clearly he did not himself think that a subject, in particular a foreign subject, had any right in justice against official authority. He had of course a degree of reason in his prejudice. The Jesuits were absurdly suspect for being an un-English body and there was therefore a certain reason in taking extra trouble to show their school to be an indubitably English school. But such restrictions were a pity.

There were of course the Irish boys—not quite as numerous a contingent as they would have been a few years before, now that the Free State had made the Irish language compulsory for public appointments in Ireland, but still a considerable number of them. The greater number had a curiously ambivalent attitude. They were for Ireland against England but for the British Isles against the rest of the world. They championed Irish Nationalism, and though most of them accepted the Treaty they thought it a matter of honour to support all that was done in the name of 'Ireland's fight for freedom'. On the other hand they were more ready than the average English boy to claim superiority over 'lesser breeds without the law' from Continental Europe, just as years later a priest in New Orleans told me that priests in general in that part of the world were opposed to racialism but that priests who were recent immigrants from Ireland were an exception to this generalisation. This ambivalence was shared by Jesuits of Irish origin. Rationalising their position, they would reasonably explain that it was their duty to support the established government, but that that had nothing to do with their private sympathies. At that time it was the custom to end Sunday Mass with a full-throated prayer for the royal family. '*Domine, salvum fac regem nostrum Georgium et exaudi nos in die quo invocaverimus te*' rolled out the sonorous petition. A visitor commented on the loyal vigour with which Father Richard Mangan expressed his fealty, but I could not but remember that he was in fact a strong Sinn Feiner and that I had heard him argue that it was very difficult to find objection to the murder of Sir Henry Wilson. In general the boys, when I first went to Stonyhurst, were extravagantly conservative. I was a little shocked, a few weeks after my arrival there, when I was invited to attend one of their debates. The violent denunciation by speaker after speaker of any views other than those of extreme reaction was in great contrast to the permissive chatter which I had been accustomed to hear all around me at Eton.

I went to teach at Stonyhurst in the September term of 1925 and remained there for ten very happy years. I suppose that it was for the best that I left there and went on to other pastures, but I cannot feel sure that it was so. Unadventurous as it may seem, I think that there is a great deal to be said for spending one's life in one place, and when I go back to Stonyhurst, as from time to time I do, I still have a feeling of regret for what I have lost and of envy for one or two masters who, in the manner of Mr Chipps, still remain where they have been for almost half a century. I was talking recently to a young friend who had been at an entirely different school, of which, rightly or wrongly, he had no high opinion. Of the correctness of that opinion I have no judgement, but the reason he gave me why he thought the school to be unsatisfactory was very extraordinary. He complained that there were still a large number of masters on the staff who had been at the school in his day. I should have thought that that was a point in the school's favour.

I had never before had more than a passing acquaintance with any Catholic school, and it was naturally of interest to me to compare it with Eton. Judged by examination results, Stonyhurst, and indeed any of the Catholic schools of that day, had a record very much inferior to Eton or other leading Protestant schools. My comparison was, I admit, unfair to the Catholics because the comparison was with College at Eton. The great majority of the scholarships and academic successes which Eton won were won by Collegers. Had I remembered to count in Oppidans, too, the record from this point of view would have been far less formidable. Still it was certainly true that at that date an Oxford or Cambridge scholarship from a Catholic school was a rarity. It would be much less true today when the Catholic schools win at least as high a proportion of successes as any other school. In spite of the fervour of my own religion I could not at that date avoid the feeling that, with all its advantages, strong dogmatic teaching was a discouragement to the adventures of the mind. There were so many things that a Catholic was forbidden to say or do, so many lines of speculation which the non-Catholic explored but which were forbidden to the Catholic. It might be to his advantage to be warned off forbidden paths but it did not make for the agility of his mind. How far was this prejudice justified?

Perhaps not very far. The main reason why the Catholic found it difficult to get his footing in the academic world was certainly quite different. It was simply that the Catholics were newcomers there. It was only towards the end of the last century and after the many controversies of Newman and Manning that Catholic frequentation of the Universities was countenanced. The monks and Jesuits who taught at the Catholic schools were from an era when Catholics were still newcomers at the Universities. If they had taken Oxford or Cambridge degrees they had taken them from their own Halls and not from one of the regular Colleges. They had not mixed in Oxford or Cambridge life. They were not familiar with the Dons or the Dons with them. At every ordinary school Sixth Form masters could greatly help their bright pupils to success by their own familiarity with the Dons and with the sort of questions that were asked and the sort of answers that were expected by the University examiners. Today the Catholic school authorities can furnish such hints at least as completely as any others and the result is that the success of pupils from Catholic schools are as frequent as from any other. But it was not so forty-five years ago.

This was the main reason for the comparative lack of academic success of the Catholic boys. But there were some more intrinsic reasons which had a bearing, if a secondary bearing, on the matter. The clerical schoolmaster who devotes his whole life to his classical texts, to Virgil and Horace and the turning of bits of English verse into Latin hexameters or alcaics, lives a very odd life. It is well enough for a nation's culture that there should be a few such people, 'settling Hoti's business and giving us the doctrine of the Enclytic De'. A society which has no pure scholars is a boorish society. Yet the pure scholar's life is a slightly dotty life. It is reasonable from a cultural point of view to have a love of Greek and Latin, but it is hardly reasonable to have the extravagance of the obsessed scholar. Those with scholarly interests have formed their tastes and their friendships in their undergraduate days and have in all probability preserved their contacts unbroken ever since. The priest's contacts have been interrupted for a few years by his novitiate. But apart from that, there was a degree of truth in my feeling that priests in the 1920's did not yet encourage an adventurous mind. The record of the Church in the nineteenth century and the suppression of modernism in the first decade of this century had not been pretty stories. Newman had had to make bitter complaints against the clergy 'moved as they are in automaton fashion from the camarilla at Rome'. The regimen of the Church was not at that time much like Newman's *Idea of a University*. Pius X had perhaps been right to condemn modernism but he had used for its suppression, with his secret delations and vigilance committees, methods that were essentially the methods of Dostoievsky's Grand Inquisitor.

It was far from true and a gross libel when the English Jesuits of the 1920's were accused of preserving old Continental habits of espionage and the like. A few years before, according to accounts, Stonyhurst had been the victim of a foolishly rigid discipline. The boys had never been allowed to leave their playground and busy prefects had been careful to see to it that their life was wholly without privacy. The Jesuits were obsessed with a morbid horror that two boys, if left alone and without supervision, would necessarily commit acts of immorality. Perhaps the stories were exaggerated, as schoolboy stories usually are, but such at any rate was the reputation which Stonyhurst held in the rest of the Catholic world and which some of those who were connected with it still propagated. If so, things under the very admirable First Prefect, Father Garman, had very substantially changed by the time that I arrived. It was not and did not pretend to be a permissive society, but under Father Garman's rule a reasonable degree of freedom was permitted—not so very different from other schools—and, amid the inevitable ups and downs which always accompany school life everywhere, relations between masters and boys were generally friendly. I found that I could mix much more easily with the boys than would ever have been possible for a master at Eton.

Today, as far as I can gather, at Stonyhurst, as indeed at all schools, discipline is a great deal more relaxed than it was forty years ago. Boys are allowed freely to roam the countryside and no great attempt is made to prevent the frequentation of pubs and the like. I am old-fashioned but I doubt if extreme permissiveness makes for happiness. There should be reasonable freedom, but at the same time authority should not be afraid to forbid where it is necessary. The zest of schoolboy life comes from escapades, from trying out whether you can evade authority and not get caught. If nothing is forbidden nothing is exciting, and a total relaxation of discipline is perhaps especially difficult for a Jesuit school with the Jesuit tradition of insistence on the supreme virtue of obedience. It is essential for a successful school that it should possess a number of colourful and eccentric masters, who at any rate appear to the boys to be slightly mad and provide the stuff for anecdotes. In these overcertificated days such characters are sadly rare, but they were prevalent enough, I am glad to say, in my own life both at Eton and at Stonyhurst.

Yet when we turn from escapades to ideas, it must be admitted that on the intellectual plane there was not such large confidence in liberty as there should have been. There was very little confidence that *magna est veritas et praevalebit*, or, on a more pragmatic plane, that the boys would soon in any event go out into a pluralist and largely permissive world and that therefore it was wise that they should be encouraged to come to terms with the ideas of such a world.

It was a fashion at that time, alike among friends of the Church and among some of its critics, to say, 'At least Catholics know their religion.' Many who were by no means Catholics contrasted the certainty of Catholic belief with the indeterminism of Anglicanism. Tom Kettle's saying that Catholics take their religion table d'hôte and Protestants *à la carte* was much quoted, and religious instruction, whether or not the religion was true, was supposed to be especially competent at Catholic schools. It was a half truth. Of course the boys at Stonyhurst as at other Catholic schools went to Mass. In those days they all had to go to daily Mass. It would not be so today. In the evenings they went to Benediction and on the great feasts to other services. A few reacted against too much churchgoing and perhaps, at any rate for a time, did not go again after they left. I remember one very engaging young man who complained that he was made to go so often to church during his schooldays that, when he left, he would never go again. He was soon after killed in the war. Whether he fulfilled his threat I do not know. A few on the other hand were devout. In those days a number every year joined the Society and became Jesuits, and some became secular priests or members of other orders. The majority of these persisted in their vocation. Today of course, as with all religious orders, the numbers are seriously less and much fewer join. I was surprised, and perhaps a little shocked, at the discovery of the extent to which their piety was regulated by rule. For instance some very decent boys, I found, saw no harm as an escapade in drinking as much as they could of the altar wine which they had discovered, so long as it had not been consecrated. In much the same way Belloc used to attend daily Mass but used frequently to interrupt its most sacred moments to ask where he could find a telephone. I found that such meticulous distinction between where the sacred ended and the profane began was a Catholic custom that had up till then been unfamiliar to me.

The great majority of the boys at Stonyhurst were naturally neither abnormally impious nor abnormally devout. They accepted its life as they found it and it formed in them a habit for which they were afterwards grateful. I would have said at the time that all of the boys, even the least devout, yet in the last analysis believed. I have found since from what old boys have told me that this would be a slight exaggeration, but not, I think, a very great exaggeration. I came across in later life a young man, now incidentally a practising Catholic, who has sent his son to a Catholic school. He told me how a schoolfellow had told him in his schooldays that religion was 'a load of old rubbish' and he had believed him. He was generally thought of as a most respectable member of society and I had never suspected his infidelity, but apparently the Prefect had somehow diagnosed it and struck him off the Sodality.

The services were of course all in Latin. How far the boys followed what was happening at them, how far they could give a liturgical analysis, I would not care to say. I should think very little. Where they and, I am sure, all Catholic boys were manifestly inferior to Protestants was in their knowledge of the Bible. It was the custom for Catholics to repudiate hotly as a slander the suggestion that they were not allowed to read the Bible. They were right to repudiate it. The truth was that Catholics were allowed to read the Bible, but that they very rarely did. I am not speaking of course of the few most learned biblical scholars but of the average, ordinary Catholic, whether schoolboy or priest. He heard of course the lesson and the gospel of the day read at Mass but those, even when they were read in English, were not much attended to. What purpose was served when, as often happened, they were read merely in Latin, which not a tittle of the congregation could follow, it is hard to say. But few of the boys ever sat down to read the Gospels as consecutive narratives, had any but the faintest notion what any of the Epistles said and above all knew anything of the Old Testament story. So far as they knew anything of it at all, it consisted of the story of the Garden of Eden and the story of Exodus, with perhaps a passing reference to King David. I do not think that I ever heard a word said about the books of the prophets and doubt if there was a boy at Stonyhurst who would have had the faintest notion what Jeremiah or Isaiah or Micah said. Indeed I remember discovering with surprise the total ignorance of the Old Testament of Urquhart, the Catholic Dean of Balliol, and his unashamed confession of it. 'Catholics do not read the Old Testament,' he carelessly said and dismissed the matter. It was almost invariably taken for granted that the restatement of the negative Commandments into the positive obligation to 'Love God and your neighbour' was an entirely original emendation of Our Lord. And it was not only the boys who were ignorant. I remember one day commenting with surprise on the ill-reading of a pupil to whom the word 'Laodicean' was quite unknown. The very holy and well-informed Prefect of Studies, to my surprise, confessed that he, too, had never heard of Laodicea. In my own schooldays, which were in this respect in no way peculiar, we used, as I have said, to have a lesson in Bible reading every day. Biblical phrases and anecdotes, from of course the Authorised Version, were, as Newman said, a very integral part of our life and speaking. We were not in the least religious—very much less religious than the boys of Stonyhurst—and biblical phrases and anecdotes were often used without any sort of religious connotation. But as a Catholic I hardly ever heard a sermon on the literary significance of some biblical phrases—never, as far as I can recollect, on a phrase of the Old Testament.

Yet, in spite of its biblical deficiencies the boys of course received plenty of religious instruction. The traditional pattern of Jesuit education—the *Ratio Studiorum*—played little part in the system as it had survived. The system was by then dominated by the demands of the University examinations. The lesson was, as it were, baptised by the recitation of a 'Hail Mary' at its beginning. The traditional names of the classes—Rhetoric, Poetry, Syntax and the rest—still held their titles in contrast with the Sixth and Fifth and Fourth forms. Otherwise lessons were much the same as they might have been at any secular school. The traditional holidays and their titles—Academy, Blandyke, after a Flemish village to which the boys used to walk out for an outing in their days at St Omers—were still preserved but without much enthusiasm. The greater number of the Jesuits took little interest in the traditions of the Society. The Catholic Evidence Guild at that time flourished among some of the more pious boys. They would go out into the neighbouring towns and there deliver public expositions of the Catholic faith. It was certainly a good way of teaching the boys their religion and also incidentally of teaching them how to make a public speech. Whether the mysteries of religion are capable of expression in this glib fashion of question and answer I am not sure. I have never come across any reliable estimate of the effect of such orations.

One of the most vigorous of these Evidence lecturers was a very remarkable young man, Henry John. Henry John was the son of Augustus John, the artist. Augustus John was, as is well known, a man of Bohemian habits who did not much attend to such children as he might happen to beget. He interested himself little in their upbringing and the care of Henry John's education was left to a worthy and more conscientious aunt. She sent him to Stonyhurst, at first as a Protestant, but he soon himself insisted on becoming a Catholic, fell greatly under the influence of Father Martin D'Arcy, who was on the staff there, became a very prominent member of the Evidence Guild and, after he left school, tried his vocation as a Jesuit. Tragically, he died an early death. He had left Stonyhurst just before I arrived, but I got to know him a few months later in Rome. Augustus John had of course no mind to submit himself to the discipline of religion, but its curiosities amused him. He was delighted one day when he went to Mass in Galway and heard an eloquent young priest attack the iniquities of the flesh, culminating in a denunciation of 'the damnable passion of love'.

One day driving into Ennis in County Clare he asked of a man who was serving him with petrol what was the big building that they had just passed.

'It is a school,' said the garageman.

'Is it a seminary—a school for training priests?' asked Augustus, for it had been decorated outside with a number of pious statues.

'No, it is not,' said the man. 'It is a school for education.' Augustus John was delighted at the answer.

There was on the staff of Stonyhurst then a full-blooded American, Sam Watson, as we called him, though his real name was Vincent Watson. He was a man to whom the ascetic exercises of life did not come at all easily, but he was always ready at any time to tire the sun with talking in the exposition of his various theses. He had one evening a long session over the whisky bottle with Augustus John, who found his conversation stimulating. Augustus John afterwards reported of it, 'Father Watson discussed the question, "If a man be born again"—a very curious supposition.'

Every week the boys received a class in R.D.—Religious Doctrine. Religious Doctrine consisted of an exposition of the propositions which formed the teachings of the Church. It was reasonable that a Catholic school should teach such propositions, and I have no doubt that they were competently taught. There was a certain amount of textual quotation about the authority on which the Church based its teaching. But the apologetics consisted for the most part of the quotation of a biblical text from which the teaching was derived. The Gospels, little used as coherent narratives, were freely used as quarries for particular doctrines. The business of the Catholic school, the Jesuits believed, was to teach its pupils what the Church believed. Some of them would have had little use for the mysteries and poetry of faith. At a time when it was the fashion in England to criticise the Church for its allegedly sentimental and irrational teachings, the great Lord Salisbury, the Prime Minister, much more justly made the criticism, 'The trouble with the Roman Catholics is that they reason too much. They squeeze out the mystery from religion.' The more intelligent among the Jesuits would have said that the mysteries of the faith were indeed valid and important but that such matters were not to be taught in class but must be discovered by the adventurer for himself. It was not an unreasonable position. As to the exact authority with which the Church taught, they themselves took for granted a number of propositions which would today be vigorously challenged, but that was only to be expected. Fashions have changed, but they for their time were not extravagent in their claims.

Whatever may have been the truth some years before, there was not by then, I fancy, very much of the fear of hell. I only remember one hell-fire sermon in my time at Stonyhurst. There were general petitions for grace 'now and at the hour of our death', but the general view was that the traditional doctrine of hell was so horrible that, whether true or not, it was not effective as a deterrent, since it was too fearful for the imagination to grasp it.

As for the boys' general conduct the Jesuits always very carefully drew the line between school rules and the precepts of the Church. The latter were naturally of grave importance and the violation of them much to be avoided. But there was never any suggestion that the violation of school rules was a mortal sin. Ragging and breaking of rules were, I am glad to say, common enough—neither more nor less common, I should imagine, than at other schools. In natural high spirits boys broke their rules and, if the Jesuits could catch them, they had no scruples about punishments —though punishments were quite without malice. I remember catching a certain Father hiding beneath an open window, through which he had discovered—I don't recollect how—that a boy who had climbed out of the College at night would in the end certainly return. 'I can't imagine anything more exciting than this,' he confided to me. One might perhaps see the anecdote as evidence that the Father's life was somewhat deficient in excitement, but even in a permissive age it cannot honestly be denied that the life of a schoolmaster, Jesuit or otherwise, is apt to be dull unless it is from time to time illuminated by the excitement of catching a boy out in some misdemeanour. The form of corporal punishment was peculiar but, I think, sensible—if one is to admit that corporal punishment is sensible at all, of which I am a little doubtful. The master did not go into school armed with a cane or a ferula. Father Dolan, the Prefect of Studies at Clongowes, in Joyce's *Portrait of the Artist as a Young Man*, swept thus into the class and dealt out instant justice, or injustice, to Stephen Daedalus. Such behaviour may have been tolerated among the Irish Jesuits. It would have been unknown among the Jesuits of England.

At Stonyhurst, as at other Jesuit schools, the system was that, if a boy misbehaved intolerably, the master would say to him, 'Jones, get twelve ferulas.' The master's part in the story was then finished. The boy, thus ordered, had at some time within the next twenty-four hours to go along to the Prefects' Room. The Prefects, of whom there were four, were Jesuits, especially appointed to look after discipline. The culprit would say to one of these Prefects, 'Can I have twelve ferulas, please?' He would then hold out his right hand on which the Prefect would strike him six times with a leather thong, known as a ferula. Then he would hold out his left hand and receive on it the other six strokes. The Prefect was merely the agent of punishment. He would not know, other than occasionally, what was the offence for which he was punishing the boy. Thus, it was argued, there would be no risk that he would strike in anger or with malice. Equally there would be no danger—or at least very much less danger—that the master who ordered the punishment, since he was not himself to give it, would act under any impulse of indecent sadism. The argument was, I think, just and, if you are to have corporal punishment at all, this is perhaps the least unsatisfactory way to administer it. Protestants are usually beaten on the bottom, but Roman Catholics on the hand. But, though they may have performed satisfactorily this particular task, I do not think that the system of Prefects was a good system and it has indeed by now been substantially abolished. It was not fair to a number of men of intelligence and learning, it may be, who had accepted the discipline of a religious vocation, to ask them to devote their whole lives to being petty policemen and to detecting the offences against the rule of little schoolboys. Life became almost intolerably dull if no offence was ever committed and the temptation to lose proportion and to manufacture offences was almost irresistible.

The Jesuits, for all their reputation for rigid discipline, were a body of remarkable variety and more different from one another than any company of lay schoolmasters, stamped as they are by their profession. There were some, such as Father Martindale or Father D'Arcy, who easily took a dominating place in any society in which they found themselves. There were shy, holy men who had never moved out of Jesuit circles, since they had joined the Society, had entered the novitiate straight from school and knew little about what a place which they called 'the world' was like. There were those who imposed upon themselves a discipline so rigid as to make personal contacts quite difficult. There were others who were avid for companionship and only too ready to partake of any entertainment that might be offered. Some were easy with boys, others distant from them, giving their statutory lessons and then at once returning to the solitude of their rooms. As with all religious societies, they had their internal tensions, but they always managed at least to confront the world with an appearance of unity. The Jesuit was 'one of ours', the world populated by 'externs'. A few years ago, when the Jesuits owing to the fall in numbers had to give up what had been their second public school at Beaumont, it was noticeable that it hardly occurred to them that they had any obligation to see if there was any other Catholic body who would take it on as a Catholic school. The Jesuits were something of an ecclesia within the ecclesia.

I made one surprising and disedifying discovery about religious, which I had never suspected. That was the undercurrent of rivalry between different religious orders, extending to the most petty matters. When I arrived at Stonyhurst, Stonyhurst and Ampleforth, as the leading Catholic schools in the North, used to play one another every year at cricket. One year the Ampleforth authorities felt that the Stonyhurst professional, who had umpired in the match, had given some unfair decisions. Whether he had or not I do not know, but unpopular verdicts from umpires are not a rarity at cricket, and it is generally considered even in the secular world a mark not so much of sportsmanship as of sanity to forget about the matter as soon as possible. But the holy priests took up the dispute about this umpiring with a vigour as if they were Yorkshire or Lancashire professionals and in a manner that was hardly sane. Letters passed to and fro, from the one school to the other, and as a result for a considerable number of years the cricket fixture between the two schools was cancelled. Neither on the one side nor the other did the priests seem able to avert from the scandal that they were causing, so enormously overshadowing any rights or wrongs about the petty dispute. People inevitably said, 'What sort of Christians are these who are not even able to play cricket with one another without a mortal quarrel?' Happily this is by now all long forgotten.

As for sex, Stonyhurst had of course the same problem that Eton and all schools had at that time—only in a more intense form. Just as at Eton the boys from term's beginning to end for all practical purposes never had any dealings with a female, so at Stonyhurst, and at any Catholic school, the deprivation was even greater since the priests were all celibate. Lay masters were comparatively newcomers at the school and, since their status was not as yet properly established, their profession was not highly recommended. They were not well paid and therefore did not as a rule stay very long. As a consequence few of them were married. When

I arrived in 1925 there was only one married master. He was a convert Anglican clergyman who had been married before his conversion. The married convert who had been a clergyman in another denomination is always apt to present a difficult problem. All too often he has no money and his life has not fitted him well for earning an income in any other profession. Sometimes he has, in addition, difficult peculiarities. An admirable charity, the Converts' Aid Society, does what it can to help such people. It is humanely administered. I remember a lady of much kindliness who served on its committee. The case of a convert came up before them for examination. A reporter said, 'I am afraid that there are difficulties about this case. I am afraid that this poor man drinks.' 'Oh, does he?' said this kindly lady. 'Then of course we must give him rather more money.' It sometimes happens that acute spiritual crises make those who suffer from them very in-looking and self-centred. It was so with my colleague. He was so concerned with the problems of his own soul that he had little leisure for the consideration of other people. The letters for the lay masters used to be delivered in the morning on to the table of the Common Room. I have seen him going through the pile of them, removing those that were for himself, and unconsciously and without compunction skimming off into the waste-paper basket any that might happen to be for other people.

After I had been there a year this colleague left and for the next four years none of the lay staff were married. I then myself got engaged and the Jesuits built for us a little house some quarter of a mile from the college. My wife, like I, was by origin of the Anglican establishment. She was the daughter of a clergyman and at the time of our marriage still an Anglican, though a couple of years later at the time of the arrival of our first child she became a Catholic. A happy marriage and a happy family are the greatest of all possible blessings. As one looks around the world as it is today one cannot easily be very comfortable. There can be none of us who do not know of many cases of marriages that have been a failure or of children who have given great anxiety to their parents. My own good fortune has been rare and, I am sometimes tempted to think, unique. Whatever may be said or should be said about such remedies as divorce, most happily such problems have never in any fashion been a problem to me. I have been blessed with a marriage that has brought me unclouded happiness and children who have been our sustainers in old age and who have never at any stage in our life given us any serious anxiety. For this uncovenanted good fortune I am indeed grateful. It has made all the incidental and small discomforts of life of very secondary and trivial importance. Anne Scott-James, engaged on some article for a woman's paper, once rang me up to ask what troubles and anxieties I had had in the upbringing of my children. I replied that I had had none. She said that she had never before come across such an answer, and I noticed that when the article appeared, with its multifarious complaints about the generation gap, there was no reference to my reply. Evelyn Waugh who had been recently received into the Church and who was at the time matrimonially unattached then lived with us for much of the time and did much of his writing at Stonyhurst. He received and greatly enjoyed the friendship of the Jesuits and congratulated me on my wisdom and good fortune in working for 'decent employers'.

It was our custom to ask some of our pupils down to our house for meals and I think that in doing so we made a little contribution to their education. One respect in which the Etonian was most certainly at an advantage over the Stonyhurst boy was the very generous hospitality which the Etonian received from the masters and of which I have already spoken. It gave pleasure and it also taught them a bit about manners and social graces which was of advantage to them in later life. The Stonyhurst boy got little of that, and so long as he was ruled by clergymen who had taken a vow of poverty and who ate all their meals in a refectory, and so long as there were no women about the place, it was not easy to see how this defect could be remedied. The austere Rector of the day seemed to me strangely insensitive to the fact that it was a defect. It was, he thought, the duty of a Jesuit College to teach boys how to avoid sin —not to teach them how to balance a tea-cup while making agreeable conversation. As Dr McAfee Brown, that very sensible Presbyterian divine, said of them ,'I love the Jesuits but there are some things about them with which I cannot agree. I could never let my daughter marry a Jesuit.' But I think that the Rector was in error and we did something to add a veneer of civilisation to the boy's lives.

As I say, ours was at that time the only married house around the premises. Later, with the growth in the number of boys in the school and the decline in the number of Jesuits following the decline in vocations, the lay masters increased in numbers and established for themselves a much more regular status. As a result now a number of them are married and modern custom encourages joint dances and the like with girls' schools in the neighbourhood, which in 1925 would have been quite unheard of. But I speak of forty-five years ago. As I say, the boys for all intents and purposes then never saw a woman. A consequence was, inevitably, an amount of half-comical, half-serious affection between big and little boys. Naturally enough to the Jesuit it would have been a matter of great concern had they suspected that such affairs would lead to really serious consequences. The more sensible majority of them at any rate did not think that this was likely to happen and indeed very sensibly took the line that such consequences were the more likely to happen if such affairs were treated with excessive seriousness. They would not thus be extirpated. Total extirpation, human nature being what it is, was not possible. The best policy was, while not formally recognising such affairs, to treat them lightly, as to a large extent a joke, confident that, if the boys were not too heavily rebuked for actions which were inevitable and innocent, their religious principles would prevent them from carrying things to a guilty conclusion. As the very wise old Spiritual Father, Father Michael King, more than ninety years old, once said to me, 'There is no more serious sin than for a confessor to be stricter than the mind of the Church.'

That was the policy. I would have said at that time it was wholly successful and that no harm came of such affairs. Later experience was to teach me that this was not quite true and, though human nature does not allow for total success in such policies, yet the way in which the Jesuits handled them was more nearly successful than any other that could have been evolved.

As for myself I made no pretence to great or accurate scholarship, and would certainly have not been fitted to handle the academic control of young boys. It was for others to provide the solid and accurate scholarship. But I had in some ways a wider experience of life and travel than those who had passed straight from school into a Jesuit novitiate and thence into the classroom and I was able to stimulate a certain interest in that wider life and a certain *savoir-faire* into the boys who might otherwise have missed it. I was able to get on friendly terms with the great majority of my pupils and am happy to think that I made among them a number of friendship which have survived the relationship of the classroom by a good third of a century.

CHAPTER FOUR

Full of Strange Oaths

I

NOTRE DAME

In 1935 I received a letter from Father O'Hara (then President of Notre Dame University in Indiana and afterwards Cardinal O'Hara of Philadelphia) who asked me if I would go out there for a year to take up some temporary teaching. Troubled as were so many other people at that time by the obscene paradox, as it seemed to us, of the coincidence of unused raw materials and large unemployment and poverty, I had written a book, *The Breakdown of Money*, in criticism of the monetary system. America had of course recently passed through a financial crisis even worse than that of Britain, and the Americans, who like St Paul's Athenians, are always ready to hear any new thing, and make it a fashion, were at that time very easily receptive to anyone who had policies of monetary reform, valid or nonsensical as the case might be, to offer in criticism of traditional and orthodox policies. It was in America the age of the New Deal. It was in consequence of my book that on the suggestion of Orlando Weber, who had recently resigned from the chairmanship of Allied Chemicals, Father O'Hara invited me to go to Notre Dame. Father O'Hara was at the time paying his first visit to this side of the Atlantic. He was travelling from London to Dublin and invited me to go over to Chester where he was breaking his journey. I did so with my wife and he made me an offer of a salary that was a great deal more generous than any which Stonyhurst could afford. I accepted, though with a little reluctance, for I was wholly happy at Stonyhurst and had no wish for its own sake to break my life there. It is true that the original offer was merely for a visit for one year, but I had a suspicion that if I once left Stonyhurst, I would not return to its staff, and this indeed proved to be so, for after I had been at Notre Dame for a little time Father O'Hara invited me to extend my visit and indeed I went out there every year for the succeeding years up till the coming of the war.

As I have said, in my previous visits to America as an Oxford Union debater we had been in the hands of the Carnegie Foundation who had been careful never to send us to a Catholic College. I therefore knew little of such institutions and indeed had no experience of the staff or faculty of any American University.

South Bend was a city of Polish workers who at that date made Studebaker cars. Chesterton, shortly before, had given offence by describing it as 'a little Polish town'—a description which in Chestertonian vocabulary was intended as a compliment but which was not taken as such by the inhabitants. Yet it was certainly in the class of nondescript American towns, and the flat plains of North Indiana are perhaps the dullest of all parts of the United States, the climate, unbearably hot in the summer, unbearably cold in the winter, the least attractive.

I found the University system very different from any to which I had been accustomed at Oxford. There was of course no tutorial system. Arriving there, I found that the arrangement of classes was most casual. There was no sort of supervision of the way in which I conducted my classes. I could have taught them anything or in any way I liked and no authority, so far as I could see, would have been any the wiser. Some twenty or thirty young men had 'registered' for my class. They received 'credits' from the mere fact of attendance. My first task was to call the roll and mark in all who were present. Any students who were absent more than a certain number of times failed in the course. I forget in what way I had to report the names of absentees. It was the custom from time to time—about, I think, once a fortnight—that I should give the students some sort of test on the topics on which I had been speaking. (I caused, I remember, amusement and bewilderment by speaking of these assignments as 'fortnightly'. The word 'fortnight', I discovered, was unknown in America.) The idea of giving periodic test papers was reasonable enough, and, if it was the custom, there was no harm in giving marks for the papers, even though the Oxford system was of course to mark by Greek letters rather than by numbers. But what was curious was the enormously high marks which it was customary and almost obligatory to award. I found that students would complain bitterly of a mark of less than 90 per cent for quite ordinarily competent work.

The predominant political opinion among the Faculty was Democratic and supported the Roosevelt New Deal, but the authorities paid extreme attention to the wealthy capitalist trustees and were very sensitive to any doctrine that might be termed 'Socialist'. They did not perhaps much approve of Roosevelt personally but they approved of men who held high official position. Therefore in November, 1935, Roosevelt and Carlos P. Romulo, the Philippine leader, were duly honoured by a reception and an honorary degree. Of the general social teachings of the Church little was known either by the professors or their students. 'I don't think the Popes know very much about America,' said one of the priests to me, thus dismissing Pius XI's *Quadragesimo Anno*. Yet he was almost slavishly obedient to papal edicts about personal morals. *Casti Connubi* ranked much higher than *Quadragesimo Anno*.

The state of religion I found very difficult to assess. The standard of information about the Christian religion was almost unbelievably low. 'What does the word "crucified" mean?' a boy asked. There was a crucifix behind the professor's desk on the wall, as there had doubtless always been similar crucifixes behind the desks of the masters who had taught him at the various schools at which he had received his previous education. 'What do you think that is behind my chair?' He had never noticed it. 'How do you think that Christ died then?' 'Guess he was kind o' beheaded.'

It was orthopraxy rather than orthodoxy that they valued, though they would not have said as much. They obeyed. They thought doubtless that they believed, but they did not know what they believed or much care to inquire. Religion was to them a business proposition. They had not much sense of its mystery. It was a matter of mathematics rather than of poetry. Undesirable literature was freely confiscated and burnt.

Yet in a military sort of way the standard of religious practice was extraordinarily high. A bulletin about the doings of the University was published, and in it was contained the statistics of the number of students who had received communion voluntarily on every week-day. The number was always high. The University had at that time a most notable football team led by four great footballers who were known as the Four Horsemen of the Apocalypse. It was as a football school that Notre Dame had won its national reputation. When during a match—or game as the Americans call it—the players were in a huddle prior to making a play it was the custom for the captain to recite to the rest a Hail Mary for success. On the morning of the game it was expected that an especially large number would take communion, and anyone who did not do so was liable to be 'hazed' in some form or other by his companions.

But what was the degree of belief that this strange combination of ignorance and fervent practice betokened? I am not at all able to say. I would be interested to see some reliable estimate of how Notre Dame boys of that generation made out in their religious practice in later life. I had never seen one. There was no custom of the professors ever inviting the students to their houses or offering them entertainment, and I never had any chance of getting to know many of them in the way that I easily got to know so many of the boys at Stonyhurst. The professors gave their classes and then went their ways. There was very little contact between the professor and his pupils.

Such discoveries were for me interesting, if not of particular moment. What was important was the novelty of living in an atmosphere that was entirely un-English. I had never thought of myself as a British imperialist. I had been willing to criticise the various British governments that ruled over me, and in particular had been from my early youth an Irish Nationalist. But, like most Englishmen of the day, I had grown up in an atmosphere that took the British Empire for granted. Some of the means by which the Empire had been acquired may have been questionable, but there it was. That was the way in which the world was ordered. It might be ephemeral and destined to come to an end some time. But I had never thought that it could come to an end in any near future or in my lifetime. Britain was one of *the* countries of the world and what Britain said must always be of very crucial importance.

The America to which I returned in 1935 was in a number of ways a very different place from that which I had left ten years before. The confident Republican domination had been broken by the Depression. The Democrats under Roosevelt were in power, and this meant in the curious confusion of American politics that in the Southern States—in the Bible-thumping Protestant States—the white Anglo-Saxon Protestants—the W.A.S.P.s—were in power and in the Northern States the cosmopolitan immigrant Catholics had influence. Prohibition had vanished, and though Americans still drank in the barbaric fashion of filling themselves with highballs before a meal and then filing into the diningroom to chill themselves with iced water, still it was possible now to sit around freely in something that could be called a pub and which was in fact called a saloon, without the feeling that one was a degraded schoolboy wondering if one would be caught by the master. Above all the bathtub was on the way out. It was by then almost impossible to get what civilised people called a bath—a tub in which a man could lie down. Nothing but showers were available. In all the country there was no public urinal except one in New York.

In some ways the America of 1935 differed equally drastically from the America of today. America has always been a violent and lawless country and it was the violence of its gang warfare which was largely responsible for bringing prohibition to an end. Our house in Mishawake Avenue was about a mile distant from the railway depot. We had no car and, as I went round the country lecturing, I often had either to leave from or to arrive at the depot in the hours of darkness. It never occurred to me to hesitate about walking home in the dark. Last year I finished a radio performance in Denver a little before midnight. They asked me how I would return to my hotel a few hundred yards away. I replied that I would be willing enough to walk. 'Are you mad?' they said. 'You won't have a hope of hell arriving in safety,' and they insisted on driving me the short distance in a car. Even then the chauffeur would not allow me to take the risk of walking across the street, but insisted on putting me down on the same side of the street as the entrance.

There was thus very little contact at Notre Dame between the professor and the student. Nor was there much personal contact between the priests and the lay teachers. The lay teachers were for the most part (though not all of them) Catholics, but they tended to be rather anti-clerical, looking on the priests as hard and rigid employers. I remember a poor, inoffensive little man who taught geography. He had been so ill-advised as to have only two children, and they a considerable time ago. He was sent for one day and questioned to make sure that this defect was not the consequence of any contraceptive practice.

The scholarly standing of Notre Dame has very greatly improved since these times, now thirty-five years ago. I cannot be pretended that it was then very high. A young man can get as good an education in the United States as anywhere in the world. With American financial resources it would be surprising if it were not so. But he cannot get it as an undergraduate. I remember a nice Mexican colleague whom I had at Notre Dame. He had taken a course in France at the Sorbonne and was loudly contemptuous of any pretence that there was any comparison between the states of European and of American Universities. The American ideal is that every boy and girl should have a college education and thus many receive such an education who have no academic bent at all. As Mr Kingsley Amis puts it, 'More means worse,' and eccentric foibles must be catered for. I remember when on a false rumour that my mother-in-law was dead two young men called on me, avid for business. They offered their services for which, as they told me, they were well qualified as they had majored in 'morticianary services' at the University of Texas. He who wishes to equip himself as a fully educated person in America does so by his post-graduate work. But post-graduate work in the late 1930's was only just beginning at Notre Dame.

Notre Dame differed in some ways from most American Universities. It was of course Catholic, run by an order of French foundation but whose members were now predominantly Irish. The students all lived on the campus. There was no fraternity system such as at that time existed at most American Universities. Hazing, or the beating up of freshmen by their seniors, not as a punishment for any offence but simply to teach them to know their proper place in life, now generally discouraged but then widely practised in many American Colleges, was never admitted in any violence at Notre Dame. The students all lived in halls on the campus—halls that were not unlike houses at an English public school. They ate in the dining hall or in the cafetaria. The Church and the Golden Dome over the University building dominated the not especially impressive Campus. Unlike most American Universities, it was wholly male. The woman's college a mile away on the other side of a busy motorway was presided over by a remarkable nun and poet, Sister Madeleva.

Arriving at Notre Dame, I found myself for the first time in my life in an entirely different atmosphere and one that I had up till then hardly understood to exist. Notre Dame was an Irish University. The nickname of the football team was the Fighting Irish. Those who played in it were either Irish or German or Polish. The Fathers were almost all Irish. In the previous war they had been strong advocates of neutrality until America actually came into the war. In the Anglo-Irish quarrels of the years after the war they had been to a man strongly on the Irish side. Great friends of mine with whom I frequently drank—an exuberant black-haired architect, Vincent Fagan, and others—had subscribed considerable sums to buy machine guns to equip the Sinn Feiners who were fighting against the Black and Tans. The battle between Catholics and Protestant was to them simply a battle between Irish and English. I remember being taken home by a kindly host after Christmas Midnight Mass. He had picked me up in his cups and had no idea who I was. When I explained that I was an English Catholic he flatly refused to believe me. 'You can't be,' he said. 'The English aren't Catholics.'

There was no especially acute Anglo-Irish contention at the time when I arrived at Notre Dame and Englishmen—though not the British Empire—were reasonably acceptable. The air was filled with the rumours of Mussolini's intention to invade Abyssinia. I knew nothing about Abyssinia save what I had heard from Evelyn Waugh, whose accounts of the ineffectiveness of Haile Selassie's attempt to reform the country published in *Waugh in Abyssinia* were highly amusing and, I was prepared to believe, true. In the Cathedral library at Wells there had been an early renaissance *History of Abyssinia*, which began with the words, 'Now the first Emperor of Abyssinia of whom we have any certain knowledge was Chus, the son of Cham, who took possession thereof immediately after the Flood.' I had introduced Evelyn to this and he included this quotation in his book. Yet my lingering faith in the League of Nations caused me to be much concerned at the proposal of a member of the League to seize by force of arms the territory of another member. If such acts of aggression were to be allowed there was no saying to what straits we would come in a few years' time. I did not greatly like the imposition of sanctions but, if told as much by those better entitled to an opinion, I was prepared to think that sanctions were necessary. At least I did not doubt that those who advocated them did so out of a disinterested devotion to peace, and I did not doubt that if the League of Nations declared for sanctions, they would be effective. I did not take in how many others there were of quite different opinion. It was therefore a great surprise to me on my arrival at Notre Dame to be confronted with an entirely different category of judgements. I was told that it would be purely hypocritical for the British, who had so much, to object to the acquisition of a colony by the Italians. It was taken for granted that the British only objected to Italian acquisition because they were planning to acquire the territory themselves. The League of Nations was a British-dominated organisation. The British with characteristic perfidy used the pretendedly international organisation in order, when it suited them, to pursue their own policies. France being also a member of the League of Nations was, it was recognised, in a position of some difficulty. She was naturally reluctant to allow herself to be used merely as an instrument of British policies. At the same time her fear of Germany made her also reluctant wholly to break with Britain and the League. Her conduct was tortuous but intelligible.

However there was another aspect of the problem with which I was more deeply concerned than with a defence or criticism of Chamberlain's policies. As I have said, when I became a Catholic I did so largely—too largely as I came to see—because I wished to belong to an organisation. I saw the Catholic Church as the great creative force of Western civilisation—incomparably the highest achievement of Man—and threw myself with enthusiasm into defence of every Catholic cause in the present world, defending a number of causes on which I was not adequately informed and some that were not defensible. I accepted inevitably the belief that, even when the Pope was not infallible, yet a special grace informed him. That his policies were policies of impeccable virtue I took for granted. I was not at that time acquainted with Newman's sentences written in 1871 in which he said, 'I had been accustomed to believe that, over and above that attribute of infallibility which attached to the doctrinal decisions of the Holy See, a gift of sagacity had in every age characterised its occupants so that we might be sure, as experience taught us, without it being a dogma of faith, that what the Pope determined was the very measure, or the very policy, expedient for the Church at the time when he determined. I am obliged to say that a sentiment which history has impressed on me, and impresses still, has been considerably weakened as far as the present Pope (Pius IX) is concerned.'

The challenge that troubled me was this. If there was one clear teaching of Christianity, it was that war, killing and violence were great evils. I was not prepared to assert, any more than it was asserted by the general mind of the Church, that that involved absolute pacifism and absolute non-resistance. I was prepared to admit that there were extreme circumstances where the use of a little immediate violence might prevent greater violence. It might be legitimate to use force in police action or in self-defence. But quite obviously on any Christian principle it was only then that it was legitimate to use violence—only when the whole structure of society was threatened. Now, whatever the blemishes on Abyssinian society under Haile Selassie, it was clear that his regime in Abyssinia was no threat to the Italian way of life. If ever there was an unnecessary war, Italy's attack on Abyssinia was such a war. Mussolini claimed that Abyssinia would provide a home for Italy's surplus population. This, even if true, was hardly a valid excuse for seizing the territory, and it was in fact nonsense. Therefore, if the Pope was to claim to be the guardian of the moral law, if ever there was an issue on which he ought to have spoken, it was in condemnation of that war. I did not claim to know enough about Italian conditions to say whether Mussolini's overthrow of the Parliamentary regime was morally justified. I was quite prepared to allow that there were two sides to that and to agree that the Pope was right to reserve judgement. But on the Abyssinian war the issue was clear. Yet no clear word came either from the Vatican or from the Italian bishops. The bishops were indeed far worse than the Vatican.

That the Abyssinian regime had its defects—that many people had just grievances against it and among them many Italians, I did not doubt. Equally I could see that, at any rate in the view of the Vatican, the concordat between Church and State was an advantage; that, if the Church saw fit to defy the State, the State would be likely to revenge itself by measures that made uncomfortable the life of pious Catholics in Italy. Orders might be expelled, revenue confiscated, freedom of action in many ways impeded. Reasons such as these might well be sufficient to justify a secular state turning a blind eye to some of the actions of another secular state—saying, 'It is no concern of mine.' But the Church was not a secular state. It was either the voice of God or it was nothing. If its claims were at all valid, then it had the promise of Christ that the gates of hell (whatever exactly they might be) would not prevail against it. It was proper enough to show prudence in minor matters of no moral content and not wantonly to defy the world and make more difficult the lives of private Catholics for no real purpose. But where there was a real moral issue, surely if the Church was to be anything, it must defy the consequences and take its stand. And what was a real moral issue if an unnecessary war was not one? Yet the Church did not speak. There was nothing like a clear voice saying that this was an unjust war, which Catholics should not support.

I could not but contrast the conduct of the Italian bishops towards the Abyssinian War with the Vatican's conduct in the conflict a few years before over Lord Strickland's behaviour in Malta. There, in a little island where the Church had for generations enjoyed enormous privileges, it was at least arguable that those privileges should be brought under some sort of control—that it would have been to the advantage of the Church that some of the privileges of ecclesiastics should not remain quite un- bridled. Lord Strickland, himself a Catholic, made certain suggestions which were at any rate, one would have thought, arguably desirable. Yet then, when a voice was raised against ecclesiastical privilege, the Church had, it seemed, no sense at all that there might be two sides to the question, that it might be a matter for debate and compromise. Its verdict was instant and without qualification. Lord Strickland's policies were condemned. The contrast was very disturbing. It was hard not to reach the conclusion that, when the Church spoke of itself as the upholder of the moral law, what it was really concerned to do was to uphold the rights of the Church—the rights of the Church to its property. It was concerned with the rights of Catholics to practise their religion—but it was much less deeply concerned about the rights of non-Catholics.

The same lesson seemed to me to be taught by events in Germany. Hitler came to power in that country. Before the National Socialists had got into power the Church and the German bishops were outspoken in their opposition to them. Catholics were forbidden to belong to the party. Yet, when it came into power, we learnt to our surprise that, far from condemning its government, the Church had signed a concordat with it. The Catholic Centre party in the Reichstag joined with other political parties in giving it their support. I was not very deeply concerned as to what the Centre party did, for they were only a political party, compelled by the nature of their being to indulge in political party manouevres if they were to survive. For that reason I was very doubtful if it was desirable to have a Catholic political party, but that was another matter.

The whole policy of the Church ever since Consalvi and the Congress of Vienna had been based on the formula of the Alliance of Church and Altar—the belief that the desirable relation between the Church and State was one of formal amity and of the recognition of the Church as the possessor of special privileges through a concordat. Political Catholics must do as they could do. But that the Church should give official recognition today to that which yesterday it had condemned as immoral just because it was momentarily successful was more disturbing. The argument that was used was that the Nazi regime was a ruthless regime. It would give a measure of toleration to those who agreed to cooperate with it. It would not hesitate to persecute those who stood out against it. Therefore for the comfort of the Catholics it was necessary to make a compromise with it. I could appreciate this argument. Whether if the Church had stood out against Hitler from the first he would have been strong enough to take these measures against it, I could not be sure. But in any event I was in no position to take a decision on this. I could appreciate the argument—I was no expert on German affairs, did not know the language and had only very infrequently visited the country. I had not at that time read *Mein Kampf*, and if a well-informed critic had put to me the question why the Pope should condemn the Nazis I should doubtless not have come with any competence out of the cross-examination. The Nazis might or might not be right in wishing to overthrow the parliamentary Weimar system, but that was not an issue on which the Pope was called on to take a stand. The Church had very often worked—and rightly worked—with non-parliamentary governments. Indeed, if we accepted the *Syllabus Errorum* as an authority it would be easier to make a case for it that Catholic tradition condemned a government for being democratic than for the reverse. It was certainly no business of the Pope to condemn Hitler because he protested against the Treaty of Versailles. Most English liberal opinion, in which I had been brought up, had been doing just that for a decade. It was hardly for the Pope to protest when Hitler reintroduced conscription. He might be right or he might be wrong, but the Allied powers at Versailles had disarmed Germany with a promise that German disarmament would be a preliminary to their own disarmament. The French had made no attempt to fulfil that promise and it was understandable of Hitler to say that, if the French will not disarm, then we will rearm. I did not feel the competence to enter into these arguments but it required no expert knowledge to be puzzled by the question.

Desmond Fitzgerald was my colleague as a visiting professor at Notre Dame. I had first met him at luncheon with Lady Lavery in company with Douglas Woodruff and Denis Gwynn, the son of Stephen Gwynn, critic of Conrad and Nationalist Member for Galway. Hazel Lavery in those days of the 1920's was one of my closest friends. She combined the roles of social lioness and ardent Irish patriot. Guests from both camps were to be found at her bounteous table. She entertained the Irish delegates when they were over for the Treaty negotiations and I remember her telling how at the time Lady Londonderry, seeing her at a reception, turned her back on her in protest against her keeping company with murder and treason. I could not pretend to belong to the high social set nor yet to be an Irish patriot. Yet with generosity she received Douglas Woodruff and me into her circle, and I saw a great deal of her during the next year and, when my daughter arrived, she became her godmother. Critics sometimes said of her that there was a certain absurdity in her patronage of revolutionaries, combined with a belief that all social life would go on unaltered, and perhaps there was something in the criticism. But she was a creature of infinite charm, generosity and piety, and possessed of a considerable artistic capacity. She survives today on the Irish bank-notes. I was a little shocked one day in Ireland to hear John Grigg ask whose was the figure on the back of the bank-notes. It was a proof of the rapidity of oblivion. She wore herself out with her unflagging social life and died, alas, at the age of thirty-nine. She was unable to rest. John Lavery said of her in explanation of her demise, 'If there was only the cat in the room, Hazel would feel that she had to entertain it.' My last memory of her was of her asking me to pray for her in her illness. 'Do pray,' she said, 'it does help.' When the Treaty came she was strongly on its side. I perhaps did not fully understand the strangeness of the mixture of company at her table—men of the most simple Irish piety, like Mr Cosgrave, cheek by jowl with the most sophisticated of the artistic world.

Desmond Fitzgerald was one of those who had taken part in the Easter Rising. The Irish at Notre Dame had therefore been prepared to welcome him with enthusiasm and were perhaps a little disappointed to meet this gentle and cultured mystic, as little like the swashbuckling gunman as could be imagined. Desmond had by then become a supporter of the Free State and an unswerving opponent of Mr de Valera. His opinions had modified into extreme conservatism and on many points he was now, in Notre Dame's view, disappointingly pro-British. He strongly supported Chamberlain over Munich. He refused to join with the demands of the faculty members for the abolition of partition. His wife was a Northern Irelander and his argument on that point was that Southern intransigence was foolish. 'If we started off,' he said, 'by admitting the right of the North, then we could perhaps have protested against their particular acts of injustice. But if we began by saying, "Whether you behave well or ill we deny your right to exist," we can hardly expect them to listen to any particular complaints.' He talked unendingly. I remember leaving him one afternoon arguing in the cafeteria about Duns Scotus. When I came back twenty-four hours later he was still there. His protagonists had supplanted one another from time to time on a relief system, but he continued unabated through it all. In particular he puzzled and dismayed Notre Dame colleagues by supporting the British policy of sanctions against Mussolini. I used to drink with Vince Fagan at the neighbouring saloon which was kept by Pete, an immigrant from Belgium, survivor from a German prison camp in the war. Pete took a great liking to me and always promised that he would leave me in his will his cabin on the shores of Lake Michigan. He has now retired there and happily there is no reason to think from latest reports that he will not outlive me. General opinion in America was opposed to Mussolini on the grounds that he was an Italian and did not believe in democracy, but the Americans had no intention at all of getting involved in the League of Nations or in the quarrel. Its attitude towards European squabbles was very much its attitude towards Wild West films. They were to be watched with amusement. They did not seriously matter. So, when the British refused to impose oil sanctions and then entirely called off sanctions after the capture of Addis Ababa, Vincent Fagan argued with me that the British had never seriously wanted sanctions to work. They were only anxious to create sufficient difficulties for

Mussolini to make it a warning to Hitler not to try any monkey tricks with Britain. I argued in reply that if that was their purpose they had most signally failed in it. The episode had most clearly demonstrated that the League of Nations was something that could be defied with impunity, and when Hitler marched into the Rhineland, he very clearly showed that this was the lesson that he had drawn.

Orlando Weber, at whose instigation I had come to Notre Dame, not himself a Catholic, was a man of German origin and temperament, a natural believer in autocracy and a strong supporter of Hitler, whose final victory he thought quite certain and on no account to be opposed. He was a self-made man. We had a tale—whence derived and whether true or not I cannot say—that he had begun his life in the music halls as a trick cyclist back in Minnesota. In any event he had prospered in life and by now was a millionaire. He was not a naturally active politician and, I imagine (though I do not remember him ever saying as much), had in the 1920's obediently, like other rich men, voted Republican. However he broke with Hoover over his failure to support farm incomes. He told me an anecdote of breakfasting with Hoover and saying to him, 'If you pursue that policy you can never be elected again to any office by the American people.' (As with so many self-made rich men the anecdotes which he related of private interviews tended always to show him as both correct and victorious.) At any rate by the 1930's he had transferred his allegiance to Roosevelt who at any rate had broken with the old foolish belief that in a depression the need was to economise, to cut down all expenditure and thus further to decrease spending power and increase the depression. Weber was an economic nationalist who thought that America was, or could be, substantially self-sufficient and that therefore, for her, foreign trade was unimportant. What was important was to increase farm incomes so that the farmers could buy more from industry. At that time he still had hopes of Roosevelt, and I was engaged to do what I could to see that these wise policies were followed. I was sympathetic enough with these policies which seemed to me sensible. What troubled me more about Weber was his complacent belief in a German autocracy. He dismissed all suggestions of workers' participation in policy as 'eyewash'. He prided himself on never visiting any of his plants about the country. He made his representatives visit him and confronted them with his elaborate diagrams from which he demonstrated how completely he knew all that was going on there. He had little sense that his plants were manned by human beings, and it could not be denied that, though he defended all his policies with powerful arguments, yet the conclusion of all of them was greatly to increase his own power. When I first went to the United States and into his service, foreign policy did not yet bulk very largely in his or in other minds. As the crisis deepened, his Hitlerian sympathies caused him to shift to antagonism towards Roosevelt and also to what he thought of as the sentimental sympathies of a power-fearing Englishman and we drifted apart. He died in the early years of the war, an impenitent opponent of America's involvement in it. He was, I must confess, always very generous to me.

At that time I was a most enthusiastic devotee of Franklin Roosevelt and, indeed, allowing for the fact that in the closing months of his life he was suffering, as we all know, both from failing health and failing judgement, I remained substantially so to the end. I was certainly attracted to him by the very undiluted malice of his opponents—those big tycoons who in the first months of his rule had lived in terror of their lives and who, when the worst of the crisis was passed, turned against the man who had saved them because in the process they had lost a little money. The American rich of the early 1930's were not a lovely lot. We in Britain certainly owe him a most deep debt for having brought his country into the war in spite of the originally overwhelming determination of the American people to stay out. Still, so much has been written in estimation of his policies and of his character that it would be to no purpose to add another estimate here. Orlando Weber's conviction at the beginning of his presidency was that, after his crippling accident, he had become convinced that he was divinely ordained for a special destiny. I think that he was always a man of burning ambition and what was remarkable was his refusal to be conquered by his disability. He was certainly a man of great personal charm, who had the gift of giving to the most undistinguished of companions the attractive impression that he was enormously interested in what he or she was saying. This was a natural gift, but it was of course one that he culvitated and used as a political asset. Without it he would certainly never have had the success which he did have. How far he was really interested I cannot say. I was not at the time so foolish as to think that his interest in such conversations as mine was more than a polite and passing courtesy. But there is a long tale of those on whom at one time he seemed to rely but who afterwards found that they had been discarded. History seems to be agreed that he was not a man of deep affections. People were valuable to him in so far as he could use them.

My interest in his policies was first aroused by the admirable Dr

McNair Wilson, the medical correspondent of *The Times*. McNair Wilson became a great critic of the monetary system, in which he was quite right. He wrote in criticism of the Money Power. But he also became convinced that autocratic government, which he called Monarchy, had been throughout all history the Money Power's unswerving enemy, which was a great deal more doubtful. Of Roosevelt he prophesied that he could be re-elected President of the United States for a hundred years. When his wife timidly objected that this would not be possible because he would die, Wilson, shaking his finger at her, like a denunciatory Old Testament prophet pronounced, 'If he will that I tarry till I come, what is that to thee?'

I do not know that Roosevelt was a great or deep reader. He preferred to learn from conversation and it was from conversation that he learnt what books were about. 'The one thing that the world today needs more than anything else is a new, rattling good life of Charles Martel,' he said one day to Hilaire Belloc. How much did he really know about Charles Martel? Would he have read such a book had it appeared, whether by Belloc or another?

He was at home in Europe—more so probably than any of his successors until John Kennedy, but his table was an American rather than a European one. The food was abominable and at lunch only coffee was served as a beverage throughout the meal in a very un-European fashion. This, though I knew nothing of such things at the time, was, as I have learnt from subsequent reading, probably due to the influence of Mrs Roosevelt.

I made also at that time through my writings another strange friend, Ezra Pound. Ezra Pound was of course an enthusiastic supporter of Mussolini and imagined—I think with little evidence—that Mussolini's attack on the Money Power was of the same kind as that which I had exposed in *The Breakdown of Money*. I soon found the enthusiasm of his argument embarrassing. During the war I had at the Air Ministry the duty of monitoring foreign broadcasts and was a little dismayed to read one day in an extract from an Italian talk by Ezra Pound, 'Who today in England dares speak of Christopher Hollis?' He obviously took it for granted that I had been suppressed in the reign of terror that ruled in war-time England—probably shot under 18B. I concealed the extract from my superiors at the Air Ministry and have never, I think, till this day, mentioned it to anyone—any more than I have broadcast how at the arrest of Vassall, the Russian spy, part of the evidence that he was living far beyond his legitimate means was a shelf of books in his flat that were photographed behind him and that prominent in it appeared a copy of my book *Eton*.

In America, as indeed in England, I found all too common evidence of a prejudice among Catholics that could not even be excused by prudence. Catholics were often strongly anti-Semitic, sometimes almost with insane violence, and more outspokenly so in America than in England, where Jews were often specifically excluded from clubs and housing districts in a way that would hardly be known in England. The Catholics argued that the Jew was a foreigner who could not be a truly patriotic citizen of the country, America or Britain, to which he professed to belong. His true loyalty was elsewhere. As this was exactly the complaint that many Protestants made about Catholics, it always seemed to me an extremely strange and extremely foolish argument on Catholic lips.

My own interest in Jews at that time was entirely cerebral. I had been brought up in the liberal atmosphere which taught that the difference between Jew and Gentile was no more than the difference between a red-headed man and a black-headed man and that it was a barbarity to pay any attention to such a difference in the according of social or religious rights. In contrast to that I heard of Belloc's thesis that the Jew was a wholly different being and had read how Herschl, a free-thinking Viennese intellectual, had, as he thought, learnt from the Dreyfus case that the Jew who imagined that anti-Semitism was dead, or would ever die, was living in a fool's paradise. The Jew, if he was to be secure, argued Herschl, must have a home of his own. But that in Herschl's mind was a purely secularist argument, and it did not greatly matter where the Jew was given his home. Sinai or Kenya or South America would do as well as Palestine.

It was only after the war when I found myself as chairman of Cardinal Heenan's Commission for the Implementation of the Decrees of the Vatican Council concerning the Jews and came to associate with Jewish friends that I acquired a certain understanding why the Jews believed what they did. I very well of course understood the Jewish reaction against Christian persecution throughout the ages and to the atrocities of Hitler. No theology was required to make that intelligible, nor to make intelligible the Jewish determination to find a home in Palestine at a time when they could not find a home anywhere else. But up till then I had always thought of the Jews as indeed a Chosen People, as was proved by their survival out of the melting pot of the old Babylonian mélange. But it never occurred to me that they had been chosen for any other purpose than to produce Christ, and, having failed in that task, they had forfeited their privilege. Even before the Second Vatican Council I had rejected as a barbarity the notion that law-abiding Jews of today, walking the streets of New York or Manchester, should be held personally guilty of the death of Christ—a view which I regret to say I had heard defended even by some of the good Fathers of Stonyhurst— but I had rejected discrimination of the Jews merely because I had rejected discrimination against anyone. It was not until quite lately that I came to understand that the Jews by no means thought of themselves as chosen merely to give birth to Christ. In all the early years of Jewish history there was no mention of Messiah. Moses knew nothing of him. He was the discovery of the much later great prophets. And even then, when they told their fellow Jews to look for Messiah, they had no conception that Messiah would be God and endowed with all the attributes of the Athanasian Son. He would be much more like Mahomet. The notion of a Virgin Birth, so far from being a notion too high for their believing, was a notion that was to them purposeless if not repulsive. The Greeks had a notion of the sacredness of virginity. The Jews had no such notion. The Jews thought of themselves as a race chosen by God not so much to produce Messiah as to guard monotheism in a polytheistic world, and from that point of view the claims of a Trinity seemed to them a slip back from monotheism to polytheism. It is in a way a curiosity that Arab and Jew should be at warfare with one another, for the two great monotheistic religions of Jew and Mahommedan are very similar to one another—much more alike than either is to the Christian. The European may suspect the Jew as an Oriental in his midst. To the Arab he is the European intruder into an Oriental world. Perhaps in a generation's time when the surplus of Asiatic and African immigration has made Palestine a Jewish but now predominantly Oriental country the problem will be soluble. To the argument of the pacifist that force is no remedy and that he should follow a policy of non-resistance, the Jew answers that he has followed such a policy for two thousand years and it brought him to Hitler's gas chambers. To the argument of the internationalist that he should rely on the resolutions of the United Nations he replies that the other nations have given him little reason to believe that in the hour of extremity they would save his nation from destruction. He prefers to rely on his own arms.

I went back to England at the end of the summer semester in June, 1936. By that time Mussolini's successful defiance of the League of Nations and Hitler's successful re-occupation of the Rhineland had already showed that there was no hope of preserving peace through the machinery of collective security. Then the civil war in Spain broke out. Catholic opinion in England as in the United States was generally on Franco's side. Catholics were primarily concerned with the attacks on churches and religion. The war seemed to them a war for the defence of religion. To the general public in both countries that issue was secondary. They knew Franco as the creature of Hitler and Mussolini, and Hitler and Mussolini were their enemies. Up till then, ever since the First World War ended, the Church had been reasonably popular. Violent anti-Catholic prejudice was looked on as an uncouth prejudice which enlightened people had transcended. The Spanish war and the Pope's championship of Franco's cause changed all that. The Catholic in liberal circles was seen as the enemy of our liberties and became at once very much more unpopular.

I had been accepted with little justification as the European authority on the Notre Dame campus. Among the blind the one-eyed man was king. On the way back to Notre Dame in the early months of 1937 I landed first in Canada and lectured in Ottawa. Lord Tweedsmuir was then the Governor General of Canada. I knew him a little already from Oxford days. I had lunch with him and he assured me that I was quite right to be optimistic and that the international situation was getting steadily better. I assumed that he knew something and was comforted. I kept that comfort as long as I could but as things developed it was not easy to keep it with any great confidence. When I returned in 1937 there were new figures established at Notre Dame. Charles du Bos, the distinguished French intellectual, was there. He was a cousin of Hilaire Belloc and I had already met him in Paris through the Bellocs. But, though cousins, the two men were very different. Belloc, for all his French characteristics, had absolutely nothing of the French reverence for a writer—for a *cher mâitre*. He despised writers and thought respect for them ridiculous. Du Bos on the other hand was a typical French intellectual with an almost excessive respect for all literary or intellectual achievements. Belloc—bluntly and not very justly—dismissed him as 'a frightful bore'.

A more potent new arrival at Notre Dame was Waldemar Gurian. This enormous German Jewish Catholic savant, who had been born in Russia but brought up in Germany, had fled before Hitler along with others of his kind and found his refuge at Notre Dame where they had given him a professorship. He was a man of vast learning in the Teutonic fashion. He had never been to England but he was enormously acquainted with all that was printed in England, as indeed in other countries. His defect was that, learning entirely through the printed word, he had no conception at all of the relative importance of the different authors whom he had unearthed. He used to bring me odd little paragraphs from the most obscure papers and wave them in my face as evidence of British policy. Nothing would convince him that Percy Wyndham Lewis's influence in England was not immense—'serious' he called him. His life had been one of shuttle between Germany and Russia and he therefore had no conception of a society in which variety of opinion was permitted and in which things were said that were quite unofficial. He prophesied with utter confidence that in three years' time Sir Oswald Mosley would be the ruler of England. He had no roots of his own. He commissioned Vince Fagan to build him a house. Vince accepted the commission but asked for more details of what was required. 'I want it big enough to take my books,' he replied 'and my wife.' (She was of ample proportions.) 'Otherwise I don't mind, I should like to go away for the week-end and when I come back find the house finished.'

He was violently opposed to the British policy that was being pursued by Neville Chamberlain and seemed to hold me personally responsible or at any rate a full advocate of that policy. It was a most embarrassing suspicion and one that it was quite impossible to remove, for a protest that really Neville Chamberlain's policy had nothing to do with me was of course met with an obviously sceptical shrug which plainly indicated that he did not wish to call me a liar to my face but that he well understood that this was the sort of unconvincing lie that one would naturally expect from a secret agent. A situation that would in any event have been unpleasant was made more unpleasant when a travelling Englishman, who lived in Italy and had become an enthusiastic member of the Fascist party, visited Notre Dame. He fell into an argument with Gurian as to whether Mussolini's government had attempted to prevent the distribution of *Non Abiamo Bisogno*, the Papal encyclical against Fascism. It ended in his making a bet with Gurian for, I think, a hundred dollars. It was shown that he had lost his bet, but he left without paying up and then wrote Gurian a not very worthy letter of apology, emphasising that he was unable to pay and that he trusted that Gurian could let him off as he would have let Gurian off had the situation been reversed. Gurian brought the letter and the story to me and explained that he was in no position to waive the debt as he had already promised the money to some organisation for the support of anti-Nazi refugees, which he assisted. I was in no way concerned with the bet and indeed had not heard about it until Gurian told me the tale. I felt that I had no alternative but to pay. Gurian accepted the money with thanks but the whole incident clearly left the worst of impressions on his mind. This was the way in which English Fascists behaved. They welshed on their bets and, when tracked down, got another Fascist colleague grudgingly to pay up so as to save them from exposure.

I respected Gurian, though I was frankly terrified of him, and his inquisitions so frightened me that if I saw him sitting in the cafeteria where we had our meals I would go out and get my food at Pete's so as to escape his attacks—a form of poltroonery that I do not remember ever to have employed with anyone else. Very great was the contrast between the overbearing Gurian and that other great Jewish refugee who during those years found his home in the United States. Einstein was the most gentle and humble of men. They had given him a home at Princeton. There his neighbour in the next house was a little schoolboy of fifteen. He kindly volunteered that, if his services should ever be of use, he would be only too glad to help his little friend with his home-work. One day his friend brought to him a Euclidean problem which he was unable to solve. Einstein promised his assistance but appeared the next morning with tears in his eyes. He had, he confessed, sat up all night wrestling with the problem but had wholly failed. He had quite forgotten how to solve it. Gurian's basic position was quite simple. Hitler was the devil. His regime was as evil as could be. There had been other evil men in history. Bismarck was an evil man. He wanted things to which he was not entitled. But Bismarck was an 'ordinate' man, as he called him. His ambitions were limited. He knew when to stop. If you granted what he wanted you could do business and make a bargain with him. Hitler was an 'inordinate' man. There was no possibility of satisfying him, of making a bargain with him. Concede one demand and he would immediately go forward to make another.

Hitler being of such a nature, the leaders of the other nations, if they had had sense or courage, would have prevented his accession to power. It was merely folly and ignorance which allowed them to be beguiled by his successive plausible justifications for the particular steps which he took, one after the other. The notion that such concessions could satisfy him was idiotic. Every concession merely led to a further demand—and each concession made it more difficult to resist the next demand. The statesmen of Europe were not men of the calibre to make against him this stand that was required. France was in disarray, 'nefast', as he called it. The only man who could have made a stand was Chamberlain for Britain, and he in poltroonery and ignorance did not do so. I remember

Gurian saying to me one day, 'Hitler will get all Europe. That is certain. Mussolini wishes to get all the Mediterranean. Of that I am not so sure.' 'But in the end?' I asked. 'Oh, he is mad and madness is sure to end in destruction,' Gurian replied. 'But he will destroy all else in destroying himself.' Since Chamberlain was not present at Notre Dame the blows of reprehension must fall on me as his representative, responsible for Chamberlain's policy.

When I went to Notre Dame at the beginning of 1937 I found the Catholics—at Notre Dame as elsewhere—supported Franco, thinking of him as the upholder of religion. Public opinion at large opposed him, imagining that the so-called Loyalists were the defenders of the constitution. It is hard, as things have turned out, to decide which opinion was the more ridiculous. But when I returned to Notre Dame for a third term in 1938 I found a new situation with Gurian installed there. On the intrinsic Spanish issues Gurian was contemptuously indifferent. He had no high opinion of the way in which parliamentary institutions had been managed in Spain in the past or in which they were likely to be managed in the future. The whole issue was no longer a Spanish issue. Its importance was as a manoeuvre for ensuring Hitler's mastery of Europe. The dress rehearsal for the world war was being fought out on Spanish soil. Of course Franco would win the war, if one chose to be beguiled by such language. What was really happening was that Hitler and Mussolini were winning it for him, and Hitler wished him to win it in order to establish on France's western frontier a puppet of his own and thus to make it impossible for France to act effectively against him when the real war came. Of course events were to prove that Gurian and, I dare say, Hitler greatly exaggerated the degree to which Franco would be willing to play puppet to Hitler's policies. Nevertheless Gurian's analysis was certainly much more realistic than that of enthusiastic Catholics who had seen the whole business as no more than a Spanish Holy War, and Gurian knowing so much more about it than I did, knew also much more than any of the Americans on the Notre Dame campus. He had a number of converts and I found that I returned to a campus bitterly divided and puzzled.

The year 1938 was a very unhappy time for me. I had my good friends and continued to assure them that there would be no war, but naturally under Gurian's withering contempt I spoke with ever decreasing assurance. My wife and family had not come with me this time and I was alone, the only Englishman on the campus, in all probability the only Englishman in South Bend. The Americans took their sides and gaily argued the toss. But it was no more than a secondary matter to them. Those of my friends who supported Franco were Irishmen who had long convinced themselves that British devious propaganda had tricked America into the last war. They were entirely determined that nothing should inveigle their nation into the next one and, therefore, since they did not intend to become involved in it their interest was comparatively tepid and academic. I said to Vince Fagan that the Irish influence in America—or at least at Notre Dame—was strong and anti-British.

'Why, hell!' he said, 'how can you talk about Irish influence? People of English origin are only a minority of the American population. Yet practically every position of importance in American history has always gone to men of Limey or at least of Ulster origin. We argue about whether America should remain isolationist or whether she should intervene. We merely take it for granted that if she should intervene she would intervene on Britain's side.'

And indeed I remembered a German American priest at Notre Dame who had argued of the First World War, 'I think we should have declared war on England,' and how the notion, even by Irish isolationists, was laughed out of court as a joke. If they had guessed what we now know about Roosevelt's intentions and secret policies, their support of him would perhaps have been less firm.

I had a certain sympathy with the isolationist point of view. I was inclined to think that, if it had not been for Edward Grey's follies and secret engagements, we could have kept out of the 1914 war, and, if it was legitimate for us to try to keep out, it was even more legitimate for the Americans. But, though it might well be that they should keep out, I did not think that they would. I remember being asked one day at a party if I thought that there was any reason why America should be involved in the next war. I replied that I did not think that there was any reason why she should be involved, but nevertheless I thought that she would be involved. The reply was greeted by some as a supreme example of British Machiavellism, by others with a shout of laughter as a proper expression of contempt for American folly.

It was no pleasure to have to estimate the dangers of Britain being involved in war in the midst of people some of whom were uninterested, some openly hostile, some following the whole story only as one follows a 'blood and thunder' at the cinema. There was no morning paper in South Bend. The *South Bend Tribune*, the town's only paper, came out in the middle of the afternoon. I used to go over to the cafeteria at about tea time, waiting anxiously for the paper's arrival, peeping at the headlines to see if they announced catastrophe. There was of course plenty of catastrophe in the earlier months of that year. One evening the undergraduate boys from the local paper came to tell me that Hitler had marched into Austria and to ask me for my comments. I was just getting into bed when they came to me with the news. I had no useful comment to make. I merely wondered with them what would happen and did not know. I had not at that time been to Austria, but I had some Austrian colleagues on the faculty at Notre Dame. It was their argument that Vienna had through the centuries been the capital of a great Empire. Austria was not only a German state but had traditionally and up till 1866 been the leading German state. Now by the 1914 war she had lost her empire and was left isolated. She had no tradition of isolation. The natural thing was for her, deprived thus of her empire, to join up with Germany. She had attempted to do that immediately after the war but had been prevented by the Allies. The vast majority of Austrians, they told me, wanted to join Germany and there was no chance of peace in Central Europe until they were permitted to do so.

The argument seemed to me coherent and plausible enough, and indeed when Hitler made his entry into Vienna the acclamation which he received was so tumultuous and overwhelming that plenty of people with very much better means of information than mine—the Archbishop of Canterbury, for instance, among them—had no doubt that the consummation of the Anschluss was an exercise in self-determination. 'The annexation,' he said, 'had the support of the majority of the Austrian people.' I dare say that it did. Certainly in the coming war even the imminence of defeat brought no breath of revolt out of Austria against Nazi rule.

But, though Hitler was so ready to use the formula of self-determination when it suited him and though it might be in general the formula by which frontiers ought to be drawn, the method in which he achieved the Anschluss—the bullying of Schuschnigg at Berchtesgaden, the brutal and sudden entry of the troops, the arrest and persecution of the Jews in Vienna—inevitably sent a chill down every spine. Where were such things likely to lead? No honest man, Gurian argued, could feel comfortable if he pretended to defend the Anschluss as a mere exercise in self-determination. No one could feel very much comfort in Goering's promise to the Czechs that the Reich had no designs against them. Naturally enough all this talk about self-determination, all this pretence of apologising for the Anschluss was the sheerest hypocrisy. It was a brutal act of aggression by a madman intent on the conquest of the world. It would, of course, if it was not resisted, be followed by further acts of aggression, each dressed up in whatever terms and pretended justifications it might be convenient to parade and, even when I feebly tried to argue otherwise, I could not deny that in my heart of hearts I no longer felt very sure that Gurian was wrong. I do not think that I had fully understood the horror of Hitler's policy towards the Jews until the time of the entry into Vienna.

I am almost a pacifist. The great majority of wars in history have indeed been fought for a reason but they have not resulted in a solution. Fought to remedy an evil, they have left the world with greater evils than those which they have been fought to remedy. I would certainly say this of the First World War. We all told ourselves that all that we needed was to get rid of the Kaiser and then we would have permanent peace. We got rid of the Kaiser (and the Czar) and what we got instead was Hitler and Stalin. All too often as between one government and another it is six of one and half a dozen of the other, and it is not worth while upsetting the world in order to decide whether, say, Alsace should be ruled by France or Germany. Dr Johnson had a good deal of sense in his refusal to give half a guinea to be ruled by one form of government rather than another. As a general rule the assassination of rulers is wicked because it is futile. You merely get rid of one ruler and put in his place another, perhaps similar, very likely worse. The Kaiser's government in 1914 was of that sort—not at all attractive but not more wicked beyond comparison than any other in the world. But what of Hitler's government in 1939? Was not that uniquely wicked—so wicked that its survival could not be tolerated even if the cost of destroying it was a world war? Assassination was in general wrong and futile, but can we reasonably think that the assassination of Hitler would not have saved a million lives? Of all the great wars of history the war of 1939 was perhaps the one that it is most difficult to oppose. Yet even there one must wonder what would have happened if the world had not fought Hitler. It would certainly have been submitted to intolerable tyranny. But Hitler must have died one day. Might not the world have then recovered some of its liberty? Would it be worse off under defeat than it is now under victory—this world in which our very survival is more doubtful and more desperately threatened than it has ever been before in history? The pacifist who pretends that the road of peace is easy and comfortable is a fool and a liar, but his may be the lesser evil.

Gurian was particularly scornful of Cardinal Innitzer's acceptance of Hitler's conquest and his ejaculation of 'Heil Hitler' at the German entry into Vienna. A little time before, when I still believed that ecclesiastics were filled by the Holy Spirit with a special grace which inspired them to give wise leadership to their people on grave moral issues, I would have attached importance to Cardinal Innitzer's acceptance of Hitler. I would have argued that, if the Church's leadership accepted the regime, it could not be in total defiance of the moral law. I was no longer able to place much confidence in the pronouncements of ecclesiastics. I did not think that they were worse than other people, but it was no longer possible for me to think that they were necessarily better. I did not think that they were more cowardly, but I did not think that they were braver. I could understand it when Cardinal Innitzer said that he must comply in order to save his flock from persecution. I daresay that that was in a measure true. But was surrender likely in the end to save them from persecution? And was his concern solely for his flock and not all for his own skin? And why did he pretend that a perhaps necessary evil was a good? It was the lying that was unforgettable.

I visited Austria after the war and went to call on Cardinal Innitzer. He was a decent enough fellow who would of himself never have done harm to anyone. He only lacked courage. I do not take it upon myself to blame him. Who can say what he himself would have dared to do in face of such a terrible threat? His conduct was by far less awful than that of the Austrian bishop who refused to allow the name of Jagenstatter, a conscientious objector who was beheaded for his refusal to fight in Hitler's army, to be inscribed on the local war memorial even when the war was over and Hitler was no longer to be feared. But, even if it be true—as it well may be—that many would not have behaved better than Innitzer, it is impossible to believe that such a man had any divine grace which enabled him to give to his flock any leadership braver or wiser than that of an average person.

It became evident even in the Middle West that the British Government was not going to challenge Hitler over the Anschluss and there would be no immediate war. It was equally evident that the new regime, far from being won to moderation by the responsibility of office, as some had hoped and even perhaps ventured to prophesy, was utterly ruthless, and not only persecuted all—and particularly Jews—whom it happened to dislike but took a positive and sadistic delight in the process, and persecuted many who would in no way have taken any action against it had they been left alone.

The months brought, as will be remembered, the first complaints and disturbances in the Sudetenland. They brought a very unpleasant few days for me as an isolated Englishman in the Middle West. My American friends without exception knew even less about the situation than I did. I could not deceive myself that their opinions, whether optimistic or the reverse, were of any importance. Apart from them was Gurian, who knew vastly more about it than I and whose opinions were unilluminated by a single ray of hope. There was a day or two of rumours that the German troops were massing at the Sudeten frontier. It was a Sunday. I went to a cinema to see some film of *Romeo and Juliet* in the hope that the scene might provide an escape from the reality about me. I came out and went to the Oliver Hotel in South Bend to buy a paper. The papers were not yet in and I had to wait some minutes for their arrival. Eventually they came. The front page was covered with headlines about a local murder—to Middle Western readers the really important news of the day—but on an inner page I found a message that the Germans had withdrawn their troops, expressing a total inability to understand what the Czechs were making all the fuss about. It seemed that there would not be an immediate war and again I breathed a sigh of relief. But again Gurian of course warned me—and very rightly—against taking any comfort from this. 'Why should there be a war?' he asked. 'There can't be a war if one side is not willing to fight.' It did not mean that Hitler had in any way abandoned his ambitions. It meant merely that he was not for the moment ready to strike. The fact that he was not, made it only the more certain that he would strike as soon as he was ready.

Depressed by Gurian's prophecies and in a state of tortured apprehension, I went terrified out to a party. I discovered that by drinking a great deal I could to a large extent and for the moment dissipate my apprehensions and for the only time in a number of days I went to bed feeling reasonably happy. I have drunk a good deal in my life, but that is the only occasion on which I deliberately used alcohol to drown apprehension.

I was back in England again when the Notre Dame semester finished in the middle of the summer and was therefore at home as the dreadful months spread out towards Munich. Dreadful as it was, it was better to live out such months in England and in the company of those who shared my anxiety than among disinterested strangers in America. My attitude was, I am afraid, quite frankly one of craven terror, but as such not very different from that of the majority of my fellow countrymen.

I knew little about Czechoslovakia. I understood that it was a composite polyglot state and indeed I did not well see how any state in that mixed part of the world could be anything else. Gurian, though of course he had contempt for any notion that Hitler could be bought off by making a concession to him in Czechoslovakia or anywhere else, nevertheless admitted that the Czechs, who had for centuries been the servants of the German-speaking, did sometimes attempt to flaunt their mastery when now at last they had got it. Policemen in Prague, he told me, would pretend that they could not speak German, though in fact they could do so perfectly well. In another atmosphere it might have been a reasonable solution to have conceded the Sudeten territories to Germany, as in fact *The Times* suggested. Indeed even in the present circumstances it might be the lesser evil, since no one could possibly imagine that Hitler would not soon find grievances in the operation of any scheme for Sudeten self-government within the Czechoslovak republic. But only the entirely besotted could believe any more that Hitler, whatever he might say, would ever accept any territorial concessions in Czechoslovakia as a final solution and that a secure peace was possible. Then came Munich. Even today I would be prepared to argue that in view of the improbability of any support from the Dominions, in view of the state of our air defences, in view of French opinion, Chamberlain was, on a miserable balance, right to accept Munich. But it was with a hard cool appraisal of gain and loss that I opened the paper the morning after Munich. 'It is peace.' I read it with a merely craven relief. We went to a celebration dinner that evening. Arriving at the party I was greeted with the news that Duff Cooper had resigned. 'But why?' I asked. 'Because of the terms,' said our hostess, Lady Horner. 'But surely the terms must have been very much what he expected.' And indeed that still seems to me true. If someone had taken on himself to say that Hitler was such a man that one could not talk with him I could have understood it but, if you agreed to negotiate with Hitler at all, you could not have expected any terms particularly different from those Chamberlain brought back.

We had no special obligation to Czechoslovakia, and we had no special obligation to Poland a year later. There were some Catholics to whom Poland, as a Catholic country, sandwiched in between Russia, orthodox or atheist, and Prussia, Lutheran or Nazi, exercised a specially romantic attraction. Poland, we were told, was the test case for the survival of Catholic civilisation. The Treaty of Versailles did well to set Poland free, but the Poles had not made especially edifying use of their freedom. They had persecuted the Jews abominably and this had not only been cruel and unjust in itself. It was a large cause of all the world's troubles, for the Jews had fled from persecution out of Poland into Germany and it was the immigration of these Eastern Jews which very largely inspired

Hitler's anti-Semitism in Germany and caused so many Germans to sympathise with it. The Germans did not so much mind Jews so long as they were only German Jews. I had been largely brought up on the Bellocian interpretation of European politics in which the Jews were always depicted as working for Germany and in which indeed German and Jew were almost identical and interchangeable terms. When first Hitler came into power the Poles made inquiries of the French to see whether they would join them in a preventive war. When the reply to that was negative, then they cooperated with the Germans, forced the cession of Vilna from Lithuania and throughout the Munich crisis acted on the German side and received as the reward for their collaboration a slice of Czech territory. Hitler pretended all through that period that his relations with Poland were satisfactory. It was only after he had dealt with the Czechs that he turned against the Poles, denounced them for their alleged ill-treatment of Germans and called for the destruction of the Danzig corridor.

II

WAR

In prospect, war had seemed terrible. In actual fact it was in its early months not so bad. Its coming after the months of uncertainty was almost a relief. Like most people in England, I had expected the war to bring immediate devastating air attacks on London. As we know, it began with one false alarm and then nothing happened in the West during all the months of the winter. In the late summer of 1940 I was sent on a mission to America. I went by boat and might well of course have been torpedoed. We were given instructions to go to bed with all our clothes on. I disobeyed these instructions and put on pyjamas. There was no sense in such folly and I should flatter myself if I called it courage. If my baseless confidence had proved misplaced as well it might have done, and we had been struck by a torpedo or a bomb, I have no doubt that I would have been as terrified as any man, but in fact, quite unreasonably, I had no fear. The Battle of Britain broke out when I was in America. A priest said to me one day in New York, 'You must be glad to be out of all this.' The remark was reasonable enough on his lips, having, as I presume, no English connections. To me it seemed extraordinary. With my wife and children at home in England my only longing was to get back there as quickly as possible—which I did, flying the Atlantic in a Clipper to Lisbon and thence in a K.L.M. aircraft with white-washed windows through an air-raid to London. The day before I flew I played tennis with friends on Long Island and astonished them by serving three let-services in succession. It was thought to be a marvellous example of steadiness of nerves. Whether my nerves were steady or not it is certainly something that I never did again, nor, I think, heard of anyone else doing. As far as fear goes I think that I was at that time more frightened of flying in an aeroplane than of being shot down by an enemy.

I went through all the air-raids of that autumn and winter in London and soon found—for no reason at all—that I merely took it for granted that none of the bombs would fall on me. I preferred a bed, even under the most dangerous circumstances, to an air-raid shelter or to sleeping in an underground station. Right up till the end of the war, though there was death all around me, London somehow never seemed to me a dangerous place.

It had been my purpose to return to Notre Dame for another stint for the Fall semester, or, as Englishmen would call it, term of 1939, but when the war came I cancelled my visit. Shortly before, the Government had asked people to inscribe their names in the Officers' Emergency Reserve. Though I was the least militarily competent of men and my total experience of soldiering had been confined to being the worst private (except for John Strachey, the Adjutant told me) in the Eton College Officers' Training Corps, yet I had obediently given my name, though quite unable to imagine any way in which I could be of effective service to the nation's war effort.

I had assumed that my offer to the Officers' Emergency Reserve would be immediately taken up and I should be called for some service—I did not greatly mind what. Evelyn Waugh had suggested that I should join him in volunteering for the regiment which he subsequently immortalised as the Halberdiers, but, though it would have been a pleasure to have served in his company, I thought—rightly enough—that the standards of living would be above the means of my purse. I pleaded therefore the Officers' Emergency Reserve as if it was an engagement and excused myself from joining up with him. But of course, in so far as I expected immediately to be called up, I was wholly in error. The nation had neither the equipment nor the trainers to make use of vast numbers of new recruits and neither I nor anybody in my position heard a word from the War Office. It was not until May, 1941 that the military authorities took any notice of my existence. Meanwhile, on the demand of Anthony Eden who was then Secretary for War, the Home Guard of local volunteers had been formed. There were contingents in every village in the country. Their exploits have been recently recited and embellished by the popular television feature of *Dad's Army*. Our local Dad's Army at Mells was in every way as ridiculous but not quite the same as Captain Mainwaring's. As far as I can recollect we did not do any drill. We had no regular officer at all. The local mine manager, Mr Berry, was nominally our commanding officer, but—for what reason I cannot recollect—he never appeared on parade or indeed had anything to do with us. We went for long route marches on Sunday mornings, which I rather enjoyed but about which others complained. We sometimes went to a local range to shoot, at which I was reasonably good, but our main task was to man a post on the top of a neighbouring hill and keep a watch from it to see if there were any descending German parachutists within sight. What we should have done had we seen a parachutist I am far from clear. Our neighbour across the road from us—who then lived in the house in which we now live—was Conrad Russell. He was our closest and most delightful friend. Some readers may remember him from the letters of Lady Diana Duff Cooper, of whom he was a very close friend and most constant correspondent. He was of the Bedford family, a cousin of Bertrand Russell, whom he considered a man of quite abysmal stupidity. He had been a stockbroker before the First War and a Railway Transport Officer during it. After the war he decided that he could never again bear the life of a city office and settled down as a gentleman farmer. He was a bachelor and possessed of a little private income, which relieved him from the need to bother much whether or not his farm made a profit, and left him free both to travel round the country and to lead a vigorous social life and also to indulge in a typically Whiggish running battle with the bureaucratic authorities who pestered him with their demands for the filling in of forms. 'I request that in future I may be addressed in a more courteous phraseology,' he wrote to the authority of the Rural District Council. Shortly before the war a company of undergraduate actors came to present *The Merchant of Venice* in the Manor Gardens. They were billeted out among us, the inhabitants of the village, and two were assigned to Conrad. 'I am instructed that I should offer them a meal which is known as High Tea,' he confided to us. 'Pray, can you tell me what is the nature of that meal?' He was a tall, handsome man with a very fine mop of noble grey hair. We, a large family, lived in what should have been the farm-house with the farm buildings attached, he in a smaller house across the road.

This naturally meant that he was continually passing to and fro in front of our house. I was horrified one day to hear my young son, now the much respected chaplain at Oxford University but then a boy of four, say to him as he passed, 'Good morning, Russell.' I rebuked him, 'You should say Mr Russell,' I objected. 'I call him Russell,' my son replied.

Evelyn Waugh one day visited us and after luncheon my wife showed him the garden. He made no comment on the flowers but, observing the garden boy who was brushing up some leaves, said of him in his hearing, 'What a pretty gardener you've got!' Conrad commented, 'I am afraid not quite a gentleman—not quite—not quite.'

Conrad Russell was at the outbreak of the war already over sixty. Nevertheless on a rumour that his cousin Bertrand was opposed to the war—as it turned out, a false rumour—nothing would dissuade him from offering himself at the recruiting office. His appearance there was, as he reported, 'greeted with a loud burst of laughter, in which I joined'. He finally found his service in the Home Guard, in which I was his colleague. He was told that he was to be a section-commander and that his men were all to fall in on him. He took up his position at the end of the line, but no supporters showed any inclination to join him. 'But I haven't got a section,' he pleaded pitiably. As I have said, we had no effective officers in our company. Our only instructions were that in the event of a German invasion I as the swiftest runner was appointed 'Get Away Man'. I was to take to my heels and report that Conrad had died fighting bravely. To whom I was to report was not very clear. It was assumed—probably correctly—that without my report the authorities would never receive any news of the German invasion.

In order to perform this onerous task we were issued with uniforms not unlike those of a private soldier but notable for what in civilian language would have been known as spats of the type commonly worn by the characters in P. G. Wodehouse's novels but which the military authorities for some reason preferred to call anti-grapelos. (The etymology of this curious word I never learnt). Thus accoutred, Conrad and I would patrol the neighbouring roads at night, looking for descending parachutists. 'I am amazed at the futility of our occupation,' he said to me. But some of the old ladies of the village were kind enough to report to my wife, 'There, we hear them walking past our houses and we feel that we can sleep safely in our beds.'

One day we were inspected by Lord Birdwood, the commander of the Gallipoli campaign, who was then our neighbour. Lord Birdwood passed along the ranks and embraced all those members of the Home

Guard whom he judged to belong to the upper classes. 'And what are you in private life, my man?' he said to Conrad. 'I'm a farmer, sir,' Conrad replied. 'No, he's not,' said the adjutant ('as I thought most unnecessarily,' commented Conrad in reporting the incident), 'he's one of the idle rich.' On hearing this good news Lord Birdwood embraced him warmly a second time.

Then eventually in May, 1941 the authorities of the Officers' Emergency Reserve at last found a use for my services. I was, I believe, a member of the last batch of those who were given commissions without going through the ranks. I was detailed to the R.A.F. and commanded to go down for a three-week course to Uxbridge. It was three weeks of hard square-bashing. Naturally I had no knowledge at all of drill and no natural capacity for smartness. What little I remembered of my days in the Officers' Training Corps, when we still used to form fours, was now wholly out of date. I was rebuked one day by the Commanding Officer for coming on parade with my buttons insufficiently burnished and another day by another officer for having one of them undone. But I did my best and on the passing out was congratulated by another officer with, 'I can see you have not found it easy, Hollis, but you've tried very hard and done well.' I was content.

When I had joined the R.A.F. I had done so on some sort of vague understanding that I would be posted to a job of liaison with the Americans. For that I would at least have had some sort of qualification. But, whatever that job was, it had not, in common military fashion, eventuated. Instead I found myself posted to Blackpool and detailed to the training of a company of recruits on the sands. For that of course I was entirely incompetent and was wholly in the hands of my sergeant who belonged to that strangest of all the creatures of mankind, those consumed by a passion for drill as the most satisfying of human activities. I did not expect that the whole machinery of the war would be arranged to suit my convenience. Nevertheless I did not see why I should not pull strings in order that I might do something a little bit more sensible for my capacities and after a few weeks I succeeded in getting myself transferred to a department of the Air Ministry known as A.I.6. This department, which was under the command of Lionel Heald who was afterwards to be Solicitor-General in Winston Churchill's government of 1951 and to be my colleague in Parliament, had two duties—to compose the communiqués which had to be issued every day on Allied or enemy air activities and to censor all manuscripts submitted for publication by members of the 'R.A.F. serving personnel', as they were called. We worked in collaboration with another department, A.I.5., which was stationed at the Ministry of Information and at which Ben Travers, the dramatist, presided; A.I.5 was concerned with material submitted by journalists. We were of course in no way moral censors. Our duty was solely to enforce strict rules about what aeroplanes and the like were on the secret list and ensure that their existence be concealed from the enemy.

I have never before or since been in any general company of barristers. They were most pleasant and kindly people—enormously more accurate in censorship and more ready to learn about aeroplanes—which was our business—than I was; at the same time, for intelligent people who had been for the most part to good schools, they were strangely bereft of general reading. They had no religion, but at the same time no hostility to religion. There was a genial, rather roguish old Yorkshireman, Percy Showan, now, alas, dead. He lived in Hampstead and he told me one day how he was seeking for a male servant. A young Frenchman answered his advertisement. He liked the post and was prepared to discuss conditions of engagement. 'You are a Catholic?' said Percy. '*Vous êtes catholiques?*' '*Ah, oui Monsieur,*' said the Frenchman. 'Ah, then we must arrange your duties so that you can attend Mass. I think that that can be managed all right.' 'Ah,' said the Frenchman, properly shocked at such a proposition, '*je suis catholique mais pas enragé.*'

I had no sort of natural knowledge of the difference between one aeroplane and another and could not boast of any essential competence for the job. But I managed to perform it without disgrace and to perform it in the company of very pleasant comrades. That most of the information that we conscientiously blue-pencilled was well known to the Germans and of little value to them I have little doubt, but there was always the possibility that—perhaps in the most casual and unexpected of places—some vital secrets might be revealed. This is the justification— and a valid justification—for military censorship in war. But the necessary price to be paid for it is that censors tend to become too pompous and self-important. We were very strictly instructed that, in all communiqués, the phrase should be 'weather' rather than 'weather conditions', and we obeyed the instructions with great seriousness. Security precautions were very strong but not very efficient. No one was supposed to be allowed into the Air Ministry unless armed with a pass, but one day I found John Betjeman at the front door. 'Your pass, sir, please,' said the janitor.

'I've not got a pass. I'm a German spy,' said Betjeman.

'Oh, I beg your pardon sir, I beg your pardon. I didn't know. Please go in. That will be quite all right.'

At the height of the submarine campaign the brother of General Donovan, the head of the American O.S.S., was sent over to England armed with very important despatches. Having evaded all the torpedoes, he at last reached England and attempted to put through a call to announce his safe arrival, and deliver his message. He gave the Air Ministry's number. There was a long silence from the exchange and eventually a confession: 'I'm afraid there's no reply from that number.'

The Director of Public Relations, to whom we were responsible, was Lord Stansgate. His deputy was Lord Willoughby de Broke. Two peers in more stark contrast to one another it would be hard to imagine. They might have been the two characters in a stylised play, representing the Right Wing and the Left Wing peer. Lord Willoughby de Broke was the son of the backwoods peer who had taken so leading a part in fighting the passage of the Parliament Act through the House of Lords before the First War. His main interests were in the turf. Lord Stansgate was of course Wedgwood Benn, the former Liberal Member of Parliament, now turned Labour. He had had a most gallant record flying in North-West India during the First World War. He had, I believe, been offered office when Lloyd George had formed his Government but had refused it, discovering that most of those with whom he acted sided with Asquith. He had the great distinction in the 1918 election, when catastrophe overcame so many Asquithian Liberals, of being the only member to gain a seat—Leith Burghs—for that party. For a number of years he remained faithful to the Liberal cause but, subsequently despairing of it, turned to Labour. The change was little more than a change of verbal allegiance. I often talked with him both then and subsequently in Parliament. He was, as he told me, 'no Marxist'. Indeed he had not, I think, much interest in theoretical schemes for the organisation of society and his policies were certainly very different from those which his young son has subsequently espoused. His main interest was in fighting attacks on the civil liberties of individual citizens and on the political claims of totalitarian regimes. It was in a way strange that he should have the overseeing of a department concerned with censorship, for censorship was something to which he was by temperament opposed. He did not of course deny the necessity for purely military censorship in time of war in order to prevent information from getting to the enemy, but clearly even in that field he thought that we in our department took our duties a great deal more seriously than they deserved. He had 'God's scorn' for all men governing. He took an impish delight in mocking at what he thought of as the elephantine pomposity of Sir John Anderson. It had of course been Sir John Anderson, afterwards Lord Waverley, who as Home Secretary had been responsible for incarcerating under 18B in the Isle of Man those who were thought to be in some way a danger to the State. Lord Stansgate, though the most vigorous of opponents of Fascism, thought that the Government in panic shut up a great many people whose incarceration was not really necessary. He was delighted when he heard the story of a lady whose husband was arrested under these orders and who wished to sell her house. Lady Waverley was interested in that house and had come to inspect it. Her hostess showed her the house. She then asked her to inspect the garden. Lady Waverley consented. Then she asked her if she would care to see the hen-house. Lady Waverley was not greatly interested but her hostess insisted and, as she bent down to look at the hens within, gave her a kick on the bottom which sent her sprawling in among them. Sharply she turned the key on her and said, 'Now you know what it feels like to be locked up under 18B.'

Stansgate was not partisan in his comments. He was as critical of Herbert Morrison, of his own party, who succeeded Sir John Anderson as Home Secretary, as he had been of Sir John himself. He thought that Herbert Morrison was incapable of considering any problem except in terms of its electoral advantages or disadvantages. Stansgate was a man of religious interests and sincerely concerned about their truths. But of Herbert Morrison's view about the future life he opined that 'his idea about hell would be solely concerned with wondering whether there was an increasing demand for it in the marginal parishes'. He was a teetotaller but happily under the impression that rum was a teetotal drink.

He was, as I say, a man of genuine religious interests and, I think, some sort of Nonconformist. I still from time to time have the pleasure of seeing his widow at meetings connected with Jewish-Christian relations. He was a friend of Niebuhr who was, I think, godfather to his son. It was a great pleasure to him to expose the religious ignorance of prominent men in public life. But his exposures were not always successful. One day he met me in high excitement to explain that Field-Marshal Smuts had said that France would rise again, like Lazarus, from the tomb. He proposed to write to *The Times* to expose such ignorance and asked me to draft a letter. For, he said, 'every one knows that Lazarus was in Abraham's bosom'. I explained that it was indeed true that Lazarus was in Abraham's bosom but that there was another Lazarus who had been raised from the dead. 'What? Do you mean to say that there are two Lazaruses in the Bible?' I confessed that this was indeed the truth. 'Oh,' he said, burying his head in his hand, 'I shall never get anything right.' Eric Kennington, who as an official war artist used to hang around the office flaunting an unexpurgated edition of T. E. Lawrence's *The Mint*, described Lord Stansgate as a zombie but this, I think, was unfair.

During the 1929 Government in which he had been Secretary of State for India, there had been controversy as to whether the Indians in East Africa should be recognised as paramount in those countries. Wedgwood Benn thought that the word 'paramount' meant 'equal' and as a believer in the equality of man said, 'Of course they must be paramount.' His decision caused a considerable amount of trouble.

The Secretary of State for Air during all this period was the Liberal leader, Sir Archibald Sinclair, afterwards Lord Thurso. Churchill always had a great dislike for his Conservative colleagues and a considerable nostalgic hankering after the Liberals with whom the most constructive days of his life had been lived. I have often heard it said that Lady Churchill throughout all her career never voted anything but Liberal. He was therefore glad enough to take the opportunity of a Coalition Government to give office to the Liberal leader. But to tell the truth I do not think that Sir Archibald Sinclair had very much to do with air policy or knew a great deal about air matters. He had two confidential secretaries, Roger Fulford and Reginald Maudling, and it was their duty to write his speeches for him. They wrote for him, 'It is never the policy of the Royal Air Force to seek to put a square peg into a round hole.' He read this out, but then thought that his self-respect required that he put in something original of his own. He therefore read out, 'It is never the policy of the Royal Air Force to seek to put a square peg into a round hole,' and added, 'But always to put a square hole into a round peg.' If it was not one, he thought, it must be the other.

After a time I was transferred from A.I.6 to the Air Historical Branch —a department whose duties were to prepare reports for the Air Staff on the part played by the R.A.F. in various operations. Our offices were in Lowndes Square in a very derelict old house with dangerously unmended banisters. It was by then the era of the doodlebugs, but the dangers of death from falling over the banisters were considerably greater than those of enemy action. My task was to write the report on the part played by the R.A.F. in operations in the Eastern Mediterranean. I went to Egypt and thence up to Syria to report on the fighting that there had been with the Vichy French. Thence to Malta and to Italy to the British Headquarters at Caserta and thence over to Greece when the Allied troops returned to that country in October 1944 and were awaiting attack from the forces of E.L.A.S. I wrote my reports—I hope reasonably competently. To what extent the members of the Air Staff ever studied them I cannot say. It was considered in Air Force circles a remarkable feat that I wrote so quickly. I myself could never understand how my colleagues managed to write so slowly. In the closing months of the war I was detailed to write a report on the S.O.E. droppings over the Continent. I could see that a year or so earlier it might have been of great importance to the Germans to know the details of such operations. But by May 1945 I could not see that it greatly mattered whether the Germans knew the details of the parachute droppings around D-day or not. I got into the way of taking a little casually the rules about the careful locking up of all documents in the safe before one left the room. However I learnt from experience that, just as there were drill sergeants to whom correct drill was the one purpose of life, so there were security officers to whom a document existed to be safely locked up and for no other purpose and quite irrespective of whether there was an effective enemy or not. By May of 1945 it might be worth considering whether the time had come for the publication of accounts of these operations for the information of the general public. The day had passed when it greatly mattered whether the Germans knew about them or not. However the election came along and I went off to fight a constituency, leaving my report uncompleted and no one, as far as I have ever heard, much the worse off for that.

War is good for religion but bad for morality. How much value there is in what is known as 'God with the wind up', how many of those who turn to God with prayer in the moment of danger continue with their prayers and with the service of God when the crisis is passed, I cannot say. But in general the Second World War, like the First, did lead to a certain increase in religious practice. A number of people started to go to church who had never done so before, and, though a number of them have doubtless dropped off subsequently, a number have also doubtless continued.

The great difference between the Wars in this respect is that the Second World War saw the first rather feeble beginnings of what it is now the fashion to call the ecumenical movement. The First World War led to a certain religious revival but apart from the efforts of Cardinal Mercier at Malines that revival was within each particular denomination. The Second World War was different. The Nazi regime, at least as it was seen in England—and surely rightly—was an attack on all religions by a gangster totalitarian regime. In Germany it was in the concentration camp that the Catholics and Lutherans had met and got to know one another very much better than they had ever done before. In England it was the same, though under much less extreme circumstances. By great good fortune the war found the see of Westminster occupied by Cardinal Hinsley, a bluff, patriotic Yorkshireman, at a time when under the threat of German invasion public opinion would not have tolerated any other language than that of bold, patriotic defiance. Such was the language which Cardinal Hinsley naturally spoke. In his Italian days before his appointment to Westminster he had defied Mussolini at a time when such defiance was by no means invariable among English Catholics. The public was therefore willing to accept from him suggestions that it would not have accepted from any other ecclesiastic. At Canterbury there was Archbishop Temple who was also a man with an open mind, but who saw in the present crisis a total attack on all Christian values and saw that, if Christianity was to survive the threat, it must find for itself a united language. Divided, they would all be overwhelmed. So they launched together the Sword of the Spirit to combat the 'spirit of wickedness in high places'. Its success was limited. Some of the Catholic bishops —particularly in the North of England—were unsympathetic and both Hinsley and Temple were soon dead. High-faluting claims, made in some newspapers, that it would heal the rift of the Reformation were found to be wholly exaggerated. Even today, while the ecumenical movement has gone further forward under further distinguished patronage, it has as yet achieved depressingly little. A few absurd regulations such as those forbidding Catholics to remain in the room if a Protestant said a prayer are no longer enforced. Mixed marriages and the conditions of them are somewhat easier than they were. Catholics and non-Catholics meet together more easily in social life and in various societies. But the obstacles to inter-communion have not yet been overcome and the reunion of the Churches is still far distant. Hinsley's Sword of the Spirit, if not the beginning of the end, was, as Churchill would have said, the end of the beginning.

Yet war, as I say, is good for religion but bad for morality. It was not easy in the ordinary affairs of war-time life to think that men's main concern was with the reunion of the Churches. Very different matters appeared to be occupying the mind. A life of tension makes people more likely both to commit sins and to repent of them. Only those who have spent all their lives in libraries or reading text books will find these two activities incompatible with one another. 'Sir,' said Dr Johnson, 'are you so grossly ignorant of human nature as not to know that a man may be very sincere in good principle without having good practice?' War invited, and throughout history has always invited, great looseness of conduct for a variety of self-evident reasons. The tension under which the soldier lives tends to make him seek for a violent relaxation. The fact that he is here today and gone tomorrow and will never again see, or have occasion to see, the object of his attentions invites him to treat her with lack of consideration. He is separated from his wife and therefore from legitimate indulgence. I was in the R.A.F. at the time as a very chocolate soldier. When it was towards the end of the war and after the conquest of Naples by the Allies, life under the Allied occupation was very shocking. The rations allowed to the Italians were very insufficient—less than they had received from the Germans—and it was the common custom of well-fed British and American troops to supplement the rations of Neapolitan girls in return for their favours. Some parents naturally took every measure that they could to protect their daughters from such escapades. Others encouraged them in the hope of getting a share of the extra rations for themselves. War is war and I have no doubt that I should have found similar stories in any other place of occupation.

Such stories were reasonably suppressed for security reasons so long as the war was on. Though everyone who fought in the war knows these or similar stories today I doubt if even now they are generally understood. Such an exposure as *Oh, What A Lovely War* or similar tales about life in occupied France are still greeted as shocking revelations—not as everyday occurences to be taken for granted.

CHAPTER FIVE

Full of Wise Saws and Modern Instances

I had never expected to go into Parliament. When I was young there had been for a short time a question of my spending my life at Eton. An impertinent clergyman, hearing it of, said, 'He should go twenty miles further east.' I was very angry. I have never had any love for any town except Leeds and certainly never thought of myself as spending my days in London, whose atmosphere I have always found particularly unattractive. I am not a citizen of Megalopolis. As President of the Union at Oxford I had sometimes, I will confess, toyed with the notion of Parliament but very much as little boys used to say that they would be engine-drivers when they grew up. When I left Oxford I took up with a career which did not in any way bring me into touch with politics. I belonged to no political party and indulged in no political activity. It has always been my peculiarity that I have been in favour of the affairs of the world being conducted with reasonable dignity and decorum— in favour of dressing up and pageantry—but have never had much wish to play a part in that pageantry myself. When I was President of the Oxford Union the centenary Jubilee of the Society occurred and it was arranged that there should be a great and public banquet to celebrate the event. I as President would have presided over it. Then it chanced that the day for which it was arranged coincided with a General Election. There was no alternative but to postpone it until the next term when I would no longer be President. Elderly Members came and condoled with me on my misfortune. 'It was too bad,' they said, 'that I should have been deprived by luck of this occasion, which it was certain, had I enjoyed it, I would never have forgotten until my dying day.' It seemed churlish not to lament with their lamentations. But I remember at the time secretly feeling immense relief at the thought that I would be saved from this to me quite onerous and embarrassing duty.

Yet when the war ended and with it my service such as it was with the R.A.F. I found myself with an undecided future. As for the political parties I had no belief at all in Socialism, which I imagined (not quite correctly) to mean the nationalisation of all the means of production and distribution, and their management by government departments. Had there been an Irish question at the moment it would hardly have been possible for me to declare myself a Conservative with its implication of being a Unionist, but the Irish question was for the moment happily quiescent. Quite frankly I thought that the pattern which I remembered from the last war would be repeated and that the Government which had won the war would be returned with a large majority. Doubtless, I thought, there would later be a reaction against it but for the moment I thought that its victory was certain. In this of course I was ludicrously in error. Yet, thinking a Conservative Government inevitable, I thought the real issue of post-war years was to see to it that we were ruled by decent Conservatives rather than by hard-faced men who had done well out of the war and who were returned to the Coalition Parliament of 1918. Sir Percy Hurd who had been member for Devizes for many years, a constituency near my home, was old and blind and did not wish to stand again. There was a vacancy. The chairman of the Association was Colonel Heward Bell, who had been the constituency's member years before at the time of the First World War. He was a brother of Clive Bell, the aesthetic critic, but, though possessed of a taste for pictures, in no sort of way resembled his brother. In politics he was a strong but not bigoted Conservative—a man who believed most strongly in the rituals of life. If he offered you a peach in his house he insisted that it be brought to you by a footman on a plate. He had had some family connection with an Italian—I forget what the story was but he once told it to my wife—and this Italian had behaved very badly. This gave him a great prejudice against all Italians—and, I fancy, pretty generally against all foreigners. Whatever his religious prejudices, he never spoke of them to me or allowed them to betray him into any hostility. He once warned me against writing to a constituent on the notepaper of *The Tablet*. 'It would not matter if you did it to me because you know I wouldn't mind,' he said, 'but you know what people are.' G. M. Young, the distinguished historian, who lived in the constituency at Oare just outside Marlborough and was at that time engaged in his not very happy biography of Baldwin, once related to me that Bell had said to him, 'I'm not a Christian but thank God, I'm a Protestant.' Young professed not to know what he meant, but to me it was clear enough. It meant that he had no use for Italians or other foreigners.

Colonel Bell suggested that I should offer myself for the vacant candidacy. I thought that it would be interesting to make the experiment and to see what Parliament was like from the inside. I offered myself, went down to a selection committee in Marlborough, addressed the company along with six other aspirants and, much to my surprise, was selected. I became the candidate. Thus my entry into Parliament was abnormally simple. Whether I would have persisted if, like so many would-be candidates, I had been compelled to hawk myself round from selection committee to selection committee, I cannot say. There was no reason why I should have been spared such an ordeal.

I was fortunate and when the election took place in June, 1945, I was duly elected. The Devizes constituency, with only Devizes and Marlborough with populations in the four figures, was, with the boundaries as they then were, as little industrialised as any in the country, and was comparatively unaffected by the Labour wave which at that election swept the country in general. Indeed travelling round its placid villages I did not even guess how opinion throughout the land was veering. This first election campaign was an enormously interesting and enjoyable adventure. One of the great treats of being a candidate in 1945 was that one received an adequate petrol allowance and nobody else did. Motoring today is hell, but to drive around the beautiful Wiltshire countryside from village to village on empty roads was like riding through the avenues of Heaven. Before the next election the boundaries of the constituency had been altered to take in a suburb of Swindon and the constituency was a much harder one from the Conservative point of view. However I succeeded in holding it in 1950 and again in 1951, though with a reduced majority, and indeed up till this day Devizes has never returned a Labour member.

I did not attain to any sort of distinction in the House of Commons. Neither office nor title came my way. As far as title went I had no regret. For the English preservation of titles when all the rest of the world has ceased to create them has always seemed to me a relic of infantilism. I cannot well understand why anyone should wish to have a 'Sir' before his name or a few letters after it and would certainly abolish the flummery if I had the power. As for office there are only a small number of Members of Parliament on either side who have any real influence over policies. I cannot pretend that I ever had any prospect of being of their number. As for a post of some sort—an under-secretaryship or what have you—everybody gets something sooner or later—so long as he stays there long enough, and I dare say that eventually some sort of recognition would have come my way. I would have been appointed to some post and in due course have been dropped again in a government reshuffle. It requires no special ability to hold some subordinate post and I suppose that I could have managed it after a fashion. On the other hand I can make no claim to any great administrative talent and cannot flatter myself that I would have performed it with any of the marked success which would have qualified me for higher promotion. I soon found myself in a curious position. I approved of the party system. There were undoubtedly extravagances in the way in which it was operated but I agreed that government through two opposing parties gave on the whole the least unsatisfactory government and was to be preferred to the competing personal factions of the eighteenth century which were the only alternative to it. On the other hand I felt no readiness to commit myself irrevocably to either party. I did not think that either had the monopoly of wisdom or the monopoly of folly. I had not been brought up in any atmosphere of party politics and did not find total party loyalty at all an attractive emotion. Only those who have never fully matured—the permanent schoolboys—are capable of such loyalty. Therefore, Parliament being as it was, I was really inoculated against success. I do not say that I did not want success, that would be an exaggeration; but I think that I can truly say that I did not want it intensely and exclusively in the way that its real worshippers pursue it, and competition is so keen that those who do not want intensively do not succeed.

In any event I was glad to have been in the House of Commons, glad to have seen things from the inside. I stayed there for ten years, but I had no wish to stay any longer. Members complain a lot—and I dare say justly—about the lack of amenities in Parliamentary life. They complain less frequently of its greatest inhumanity—that it is virtually impossible to have a decent family life. In every other profession the man comes home to his wife in the evening. Husband and wife have the week-end together. At Westminster, members are detained, to quote Trevelyan, 'to an hour when all honest men should be in bed, to an hour when, if we are to believe some cynics, all honest men are in bed'. Husband and wife are separated during the week. Even at the week-end the wife has to motor out and sit by her husband's side on the platform at some meeting. It is not surprising that broken marriages in politics should be more common than in any other profession except, it is said, among county cricketers. The life makes demands on a wife which no woman should be asked to bear.

It is common enough among politicians to complain of the demands of constituents, and journalists, parading their plans for Parliamentary reform, often see it as one of their main tasks to find ways of relieving the member of the chores of a welfare officer. For myself I had no belief in Socialist theories, nor that workers would suddenly become more industrious if they were told that they were working for the State. On the other hand some of the assumptions upon which the capitalist system were based were very unlovely and some of its practices equally unlovely. I did not think an absolute equality of wealth was possible without a total destruction of liberty and in all probability not even then. But I detested those who complacently accepted for themselves this great inequality, and were not ashamed to be inordinately rich, and an unpleasantly large number of Conservatives appeared to be thus. The fault on the left I found to be its lack of independence of mind. Those who repudiated orthodoxy and the Establishment so often adopted in their stead a monotonous packet deal of exactly identical unorthodox opinions, falling to what Boswell so well called *la crédulité des incrédules*. The fault of the Conservatives on the other hand was their utterly complacent assumption that all people of sense must necessarily agree with them. The pretence of irrepressible conflict between the two parties to which both leaders pretended in public was self-evidently false, and it became increasingly difficult to bear with patience the so highly synthetic party debates to which we were daily subjected, or to make speeches in which we had to pretend that one's own side was wholly right, the other side wholly wrong.

Only the tip of the Parliamentary iceberg shows itself in the Chamber. There are at Westminster endless hours of hanging about, waiting for a division bell to ring; the most important times spent there are those out of the Chamber—in the smoking rooms or the bar—and the most important lessons learnt there are the lessons about the nature of men of wholly different origins and professed opinions from oneself. I saw members who had been belabouring one another in the Chamber going off afterwards to have a glass of beer together. I was not brought up in a political family, nor brought up with any natural knowledge of the workings of the corridors of power. Devices which others took for granted as manoeuvres of the game were quite beyond my imagination. When I made my maiden speech I was congratulated by a fellow member on my astuteness in having chosen to make it from a seat on the extreme back-bench from which I could triumphantly look down on the other members beneath me. It had never occurred to me that there was any such advantage. I had merely spoken from that seat because it was the seat in which I happened to find myself. So after I had been a few years in Parliament, Cross-Bencher in the *Sunday Express* one day carried a paragraph in which he announced that I was attempting to bring about a National Government. In that attempt he said that I was supported by Anthony Head and Toby Law. The suggestion was so preposterous that to this day—perhaps mistakenly—I have never bothered to contradict it. Whence the writer derived his information I cannot imagine. I should have had no faintest notion how to set about organising a movement for a National Government or indeed any other purpose. Such manoeuvres were, and are, wholly beyond my capacity. I was intensely embarrassed when one day a colleague confessed that he employed a publicity agent to get paragraphs about him into the papers. I do not know that it was a particularly wicked thing to have done but I would have died sooner than do it.

Apart from working at Westminster and in the constituency Membership of Parliament brought a number of foreign journeys, whether as member of Parliamentary delegations or indirectly as lecturer for such bodies as the British Council. As with other members such assignations have caused me at one time or another to visit most parts of the world and, though there comes a time when such travelling is no longer welcome, its opportunities add greatly to the zest of life in youth. Parliamentary delegations were of course all-party affairs. There has recently been some criticism of the expense which members charge up to the public purse for these jaunts. Whether or not the criticism is justified I cannot say. Doubtless ten days' travelling over a country did not make a member expert in all its problems and only fools would imagine that it did. The very real value of such trips to the member was to my mind the opportunities that it gave to get to know better one's fellow members.

In particular I valued the opportunity for a number of years to serve as one of the British Delegates at the Council of Europe at Strasbourg. The Council of Europe which was formed as a response to the demand for European unity which Churchill raised after the war did not establish itself as the Parliament of Europe for which enthusiasts had hoped. Its constitution did not correspond to any of the bodies of international government which were then able to establish themselves. The British and the Scandinavian countries refused to join the Economic Community. The British did not join the Coal and Steel Community. The Swedes would not join the military N.A.T.O., the four-letter word, as they called it. As a consequence Strasbourg could never become much more than a debating society but as such it was admirable, and the educational advantage of meeting and making friends with members from all the European countries was very great. There was a good deal of most pleasant international entertaining.

The Turkish delegation one day gave a luncheon. At it I found myself seated next to the permanent Turkish member of the secretariat. In order to make conversation I asked him how he liked living in Strasbourg.

'I do not like it at all,' he replied. 'The ladies of Strasbourg are not at all convenient. When I wish for a lady I have to go to Switzerland.'

A colleague across the table objected, 'But you have your wife with you,' whereat he hunched up his shoulders, spread out his hands and enunciated a curious 'Pouf, pouf' noise as if he never heard any observation more ridiculous or more clearly irrelevant.

It is true that the very ineffectiveness of the Council meant that the representatives one met there tended to be not quite of the first rank. One met there Paul Reynaud who had been in power in France at the moment of her defeat; Chaban Delmas, who was to be Prime Minister of France and then dismissed from the post under circumstances that were not so very glorious; Herr Kiesinger, the last and not very successful Christian Democrat Chancellor of Germany. Though Churchill came to its inaugural meeting and though we were later addressed by Dr Adenauer and M. Mendès France when he was Prime Minister of France, it was not as a rule worth the while of the rulers of quite the first rank to waste their time there. There was General Koenig who was, I think, the Gaullist Deputy for the city of Strasbourg itself. He was an apostle of an exuberant nationalism that is not perhaps today very fully in favour. 'One fights for France—bon,' he said one day. 'One fights for England —bon. One fights for Europe—bloody hell.' Still, politicians who are not quite successful are on the whole nicer and more interesting than those who are right at the top of the tree and so we were not necessarily the worse for being addressed by those of the second class. The British Labour Government, still in power when the Council was first formed, was always a little suspicious of it. They suspected that Churchill, at that time under defeat in British politics, used it as a platform where he would be able to win victories that he was denied at home. Herbert Morrison was then the leader of the Labour delegation and behaved with some pettiness. Churchill, as a full delegate, had under the Strasbourg constitution the right to appoint an alternate who could represent him when he was not present. Churchill appointed John Foster as his alternate, but both attended the session together. Morrison challenged this and objected that both Churchill and Foster were drawing the daily subsistence allowance of a thousand francs—worth then £1. He publicly challenged Churchill on this in the bar. Churchill of course knew nothing about this allowance, which was drawn for him, if it was drawn at all, by a secretary. To him it appeared the sort of sum one would give to a taxi-driver as a tip, and he was contemptuous of Morrison's pettiness in raising the matter. He advised Foster to refrain from drawing his allowance.

As for my own activities in Parliament at Westminster, naturally enough, like all other members, I spent the greater part of my time obediently traipsing through the division lobbies at my whip's command. 'Parliament is a place where a man can neither work nor relax truly,' said Gladstone. 'Most of the duties of a Member of Parliament could be better performed by a fairly intelligent poodle dog,' said Lecky, the historian, himself a member. Only twice did I play a part of any prominence or independence—over the American loan and over the abolition of the death penalty.

During the war we had of course lived on American lease-lend. Very soon after the war the Americans brought that arrangement to an end and the British were left in a desperately dangerous position. In order to survive the Government applied to the Americans for a loan to tide us over till a time when we had been able to rebuild our export trade. After difficult negotiations the loan was at last arranged, but the Americans dictated harsh terms. They made no concealment of the fact that they thought Socialism was an evil policy and that they intended to use their position of advantage in order to try in every way that was possible to force the British back from their policies of Socialism to what they called Free Enterprise. Also, while they had good will towards Britain, they had none towards the British Empire, any more than my friends had had at Notre Dame or in Denver before the war. They thought imperialism an evil system. They intended to use their advantage in order to hive off Britain's colonies from the mother country. They made it the condition of their loan that Britain should be committed to freer trade. But the particular way in which they phrased their demand was for the reduction of tariffs but at the same time for the elimination of preferences. I had inherited from my monetary studies of before the war a strong faith that, while both stable prices and stable exchanges were in themselves desirable, yet, if you had to choose between the two, stable prices at home were more important than stable foreign exchanges. I therefore was from the first a critic of the Bretton Woods arrangement and Bob Boothby and I joined together in opposing the loan arrangement which

committed us to Bretton Woods and which was supported by the Labour
Government while the official Conservative policy was one of abstention.

Whether we were right or not it is hardly now very interesting to
inquire. Certainly most of those who accepted the loan did not pretend
to like it. Dalton confessed in the House that there were moments when
the negotiations were very close to breaking down and Stafford Cripps,
meeting me in the lobby, very courteously congratulated me on my
speech in opposition. Nor has the attempt of Bretton Woods to impose
fixed exchanges been very happy. As we all know, countries have over
the subsequent quarter of a century been constantly compelled to change
the value of their currencies and a pretendedly fixed currency that has in
fact to be constantly changed would seem to have no advantage over a
floating currency. On the other hand it could be plausibly argued that
we had really no alternative but to accept whatever terms were offered
to us. The money was desperately needed. On looking back I do not
know that my opposition was altogether quite responsible. In fact, of
course, the original loan was rapidly spent without establishing any very
notable recovery and then a few years later America came a second time
to our and to other people's rescue with Marshall Aid on much more
generous and less exceptional terms.

My other excursion was on capital punishment. A bill for the reform of
criminal justice was being brought in by the Government. The bill itself
contained no provision about the death penalty, but there was a strong
body in the House—predominantly though not exclusively on the
Labour side—which was in favour of abolition. It was agreed that the
abolitionists should move to add a new clause in favour of abolition to
the bill and the whips on both sides should allow a free vote on it.
Sydney Silverman, the pertinacious, able little member from Nelson and
Colne, moved the clause and I seconded it. My attitude towards capital
punishment was that to a Christian the taking of life must be most
repugnant. I was not prepared from that principle to say that capital
punishment could be abolished without any considerations of the evidence, any more than I was prepared to be an absolute and unconditional
pacifist. If I could be convinced that hanging was an uniquely effective
deterrent, that if hanging was abolished more murders would be committed and therefore more people killed on the whole, I would be prepared
to accept hanging. But all of the evidence seemed to me to show—and
Ernest Gowers's subsequent commission has confirmed—that it was not
such an uniquely effective deterrent, that other methods of punishment

were at least as effective, and, if that was so, I was not prepared to give my vote for hanging. Nothing short of the absolute necessity would in my opinion justify it. It should not be accepted if it was merely equal in its deterrence to an alternative.

We carried the vote, greatly to my surprise, in the House of Commons, though it was thrown out in the Lords and it was more than twenty years before capital punishment was finally taken off the Statute Book. The public reaction to the proposal was to me surprising and unpleasant. I had thought that the man in the street who had never given his mind to the study of evidence would at least have thought that the matter was doubtful and probably one best to be left to those who had studied it. I was quite unprepared for the utterly violent outburst of public opinion both in my constituency and throughout the country. It was clear that perfectly sane people took it for granted that, with hanging abolished, murder would become almost at once universal. 'We shall all be murdered in our beds,' they claimed. As for other countries that had abolished capital punishment, the people were unaware of any that had indulged in such an eccentric policy and did not believe therefore that sensible conclusions could be drawn from their experience. Had a vote been taken in my constituency there was no doubt at all that the majority in favour of hanging would have been overwhelming and the same would have been true of any other constituency. My association treated me very well. I had to explain my vote to them. They made no pretence of agreeing with me but they recognised that the vote was a free vote and they were not prepared to censure me for, as they put it, having followed my conscience. I could not ask for more. Sir Geoffrey Fry who had been Baldwin's Private Secretary was among the members of my association. At about the time of Munich he had passed through a phase of profound depression—so much so that some of his friends even began to feel that he might do away with himself. Father Leicester King was persuaded to go and see him and wrestle with him for his soul. But Father King was a man of sturdy and jingoistic patriotism. He was not profoundly shocked on learning that Sir Geoffrey supported Munich, and the conversation which began by him urging Sir Geoffrey that he should not commit suicide ended up by him saying that if he held such views he should certainly be hanged. I received during these months, as did other abolitionists, particularly those of them who were Conservatives, a generous volume of abusive letters from constituents and others. A few even expressed their devotion to capital punishment by threatening to murder me, presumably under the hope that they might afterwards vindicate their principles by getting hanged. A larger number contented themselves with expressing the hope that I might be murdered without themselves volunteering to take a part in the operation. On the evening of the debate in the House of Commons a fellow member, who both before and afterwards was always friendly, said to me, 'I hope you get murdered on the way home tonight.' It was, I think, the only occasion of my life when I have received such a direct, face to face, expression of ill will.

What interested me about my correspondence was that with very few exceptions the writers made no attempt to base their conclusions on evidence or reason. They simply took it for granted that there would be more murders if there were no hangings, did not imagine that I even questioned that, but assumed that I had opposed hanging because of some strange perverted principle, probably religious, and had voted for its abolition to satisfy this whim of conscience and in indifference to the fate of the writers whom I left callously to be murdered as they went about their lawful business, as they certainly would be. The argument was a curious one and I discovered that to a number of people there was a positive attraction in the thought of a few people being hanged from time to time. Life, as Denis found in Dickens's *Barnaby Rudge*, would be duller without its pantomime.

Now of course, as I have said, the vote by the House of Commons was reversed by the House of Lords, and for the moment there was no change. Yet the issue remained alive and was raised again by Sydney Silverman. First we got a modified change in the law with the substitution of degrees of murder for the previous absolute verdict. Then eventually about twenty years after the original vote Parliament accepted total abolition, which we now have. There, is, I think, little doubt that even now public opinion has not been converted to abolition. Parliament has perhaps been converted and in particular it is much more broadly favoured by Conservative members than it was in the years immediately after the war, but the polls still seem to show that if the matter was submitted to them, the majority would vote for a return of hanging. The majority would certainly be much less than it was in 1947, however. And what is more interesting, it would certainly be much less violent and more reasoned. In 1947 to most people the suggestion of abolition was an entire novelty and they reacted against it with total unreason. By later years they had become familiar with the idea. They thought of it as an idea that was in the air. They knew by then that other countries did without capital punishment, that a distinguished royal commission was not convinced that hanging was an uniquely effective deterrent. Doubtless only a small minority had actually studied the statistics of the rise and fall in the murder rate in other countries and the like, but they were aware that such statistics existed. They had come to think of the matter as one for debate. The era was one of great violence and of increasingly prevalent crime. Abolitionists claimed that murder was a crime apart and that, while the rate for other crimes had increased, the murder rate had remained significantly much more steady. Others denied this. There was dispute about the statistics. The man in the street was perhaps more inclined to ask what the statistics proved than directly to challenge them. If the murder rate had not changed, while the rate for other crimes had greatly increased, what did this prove? Did it prove that murder was absolutely a crime apart, and could we be confident that the murder rate never rises? Or was it rather that the criminal looked on murder as the most serious of crimes? He could take to other crimes more easily but in the end, in conditions of a general moral collapse of law and order, would he not, escaping effective punishment, progress from the other crimes to murder? Whatever the conclusions of such arguments, they were not in themselves unreasonable arguments. They were urged by reasonable people in a reasonable fashion. It was recognised that there was a balance in the argument, but those who advocated abolition no longer had to fear that they would be assailed as cranks, lunatics and moral degenerates.

My other great problem was with the declaration of the Irish Republic. As I have said, I had from my youth been a very strong supporter of Irish Home Rule and should have found it difficult in any way to have associated myself with the British Conservative party had there been any very lively Irish issue at the time of my candidacy. Fortunately that was not so. The Irish had been neutral during the war. Churchill had immediately after the war's end made a violent speech in denunciation of de Valera's policies. Perhaps the majority of British opinion was hostile to Irish neutrality but few thought that there was much sense in Churchill's protest against it when the war was over. In general, though people had no wish to become involved in Irish politics, Ireland immediately after the war was voted a very pleasant place by Conservative politicians and many, including myself, were frequent and happy visitors there.

In 1948 there was an Irish election as a result of which Mr de Valera fell from office and was succeeded by a Coalition Government under Mr Costello. Mr Costello's son, Declan Costello, was a very great friend of mine and I had often been entertained by his father. Much to most people's surprise this Government proceeded to declare a republic, though there had been no mention of such an intention in their election campaign. Considering the fuss that a suggestion of republicanism had caused only a few years before at the time of the Treaty it was remarkable how little excitement was caused in British opinion by this action. Attlee's Government however thought it necessary to bring in a bill to define the British attitude towards the new arrangement. I had always been an 'Irish Home Ruler', but it seemed to me that the arguments that justified Dublin's claim to be free from Westminster equally justified Belfast's claim to be free from Dublin. The Government decided to bring in a bill to guarantee that Northern Ireland should not be deprived of her rights under the partition bill, save by the consent of the Stormont Parliament.

Now I was one who would have liked to see the union of all Ireland. What sane person could wish for its own sake to see this small island saddled with the expense and absurdity of two governments? Still I could not see how it was either right or possible for the South to impose its government on the North by force. Besides Mr de Valera had to my mind his considerable share of responsibility for the division of the island. Whatever the threats of Carson it was the Sinn Feinners who had used the gun in Irish politics and, the battle having been taken to the gun, it was perhaps inevitable that the international war between Irishmen and Englishmen would be followed by a far more bloody civil war between Irishmen and Irishmen—a civil war in which Irish killed many more Irish than Irish in the previous years had ever killed English—and it was not unnatural that Northern Protestants when they read of the killing of Michael Collins at republican hands should have concluded that their own lives would not be safe in the hands of any Dublin Government. Nor, when less violent times came round, did Mr de Valera follow policies which made the reconciliation of the six counties with the twenty-six any easier. On the contrary, by his claim of special status for the Catholic religion, by his refusal of facilities for divorce and contraception he dug much more deeply the ditch between North and South than it had ever been dug by any British policies of partition. So, remembering Desmond Fitzgerald's warning to me at Notre Dame, I concluded that the only hope of ever ending partition lay in frankly and freely recognising it. So I joined with the rest of the Conservative party in voting for the bill.

But there was of course one great difference between the position of Protestants in the South of Ireland and the position of Catholics in the North. The Protestants in the South were an inconsiderable minority;

they had come to recognise and accept the change and received a great deal more than their fair share of positions of responsibility in Southern life. They could not make any reasonable claim that they suffered from any discrimination. The Catholics in the North formed a third of the population. In two counties and in some areas they were a definite majority. In employment, in housing, in local government and in every other way they suffered under blatant discrimination. It was the declared policy of Stormont's Prime Minister, Lord Craigavon, to preserve the North as 'a Protestant Government for Protestant people'. At this very time I was in correspondence with Connolly McCausland, an officer in the British Army, of a distinguished landowning family at Limavady just outside Londonderry. He had recently become a Catholic but wished to continue as a Unionist and to appear on Unionist platforms. He found that Protestant Unionists would not allow him to do so. In the last sad months his son has been brutally murdered after being tortured by the I.R.A.

The Catholics in the North had of course many just grievances. It could not be pretended that a regime in which one party was always in power and was prepared to use any sort of device to remain in power was in any real sense a democratic regime. Democracy requires not merely that the majority should be in power but that the minority should be treated with justice. Successive British Governments were certainly to blame—I myself no doubt had my share of fault—in that we were content to think that we had solved the problem by having established a government at Stormont and did not take sufficient trouble to see that the Government was ruling with any sort of decency. Still I could not think that violence was any remedy. The only hope of a solution lay in the growth of a greater spirit of decency and tolerance among the ruling people. I had from time to time visited Queen's University at Belfast and had been entertained there by undergraduates who were always careful to explain that they belonged to a generation to which the sectarian battles of the past were a relic of barbarism and that, in their societies, members were elected to their various offices strictly on merit and with no attention to creed. I had attended a luncheon in Belfast in favour of European unity in which Catholic and Protestant sat down together in apparently perfect amity. I had attended a week-end school for the same purpose and of similar constitution at Bangor. A very wise priest, Monsignor Ryan, chaplain at the University, warned me against undue optimism. The undergraduates were, he told me, generous and ecumenical in their youth but in a few years' time they would be out in the world, seeking for jobs. It was hardly to be believed that they would not use sectarian slogans in order to defeat their competitors. Still, though I did not doubt that progress in that strange and unlovely atmosphere could only be slow, I ventured to hope that there was progress. I hoped, as did so many others in England, that Terence O'Neill's bid for transcendence of bigotry would prove successful. Alas, we know, I was wrong. But even now I still think that I and the government of the day were right in supporting the bill to guarantee the North its self-government. The appeal to violence would not lead to a solution. It could only lead to counter-violence in which the Catholics, as the poorer and the minority, would inevitably get the worse of it.

But I was not prepared, any more than I had been prepared over the capital punishment controversy, for the extraordinary outbreak of violence with which my vote was greeted. I received letters of the most unrestrained abuse, threatening me with my life and written under the assumption and apparent impression that I was an out-and-out Unionist who would oppose any rights of self-government for Irishmen, though I had spent my life in writing and speaking against the Unionist cause.

Religion has always been to me a private affair. I admitted the need for authority. Without it, history and my own experience showed that we fall into strange extravagances. But religion, though indeed it teaches that we are members one of another, ought to be derived fundamentally from our own personal experience. Authority should be no more than the exceptional regulator, required to step in only when it is absolutely necessary. I had none of Wilfrid Ward's ambition to receive a papal bill every morning with my breakfast mail. I had of course got to know very intimately and to like the Jesuits at Stonyhurst, but I knew nothing of bishops. The only bishop that I knew was our local bishop at Clifton, Bishop Lee, as he then was. He was a man of most unrestrained bonhomie and my dealings with him, such as they were, were by no means exclusively theological. The monks of Downside had an excellent and generous habit of offering at Epiphany time a dinner to a fortunate selected company of their neighbours. One sat down to dinner at seven-thirty and, since the good Fathers had to be up in the middle of the night for their offices, it was naturally customary to leave at a fairly early hour. When the time came to go, Bishop Lee was by no means ready for such a move. He had got himself ensconced in a comfortable chair behind a table with a whisky and soda before him and, seeing me, he called me to join him. After a time it became evident that the monks were anxious for him to go; it was equally obvious that the Bishop had no intention of doing anything of the sort. Eventually the monks were reduced to pushing chairs to and fro along the floor as waiters do when they are anxious to clear their restaurants of inordinately lingering guests.

Before I went into Parliament I was, as I say, in no sense a leading Catholic layman. Perhaps I used at times to repeat without any very deep consideration Bellocian gibes about the anti-Catholic prejudice that ruled in the political world but I never had any occasion seriously to see how far they were true. It was only when I came to offer myself as a candidate that I had the opportunity to test them. The ways of selection committees are notoriously unpredictable. It is quite impossible to fore-tell what considerations, whether they be political or religious, will sway votes for or against a candidate. Men of the first ability have been turned down by constituency after constituency. Surprisingly unworthy aspirants have met with instant victory. As for whether Catholicism counts against a candidate, that is the purest chance. The great majority of those who serve on selection committees doubtless have no pre-judice in the matter. Very likely the question will not be raised. But there is always a chance that the committee will contain one obstinate member. He, or it may well be she, will probably not confess to prejudice. He will say, 'Of course I am not bigoted, but we have to face the fact that if we select Mr X his Catholicism will lose us a number of votes. Mr Y is a Protestant.' If it is true that X and Y are about equal in ability, it is likely enough that this will swing the votes of the indifferent generality of the selection committee. It is probably in the strongly Catholic con-stituencies of Lancashire and Cheshire that the anti-Catholic argument is most frequently displayed and most frequently effective.

However that may be in another part of the world, in central Wilt-shire Catholics were negligibly few on the ground. I suppose that the members of the selection committee had somehow heard that I was a Catholic but the matter was never raised at the committee's meeting and I was adopted on quite other grounds in preference to five other candidates all of whom were Protestants. During the campaign there was some strange little society in London—not in the constituency—which pestered voters with some ridiculous pamphlet accusing the Pope of having been pro-German in the war, but the candidates opposed to me repudiated it and I have no reason to think that any voters allowed their votes to be swayed by it. If anything I should think that it did me a little good as the predominant mood was certainly one of dislike of bitterness and bigotry.

Two years later, when the controversy about the abolition of capital punishment came up, a good friend of mine, a stout old farmer, did ask me whether it was the teaching of the Catholic Church which compelled me to give my vote for abolition. I was able to assure him that there was no dogmatic teaching of the Church on this point and that indeed a large number of Catholics, both in the House of Commons and elsewhere, were strong supporters of capital punishment. This, I think, satisfied him. But a not very popular Anglican clergyman did write a letter suggesting that it was a scandal that a Protestant constituency should be represented by a notorious Papist and that if I wanted to go into Parliament I should more decently find a constituency in some such place as Liverpool. The suggestion was surely as inept as could be imagined. The one thing that we do not want in the country is the creation of conditions similar to those of Northern Ireland with Catholic districts returning Catholic members and Protestant districts returning Protestant members. 'If he wanted to attack Catholics he would have been much better advised to demand the repeal of Catholic Emancipation,' said a sensible constituent.

At the election of 1951 some newspaper published a rumour that if the Conservatives were returned I would be appointed Minister of Education and a small group of Low Churchmen attempted to make of this an argument that I should not be re-elected. But there was no sort of authority for the rumour and indeed it was so manifestly improbable that their campaign had as little effect as that of the gentleman who accused the Pope of being pro-German in 1945. When Attlee formed his Government in 1945 he did not include any Catholic in it, nor later did Churchill. But this was not, I fancy, on account of any anti-Catholic prejudice. I doubt if either of the Prime Ministers were aware of the omission. It was rather that Catholics—Dick Stokes, for instance, and Hugh Delargy in the Labour Party—almost always stick more loosely to party allegiance than others and are unable to see in party regularity a sort of religious obligation. Rigid party loyalty is a virtue of non-Christians.

At Westminster I never heard a single word of insult to the Catholic religion or to myself for holding it. My most excellent friend, Sir William Darling, the most large-hearted and kindly of men, a member for an Edinburgh constituency, the licensed jester of the Conservative back benchers—'I do congratulate you on your Darling,' a Labour member once said to me on the way home—himself a Protestant but who had, when Lord Provost of Edinburgh, defied Presbyterian bigotry by insisting in spite of stone-throwing on attending Mass, warned me in all friendliness not to exaggerate the importance of this courtesy. 'You know what the English are,' he said. As a Scot he had for them a contempt. 'Of course they never say anything to your face. But the moment that a Catholic leaves the room, they always put their heads together and say, "Why did he say that?" "Oh, Catholics have to say that. Their priests tell them to." '

And indeed it is the real disadvantage from which a Catholic has to suffer in England that, however independent, indeed perhaps however heretical an opinion he expresses, the know-alls get together and say, 'Of course he had to say that because he is a Catholic.'

William Darling warned me that a Catholic could get most of the posts of state. There were only a few which were in effect barred to him. 'He could not be Lord Chancellor, of course. And he could not be Prime Minister, or Foreign Secretary or Minister of Education or Speaker.' I was surprised at the inclusion of the Speaker in the list, but that was what he said. The Ministry of Education was self-evident and I had always been very well aware that, even if I possessed every other qualification for the post (which I by no means did), it would have been quite out of the question. The position would have carried considerable embarrassments for me.

Immediately after 1945 there was happily no grave denominational issue to trouble party politics at Westminster. There was at the moment no particular Irish issue. The accusations that a few years later were to be levelled against Pius XII for his conduct in the war and his neglect to protest more clearly against Hitler's persecution of the Jews had not yet made themselves heard. The general uninformed British attitude was that he had behaved himself well throughout the war in a position of little opportunity. 'He had not done much about the war, but what could he have done?'

The only denominational issue at Westminster was that of the Church schools. R. A. Butler in the Education Act of 1944 had given to the Catholic schools what he thought of as a generous deal and a final settlement. The Catholics had to build their own schools. If they did so the State would maintain them. But it rapidly became evident that prices were rising so fast that it was impossible for the Catholics to bear the burden of building. Some State assistance was necessary and the bishops confidently looked to the Catholic M.P.'s—myself of course among them—for support in their demands. On the eve of the 1950 election they had issued a pronouncement threatening that all candidates would be submitted to a questionnaire on the Catholic schools and that those whose answers were not satisfactory would not receive the Catholic vote.

They issued the pronouncement without any consultation with the Catholic members, and it was an act of extreme folly. The voters had only one vote and the number of Catholic voters who felt so strongly on the schools question that they were prepared to vote on it rather than on more general and larger questions was small. The bishops' threat was a foolish bluff and was rightly treated as such by the politicians.

The schools controversy inevitably thrust me into the position of appearing as a leading Catholic layman. The bishops looked to me for support, if not for leadership, in their campaign, and I was not willing to refuse their request. At the same time I was far from happy in it. As a citizen, I felt that a refusal of the demands of the Catholics would be insupportable. If the State is going to impose compulsory education on its children, then their parents who pay their rates and taxes have the right to demand that the education should be of the sort that they want. The State should certainly pay for the Catholic schools as it does in Scotland. I was much more doubtful of the desirability of the reform from the point of view of Catholic interests. About half the Catholic children in the country went to Catholic schools and about half went to non-Catholic schools. Did those who went to Catholic schools turn out better, whatever 'better' might mean, than the others? Did a much larger number of them persist in the practice of their religion? Did a much smaller number find their way into prison? Was their book-learning superior? For better or worse they were destined to live in a pluralist society—to go out from school to earn their living and to live their lives in the company of people who by no means shared their faith. Did an exclusively Catholic schooling make it easier for them to keep their faith in these pluralist surroundings? Or were they more likely to keep it if, from the first, they were conscious that they held it under challenge and that it was not shared by the great majority of their fellow citizens? A theoretical case could be made out for either conclusion. It obviously to a large extent depended more on the parents than on the school. A child brought up in a strongly Catholic home would perhaps keep the faith whatever he or she was taught at school. A child brought up in a home of parents who themselves did not much value or practise their religion would be likely enough to drop it whatever the influences of the Catholic school. But at least it was important to get some sort of rough statistics on how the two sorts of children did fare in later life. The trouble with the bishops was that they had very little answer to give to any such request for information. Roman Catholics do not answer letters, and their technique in face of such requests was simply, in the good old tradition of Cardinal Wiseman, not to answer. They clearly did not know the answer, and what is more it had not occurred to them to ask the question. The battle for the schools was under the command of Bishop (now Archbishop) Beck. He was an ex-schoolmaster and well informed on the details of the problem. But the majority of the other bishops, I found, knew absolutely nothing about it. They had been taught in their seminaries the slogan of a 'Catholic school for Catholic children', and they had gone on repeating it through life. They had never inquired into it. In fact there were of course some very good Catholic schools, but there were also some very bad Catholic schools—bad in their general education and their appointments, but bad, too, in their religious training—schools from which the children were much more likely to emerge having lost their faith than having been confirmed in it, and from which, in fact, the majority did emerge having lost it. The bishops, if they were to demand public money for their schools, had an obligation to make these inefficient schools efficient. To this obligation many of the bishops paid little attention. They contented themselves with repeating the slogan. It was, and is, my experience that priests are generally in very close touch with their flocks but that is by no means true of bishops.

The House of Commons is very like a public school. On the front benches sit the Prefects, the fags behind them. Naturally front bencher varies from front bencher in courtesy and intelligence. Some are sensible enough and generous enough to see the importance of showing friendship to the lesser fry behind them. Others almost visibly resent any challenge from inferior beings—little boys to be seen and not heard. When I arrived in the House of Commons Winston Churchill, though he had just been humiliated by his electoral defeat, was of course still incomparably its most distinguished member. It was greatly to the credit of his character that he accepted defeat with as little overt bitterness as he did. He was not a man who liked being beaten. Why should he? The story is told that his wife said to him that his defeat was perhaps a blessing in disguise. 'Very well disguised,' he said, and there is no doubt that he never fully recovered from the blow. Those who only saw him after 1945 never saw him at his greatest. He was a man who of course threw himself with every vigour into the controversies that he really thought important, and it is well for England that he did so. But he hardly pretended to be above scoring quite petty points in minor matters. 'The Rt Hon. gentleman is responsible when he is in office, but only then,' John Strachey once said of him—not altogether unfairly. When asked by a junior colleague how to make a speech on some secondary issue, Churchill's reply was, 'Oh, take the high moral line. Bugger you— and all that.'

He never bothered to adjust himself to the new Parliament of 1945— this new, unfamiliar and to him unwelcome Parliament. Why should he? He never made any pretence of getting to know his new members one from another, and his second period of office after 1951 was not one that added to his reputation. He was very deaf by then and wore a deaf aid. It was his habit to wear it when he himself was speaking or asking someone a question, but then to remove it when it came to the turn of he whom he had questioned to give his answer. On the other hand he submitted himself to the great courtesy of asking small batches of us Conservative members to luncheon at his house every Thursday, thus in time working through the whole rota of the Conservative team. I do not suppose that he knew very clearly who his guests were on any particular day, but he was the most kindly and generous of hosts and he gave us an excellent luncheon. 'The population of this island,' he explained in genial fashion over his brandy and cigar, 'will be reduced by a half,' and then added with a delightful chuckle, 'And what's more, there will be a good deal of ill will about which half it is.' As a host he was also generous to his opponents. One day Sir Stafford and Lady Cripps were bidden to lunch. Lady Churchill (she was then Mrs Churchill) went down in the morning to the kitchen to explain that two of her luncheon guests were strict vegetarians. It was still rationing time, but she was reassured by being told that there were a few eggs in the house and gave instructions that an omelette be prepared. When the luncheon came the omelette was offered first to Lady Cripps, who thought that it was a personal dish for herself and therefore helped herself to the whole lot. Poor Sir Stafford was left to make his disconsolate lunch off a dry biscuit. But I dare say that that ascetic soul did not greatly mind. He certainly did not complain. There was a pleasant schoolboy side to Churchill's character which loved to rag the master. When there was a fuel shortage he came into the House of Commons, clad as for an arctic expedition, and sat on the front bench shrouded in an enormous overcoat in pretended protest at the Minister of Fuel's incompetence, though in fact it was quite bearably warm. 'Never trust a Lord,' he told me, and indeed I soon had reason to discover how necessary was his advice. One day I went to the House in a new overcoat. I left it in the members' cloakroom. When it came to the time to go home it was not to be found; I got the policemen to search everywhere but without avail and I had to go home without it. I gave it up for lost, but two days later the attendants came and told me that they had found it hanging in the cloakroom of the House of Lords. 'What did I tell you?' Churchill said, when he heard the story.

Randolph Churchill was naturally more of my own status, and my acquaintance with him was easier than that with his father. I had known him ever since, at less than twenty-one, having failed in his History Previous at Christ Church, he had embarked on a successful career as a public lecturer on Anglo-American relations. It would be idle to pretend that everybody liked him. He made many enemies, one among them Lady Pamela Barry, the daughter of Lord Birkenhead. There was an amusing scene in the press gallery in the House of Commons when Lady Pamela had been my guest and when, as she made her way out, Randolph either pushed her down some steps or at least neglected to uncross his legs so that she might get past him. The incident played its part at the time in an article which he wrote for the *Evening Standard*. There was another contretemps with Lady Violet Bonham Carter, who had been induced, a little against her will, to visit him at his house in the country. She ventured to make a remark in protest against some judgement of his, whereat he stumped out of the dining room, exclaiming, 'Am I not to be allowed to speak in my own house?' However I always got on very well with him and he allowed contradiction from me more freely, I fancy, than he did from most others. He died early, not having met with the success which he had confessedly expected and which many had prophesied for him. It is a great misfortune to have too distinguished a father. He had a pungent journalistic style and plenty of self-confidence, but it was not supported by very wide or accurate knowledge. I well remember hearing him one day pontificating at large on the iniquities of Mr Gandhi. It became evident after a time that he was under the impression that Mr Gandhi was an Egyptian. On that error being pointed out, he dismissed it as a petty point to which only a pedant would have ventured to call attention and did not allow it for one instant to interrupt the flow of his denunciation.

The members of Parliament of 1945 were with a very few exceptions a decent and friendly lot—far preferable, from all that I can learn, to the members of the 1918 Parliament, returned immediately after the First World War. The back benchers were on the whole to be preferred to the front benchers. Power corrupts, and office, or the prospect of office, is very deleterious to the soul. I can think of a number of persons on both sides of the House whom I once greatly liked but whose character has very visibly deteriorated as their political fortunes have prospered. Both front benches in 1945 were inhabited by men who had been worn down by the enormous burden of responsibility during the war. They were tired and often sick men. On the Conservative side, apart from Churchill, Anthony Eden was to prove of insufficient health to bear the burden of office. Oliver Stanley, that brilliant wit, like his ancestor the Rupert of debate, was to die before even the opportunity of new office came his way. Brendan Bracken was not to survive for long.

Eden's ill health had in fact already impaired his judgement before ever he became Prime Minister. He was not at his best a very enlivening speaker. Ernie Bevin described his oratory as 'Clich, clich, clich,' rhyming with 'dish'—he was unaware that *cliché* was a French word.

Oliver Stanley's only rival in wit on the Conservative front bench was Harold Macmillan. Both of them were masters of a witty phrase, but they differed greatly from one another. Oliver Stanley was a man brought up to breathe the political atmosphere and a very great devotee of the party system. I remember him once saying that it was never wise for a man openly to break with his party. Macmillan in his pre-war days of revolt had shown himself of a different kind. Although a consummate politician, as he showed when he rescued his party from the débâcle in which Anthony Eden had left it after Suez and brought it to unexpected victory, he was by no means merely a politician. He had been the 'C' of Evelyn Waugh's life of Ronald Knox and was, I fancy, always a little troubled in his innermost soul lest at that period in his life he had perhaps made *il gran rifiuto* in his pursuit of lower things. I was, I fancy, the only other member of Parliament at that time who also possessed the intimacy of Ronald Knox, who then lived in our village of Mells, and this gave us a bond in common.

I remember Macmillan as Minister for Housing being called on to preside at a dinner in the House of Lords in honour of Lord Samuel, who was then the Visitor of Balliol. He arrived late, obviously not having had the opportunity to do much preparation for the occasion. The gist of his speech was that Lord Samuel's highest distinction at Balliol was to have been a contemporary of 'the greatest of all Balliol men, Hilaire Belloc'. Macmillan belonged to the pre-1914 generation of undergraduates among whom reverence for Belloc's prose was widespread. But he had forgotten that in the controversies of the Marconi case Belloc and Cecil Chesterton had most violently and unfairly attacked Samuel in a fashion that cannot have left him with any great liking for Belloc. Throughout Macmillan's speech he sat silent with a sickly smile and made no reference to it in his reply. I chaffed Macmillan afterwards on his speech but he had clearly in no way recollected the Marconi controversies and did not seem in any way conscious that he had been guilty of a failure in tact.

The best companions and friends to new members on the front bench were Shakes Morrison and Walter Elliot. Neither was to receive office again when the Conservatives returned to power. Morrison became of course Speaker and after that Governor General of Australia where he died. He sat for Cirencester, the neighbouring constituency to mine, and I attended a dinner in honour of his twenty-one years of membership. It was Cripps country and most of his supporters seemed to be called Cripps and were, according to the family tradition, with which Stafford and his father alone had broken, staunch Conservatives. I was taken round and introduced to my fellow guests. 'This is Mr Cripps. This is Miss Cripps. This is Major Cripps. This is Sir Arthur Cripps.' I was told how Sir Stafford's ancestor had been Lord of the Manor when the first train arrived at Cirencester from Swindon. 'What did he do?' I asked. 'He went down to the station and told it to go back again,' I was told. I stayed with Morrison in his house and must have been one of the few people to have been awoken by the Speaker in his dressing gown with morning tea.

Walter Elliot truly loved the House of Commons. To him it was not a stepping stone to office but rather almost a shrine. He loved talking—in private or in public—on almost any subject and almost endlessly. Churchill, it is said, did not greatly like him and described him as 'a Scotch dominie'. In any event he did not give him office when he returned to power. He had an excellent sense of humour. His love of the Palace of Westminster had caused him during the war to be one of its most faithful fire-watchers. Popular rumour always used to record that, when the House was bombed, it was Walter Elliot who by breaking down the wooden doors of Westminster Hall before they had caught fire saved the Hall from destruction. As Elliot recounted the anecdote to me one evening after dinner, he did indeed break down the doors, but, when a professional fireman came along soon after, he asked, 'What damned fool has done this?' and explained that the effect would be that the fire would be dragged in as into a tunnel, to the infinite danger of the Hall. So, as Walter recounted the story, 'I then walked away whistling and murmuring, "I wonder who is in charge here."'

Edward Heath was in those days a Whip and as such of course precluded from speaking. The only observation of his that I recollect to have heard carries with it in these days a certain tinge of irony. Enoch Powell was making a trenchant attack on Aneurin Bevan's record as

Minister of Health. Heath and I chanced to be standing together at the bar of the House. 'That's the stuff the doctor ordered,' said Heath in approval of Powell's speech.

On the whole I got on better with the Socialist front benchers than with the Conservatives. This was not because of any superiority of virtue or courtesy among the Socialists, on which I would express no opinion. As almost every day's news has always shown and still shows, Socialist ranks are almost perpetually rent with most bitter internal personal quarrels. I remember when poor old Arthur Greenwood was failing in health and had at last to be dropped from the Government. Soon afterwards he died, and in the conventionally eulogistic obituary speeches we were told that even in his day of disappointment no word of complaint or disloyalty was ever heard from his lips. I remember meeting him on the night when he was dropped and he said to me of the Labour Ministers, 'You can say what you like about the beggars. I don't care.' I do not think that I can honestly remember ever having heard a Socialist member of Parliament saying anything complimentary in private about any other Socialist member of Parliament. The Socialists are like Dr Johnson's Irishmen: 'They are a fair people, sir. They never speak well of one another.' When someone commented on the mercurial Aneurin Bevan, that he was his own worst enemy, Ernie Bevin, who was his Cabinet colleague, said, 'Not while I'm alive, he ain't.' Similarly Socialist leaders are often very tough with their rank and file, but it is easier in the atmosphere of Westminster to have comfortable personal relations with one's political opponents than with one's political colleagues. There are always internal conflicts and jockeying for positions within a party. There are no personal rivalries with an opponent. Of the members of Attlee's government some, like those who had been their Conservative colleagues, were already a little damaged in health and did not survive many years. Bevin and Cripps were the most notable casualties of this sort. Others, Dalton and Morrison, survived only a little longer. Attlee, the greatest of them, outlived them all. The two nicest members of the Socialist front bench, two men who are now perhaps almost forgotten but whom we all knew and loved in those days, were Chuter Ede, the Home Secretary, and George Tomlinson, the Minister of Education. Chuter Ede had been a schoolmaster, a headmaster, and had all the qualities of a Mr Chipps. He was a strong friend of liberty. Though a teetotaller, he was opposed to local option, and, though no Buchmanite, in an exquisitely witty speech he routed those who had wanted to invoke the law for the suppression of the Buchmanites. It was a joy to see him at a county cricket match, armed with an enormous score book and carefully keeping the score and the bowling analysis ball by ball. George Tomlinson was a Lancashire trade unionist, the friend of everybody.

It was common in Conservative circles to dislike Aneurin Bevan, in particular for an unfortunate speech in which he referred to Conservatives as 'vermin'. I always got on with him very well. He was proud—it may be, a little too proud—of having other interests beyond politics and was perhaps contemptuous of some of his fellow Socialist members. '*Lumpen proletariat*' as he called them. He went with a Socialist party delegation to China. Meeting him on his return, I inquired how he had got on. 'Bloody awful,' he said. 'What?' I asked, 'didn't you like the Chinese?' 'Oh, the Chinese were all right,' he said, 'but, my God, the company.'

Bevan was an omniverous reader. He once told me that there were only two authors whom he found absolutely unreadable—Churchill and Attlee. He had no fundamental religious beliefs but he had a great liking for good reasoning. He had a great admiration for Cardinal Newman. I found him one day reading the *Apologia* over his whisky, and lecturing some fellow members on their arrogant folly in venturing to speak disparagingly of so great a writer. In 1963 I chanced to follow him round Israel on trips that we both took in that country. I succeeded him by a few days as guest at the kibbutz to the south of the Sea of Galilee. I asked him of his experience and commented on the discipline and dedication that I had found there. 'Yes,' he said, 'and the chastity—and the chastity.'

We used from time to time to invite guests to the *Punch* table for luncheon and one day we invited Aneurin Bevan. He was seated at the right hand of Alan Agnew, the very correctly capitalist chairman of the Board. They had not very much in common and for a time the party did not go very well. Then Aneurin Bevan, who was in most genial form, remarked, looking round at all of us writers, that in his opinion all journalists were much too highly paid. At once Alan Agnew perked up. Here he had discovered was a man who had got something and he most heartily agreed with him. Ever afterwards he spoke with great admiration of Aneurin Bevan. He could not quite remember his name, but spoke of him as 'that nice man who had such sensible views on economics'.

My own most vivid memory of Herbert Morrison is of an hilarious summer evening in the Place Kléber at Strasbourg. I was with Declan Costello whose father had recently supplanted Mr de Valera as the Irish

Taoiseach. Herbert Morrison had been dining with M. Spaak. I introduced him and Declan, for they had not met one another, and we went to have a drink together. But it was clear that in the mellow atmosphere of M. Spaak's dinner Herbert Morrison's memories of the developments of Irish politics were not very clear and that he imagined that Declan was Mr de Valera's son, which he by no means was. The conversation was friendly but somewhat confused.

In general Prime Ministers ever since the First World War have become steadily more and more dominant over their cabinets. Attlee is a remarkable exception to that generalisation. Where others ruled by dominating he, quietly doodling on his envelopes while they quarrelled, ruled by holding the balance. With every day it is becoming clearer how consummate was the skill with which he held that balance. The Labour party, as I have said, is by its nature a difficult horse to ride. In all its history Attlee is the only leader who has had the smallest success in keeping it united. We have only to look at its divisions under Macdonald before and under Gaitskell and Wilson after him to see his greatness. A common anecdote reports Churchill as saying of him, 'A very modest little man—plenty to be modest about.' I have always heard that Churchill very vigorously repudiated ever having said anything of the sort and I can believe it. Attlee had been Churchill's loyal supporter throughout the war and no one had a better reason than Churchill to appreciate his greatness.

It is not relevant here to attempt a criticism or appreciation of the achievements of the post-1945 Government or to estimate its politics. I am concerned with Attlee as a man. We belonged to the same club. I do not think that he ever came to the club when he was Prime Minister but, when he left Downing Street, he returned to his old haunts and was frequently there. We often talked together. His unassuming modesty was for someone who had held his position quite remarkable. Lord Longford tells the story how the two were dining together at the Queen's Restaurant in Sloane Square. When it came to paying the bill it transpired that neither of them had any money on them. Each was determined that the other should pay. 'You can give them a cheque,' said Lord Longford. 'Oh, they won't take a cheque here,' said the Prime Minister, 'nobody knows me here.' His favourite form of conversation, when he was not engaged in discussing the coming season's Haileybury cricket team ('I hear they have got a very promising young left-handed slow bowler') or Oxford's chances of 'beating the Tabs' at whatever sport might be coming up, was little anecdotes about Churchill's latest *bons mots*, the curiosity of which was that they were exactly of the kind that anybody else might have recounted about Churchill. It clearly never occurred to him that he stood in any different relation to Churchill from anybody else. 'Have you heard about Winston and the Pakistan banquet?' he asked me. I had not. The Pakistan Prime Minister had recently been on a visit to this country. They had given him a banquet at which Churchill had been seated next to him. The waiter had come round with the wine and the Pakistani had refused it.

'You don't take wine?' said Churchill.

'No,' said the Pakistani, 'I'm a Moslem, I'm a strict teetotaller.'

'Christ,' said Churchill. 'I mean to say, Allah.'

The story had travelled out to Australia and I heard it there from Robert Menzies, but I heard it first from Attlee. Menzies recounted it as a comment of proper swagger which he himself would have been glad to have perpetrated, Attlee as of a man who moved in a company infinitely above him to which he did not aspire. It was only of his own colleagues of whom he spoke with disdain. I used to write little verses on what was going on in the world. I remember a parody of John Betjeman's *Summoned by Bells*, in which I enumerated in blank verses the things that Betjeman had loved. It contained the line

'And Major Attlee and the Holy Grail.'

Attlee congratulated me on the line. Occasionally my verses would contain some little gibe at one of Attlee's colleagues. When they did he always congratulated me. Betjeman and I had to go down one day to Haileybury to take part in a B.B.C. Brains Trust there. We foregathered at the club preparatory to making the journey. Attlee was sitting in the morning room there reading a detective story and translating it into Italian verse. We went across to him and told him:

'We are going down to your old school to take part in a Brains Trust.'

'I'm going down next Wednesday,' he said, 'to speak to the Middle Fourth.'

When he was defeated in the election of 1951 he said with relief, 'Well, at any rate I shall have a lazy afternoon tomorrow.'

'Oh, no, you won't, Clem,' said his wife. 'You'll mow the lawn.'

On the evening when he received his peerage I saw him seated in a chair with an enormous waste-paper basket beside him. He was opening letters and throwing them into the basket. I asked him what he was doing. 'Letters of congratulation,' he said. 'I throw away those that I won't answer.' They were the very great majority.

His comically pedestrian prose reminds me of Cardinal Spellman's letters to his father in which he writes 'and then we came to Mesopotamia, which is so-called because it is in the middle of two rivers', a remark, said Evelyn Waugh, in reviewing the book, 'for which, if my son were to make it, I should beat him though he were the Pope himself'. Attlee had a pleasant habit of giving utterly inconsequent reasons for refusing invitations. Malcolm Muggeridge and I met him one evening at eleven o'clock at night and offered him a drink. 'I've got to go and give away the prizes at a school in South Shields,' he said in refusing the invitation. It seemed improbable that the important ceremony would take place at midnight and, as we saw him patiently waiting under the street lamp for a Green Line bus, still less probable that such a form of transport would take him there.

Great political success is always deleterious to the character, but it is much less harmful when it is wholly unexpected. Attlee had confessed that until middle age his highest hope and expectation was that one day he might be mayor of some lesser London borough.

CHAPTER SIX

The Lean and Slipper'd Pantaloon

I

FAMILIAR FACES

A year or two before I left Parliament Malcolm Muggeridge, then the editor of *Punch*, invited me to write an article for that paper. I did so and soon became a regular contributor. When I finally left Parliament I became its Parliamentary correspondent. I still had a considerable interest in political developments without having any desire for a personal political career. The post therefore suited me very well. After a time I was invited to become a member of the Table, which lunched at the paper's offices, then still in Bouverie Street, every week and settled the cartoon for the coming week. The Table had a long tradition behind it, dating back to Thackeray's time. Each member had his initials carved on the table and his photograph hung on the walls. At that time it was the custom, which was later changed, for every member to have a regular place at the Table at which he sat. Malcolm Muggeridge sat at the head of the table, on his left was Kenneth Bird—Fougasse—who had been his predecessor as editor, and I sat to the left of Kenneth. I had never previously met Kenneth Bird, though of course, like everybody else, I was well acquainted with his delicate and witty drawings. Naturally, sitting next to him each week, I had the opportunity of getting to know him very well and seldom have I met anyone for whom I had a higher admiration. He had been badly wounded in the First World War and ascribed his wholly unexpected recovery to a miracle. This miracle was, he believed, due to his faith in Christian Science, of which he was a fervent disciple and to which he devoted his life. I had never before met a Christian Scientist in any intimacy and held—and, indeed, in a measure still hold—against it the objection that a creed which asserts that suffering is only possible owing to the imperfection of the sufferer can hardly call itself a Christian creed since it is the essence of Christianity that the supremely perfect man took suffering upon himself. That incidentally a lot of disease can be cured and suffering overcome by suggestion, will power and faith I did not doubt, but one did not need to become a Christian Scientist to believe that. Such things may be. Kenneth Bird never made any attempt to convert me or, as far as I observed, anybody else to Christian Science. He went down every week to Eton to give a voluntary instruction to the boys of his faith. How many pupils he had or what he told them I do not know. His own conversation and conduct were models of kindness and charity. Brimful as he was of wit, I never heard him say a wounding word about anybody and, if he is in any way an example of what a Christian Scientist can be, I certainly learnt from him never in ignorance to speak with uncharity of that creed.

The infinite variety of Malcolm Muggeridge's career is so much public property that there is no need to recount it in detail. The son of a Socialist Member of Parliament, he was brought up in the belief that all the evils of society were due to the capitalist system and that all that was required to set the world to rights was a Socialist Government and the passage of a small number of self-evidently desirable measures of socialist reform. He was reared in youth on the Socialist Sunday School Leagues where he was taught to reject any suggestion that religion could have anything of importance to contribute to the solution of the world's problems. He went up to Cambridge and there, mainly through the influence of Alec Vidler, came in contact with certain Christian influences, but their effect on him, though they were not defiantly rejected, was not sufficient materially to change his life. He spent time in India as a sort of missionary teacher, then, returning to England, obtained a post on the *Manchester Guardian,* which he held until he found that his views had moved considerably to the left of that paper. He went out to Moscow as a correspondent and as a communist or near-communist, but the sight of the tyrannies, incompetence and corruption of the Communist regime in action cured him of all admiration for Communism. During the war he did some work in Intelligence and then immediately after it he was joint editor with Colin Coote of *The Daily Telegraph.* From there the Agnew family persuaded him to transfer himself to *Punch.* When he first arrived at *Punch* he still considered himself a Conservative and, indeed, when I announced my intention not to stand again for Devizes, he wrote to the constituency Chairman, Sir Arthur Harford, offering himself as a candidate. His offer was not accepted, nor, I think, even seriously considered, and it it was as well that it was not. For he was most abundantly filled with what Chesterton called 'God's scorn for all men governing'.

He had hated the Communists when he found them in power in Russia. He hated the Socialists and bureaucrats when he found them in power in England in 1945. The Conservatives, so long as they were impotent and in opposition, he had looked on with reasonable benevolence. But, once they themselves came into power, he turned against them. He published in *Punch* violent attacks on Winston Churchill as Prime Minister, which earned him the great hatred of my friend, Lady Violet Bonham Carter, who thought very meanly of the record of my association with 'smearer Muggeridge', as she called him. After Churchill had gone he turned his attacks on Anthony Eden and was a vitriolic opponent of Suez. His criticisms of the Royal Family won for him widespread and sometimes pretty obscene abuse. His position would certainly have been impossible had the Conservatives of Devizes ever been so foolish as to select him as their candidate.

When Kruschev and Bulganin came over on their visit to Britain Muggeridge and I held meetings at Liverpool and elsewhere in which, sensibly or not, we denounced their visit. Malcolm was never a very careful epicure but at that time he had by no means developed the extreme asceticism which makes him today so determined a vegetarian and so rigid a teetotaller. He had by then abandoned, in so far as he had once had it, his mood of indifference to religion. He talked about religion almost embarrassingly frequently, even at the *Punch* table, for instance. His attitude towards it was one of respect for what he called its meta-physics combined with an inability to accept its historical claims. He could not bring himself to believe that the Resurrection actually happened as an event of history, and, indeed, his contempt for the world and history was such that he would, I suspect, have almost thought the worse of it if he had been compelled to believe it in that sense. He was attracted to a number of Catholics, in particular to Father Bernard Bassett, the well-known Jesuit, a previous pupil of mine at Stonyhurst, who had supported his campaign against Bulg. and Krush. At that time he would have said that the Catholic Church was the superior of other Christian denominations on account of its sturdy refusal to compromise with the spirit of the age. Subsequent developments in the Church have caused him to modify that judgement. It is only since he left *Punch* that he has engaged himself in his violent campaign against the permissiveness of the age and its sexual licence. To what extent he has by now reconciled himself to the historical claims of the Christian story I cannot say, but he certainly now calls himself a Christian, though without even an ambition to attach himself to any organisation or denomination. It is common

enough for those who have least sympathy with his opinions to pay
tribute to the courtesy and kindness of his private manners, and I who
have in all his stages had a good deal of sympathy with his opinions
would certainly join in those tributes. For he has always shown unfailing
kindness both to me and to my children, to whom he has on a number of
occasions given much assistance of one sort or another. It is not for me to
criticise but it is perhaps impossible to deny that there is a certain force in
the charge that there is a tinge of Manichaeanism in his extreme hostility
to sex. After all it is not Christian teaching that sex or matter is evil. Sex
and matter are good and only the abuse of them is evil. God saw His
creation and pronounced that it was good, and though the Church has
indeed always condemned the extravagances of sex, it has not given any
countenance for the condemnation of even the abuse of sex as a sin of
sins. Paola and Francesca in Dante are only condemned to a very mild
punishment—by no means to the nethermost pits of hell. But, however
that may be, what seems to me more curious is that with his unceasing
denunciation of the mass media and the corruption of modern journalism
Malcolm should still be so constantly ready to display himself before the
public or on a screen. Chesterton said of Dean Inge, when he made a
somewhat similar complaint against self-advertising clerics, 'that he was
ready to display himself

> When earthly fame he can no more endure
> Upon a transatlantic lecturing tour.'

With Malcolm's contempt for publicity and for the television one might
have expected that he would have hidden himself in some lonely cottage
in the Hebrides or in the West of Ireland, whence he could perhaps from
time to time attack the corruptions and vulgarity of the world in a book
and where he would be sheltered from daily contact with it. There is no
such thing as bad publicity, I once heard him say, and if the object of life
is to get oneself talked about as much as possible, this is probably true.
But according to his principles this should surely be the meanest of all
ambitions. Jakie Astor once said to me, 'The secret of happiness is never
to meet interesting people,' and if by interesting people is meant people
who get their names in the papers this is on the whole true. Of Malcolm's
protests I would say that pornography is no doubt a great evil but it is
not so great an evil as publicity.

At about the same time as my entrance, Malcolm had also brought on
to the Table of *Punch* John Betjeman, and there he sat during the period
of Malcolm's editorship, contributing very greatly to the gaiety of our

luncheon but not—to be truthful—very frequently to the columns of the paper. John Betjeman had been up at Oxford a short time after me. His career there, in strict academic terms, had not been distinguished. He had failed in the examination in divinity—Divers—which it was then necessary to take, and was sent down without a degree after a year's residence. But the mark which he left on the social life of Oxford was considerable. Leading young dons such as Maurice Bowra recognised him as a man of wholly original genius and took him up. The only problem, at that time, as they thought, was how to turn his genius to practical advantage—how would it ever be possible to find a job for his most original but most eccentric gifts? It was generally thought that it might be possible to accommodate him with some work on the *Architectural Review* but the prospects were not considered bright. As we all know, his verses found a market and found favour to an extent that few had foreseen. Entirely unlike the conventional poetic habits of the age, they yet won general favour for their strange mixture of wit and serious melancholy. Readers complained that they could never tell whether he was serious or not—to what extent he liked things because he thought them beautiful and to what extent he praised them because he found them amusing. But if readers could not guess this, it is certain that Betjeman himself had no notion of the answer to that question. He founded the cult of the love of things Victorian. He substituted for the pre-war and absurdly exaggerated loyalty to public schools, and for Alec Waugh's reactions against that absurdity, a new love-hate by which he thought of schools as places of bullying and barbarity but still as places to be remembered. There were none among his acquaintances, however slight, of whom he was not careful to discover where they were at school. He taught the British public to love Miss Joan Hunter Dunn, Major Attlee and Lord Tennyson, and, as we know, has in recent years, to general approval, received both a well-deserved knighthood and the Poet Laureateship. In a melancholy world in which all beautiful things are perishing he is unaffected in his delight at the unexpected success that has come to him. His only regret, I fancy, is that it was not Lord Attlee who conferred upon him the Laureateship. That would have indeed been glory.

Betjeman is a man of infinite kindness, humour and geniality, though, as is not uncommon of great humourists, his humour is interlaced with melancholy. It shows itself in most strangely contrived jokes, as when he gave a dinner party for all the people whom he could find in the telephone book whose names ended in 'bottom'. It was only when this oddly assorted company arrived that they discovered—a little, I believe, to the displeasure of some among them—for what peculiar reason they had been bidden. His religion is deep and genuine but I do not think that he would take issue if I said that it was architecture which led him to it, and therefore since he greatly dislikes to be abroad he has never felt temptation to abandon the Church of England in favour of any other denomination. We once happened to coincide on one of his rare trips, to Denmark, whither we had both gone to deliver some lectures. Our hosts kindly gave us a dinner together. It was the evening of his first arrival in the country and he was most anxious to learn all that he could about it. He was full of curiosity about Hans Andersen. From him he turned to the Danish Royal Family.

'You have a king? And your king comes to open your Parliament?' he said.

Our hosts assured him that it was so.

'And I suppose he rides there on a bicycle.'

We finished up the evening by five of us crowding into a lift that was only advertised to hold three. As a result the lift stuck and it took a good hour for the kindly Danes to lever us out.

Betjeman used to come to lunch with me at the House of Commons, where it was his whim to pretend that the only matter of the smallest interest about the various Labour Members was the precise school of Anglican churchmanship which they professed. 'Is Dalton high?' he once asked of a fellow Labour Member.

Not the least remarkable thing about Betjeman is his most remarkable wife. Penelope Betjeman was the daughter of Lord Chetwode, the Field-Marshal, and in his time Commander-in-Chief in India, where she was brought up, and such portions of her affection as she can spare from horses she gives unstintingly to Indian philosophy. Unlike her husband she became a Catholic and professes her religion in an edifyingly literal and pious fashion. She once stayed with us and the conversation after dinner turned on the Resurrection of the Body. She was so impressed by our deployment of Christian doctrine that she insisted on going to bed with all her clothes on so that she might be well prepared should the end of the world come before the next day's breakfast.

I once served with her on a Brains Trust. One of the other members of the trust was Abbot Butler of Downside (Bishop Butler, as he now is). The last question of the evening was about the merits of modern youth. Abbot Butler and I and the rest of us gave bromide answers. The young of today, we asserted, were every bit as good as, or better than, we of our generation had been. Finally it came to Penelope to give the last word. She said that she could not agree with us. On the contrary, in her opinion the modern young were perfectly bloody. She cited the example of two young men whom she had recently asked to her house for luncheon. They arrived as if they had been 'rolling in the midden'. They had not the manners to answer any questions that they were asked or to acknowledge any introductions. 'The only question,' she concluded, 'out of which we could extract a civil answer was when we asked them where they had been at school and they both said "Downside".' With this unexpected Parthian shot the curtain was rung down. But Abbot Butler, it must be admitted, took it all in very good part.

Until she recently left her house at Wantage Penelope kept in the town a small tea-shop—King Alfred's Kitchen. Burnt cakes, of course, alone were served. She was for many years a regular reader of *Punch* but always imagined that the pictures of the advertisements in that paper were its jokes. She found them quite funny.

As I have indicated, my upbringing was on the whole liberal and, had the Liberal Party had any prospects of carrying into force its policies, I daresay that when I went into Parliament I would have gone in as a Liberal. Anthony Asquith had been at school with me at Summer Fields and then later at Balliol. I had met with Mr Asquith when he attended the dinner of the Oxford Liberal club at the time I was an undergraduate, and he had kindly invited me over to the Wharfe at Sutton Courtenay to luncheon. My connections with the Asquith family were reforged some years afterwards in a very happy fashion. My father lived at Wells, and the Horner family lived some twelve miles away at Mells. Sir John Horner, the head of the family, was by then dead, but in these years immediately before the war his widow, Lady Horner, who had in her day been one of the 'Souls' and a great liberal hostess, still lived on at Mells Manor. The Horners had had four children, two boys and two girls. Of the boys both were dead, the one dying at school, the other being killed in the war. The two sisters remained. Of them one was Cecily Lambton who had married George Lambton, the race-horse trainer. The other was Katherine Asquith who had married Raymond Asquith, Mr Asquith's eldest son. He also had been killed in the war and Katherine, thus left a widow, lived at Mells with her mother. They were kind enough to ask my wife and me over to see them from time to time and, as a result, when in 1936 it appeared that on my return from America I should require a house somewhere in England, I wrote to Katherine to ask if there was any house available in the neighbourhood of Mells. She replied that there was a house actually in Mells. After some negotiations we went into that house and have lived in Mells ever since, only exchanging the larger house for a smaller house when our children grew up and got married, and a two-story house was therefore more convenient than the more spacious three-story one. We have thus had the great happiness to be inhabitants of Mells now for about thirty-five years. My children in their earliest infant prayers always used to say, 'Please God, bless Mummy and Daddy and make Lord Oxford pass in his examinations,' a prayer that was happily answered as he went forward to gain all the academic successes that are customary in that family.

The old Prime Minister had, along with other Liberal leaders, been a very regular visitor to Mells in the days of Lady Horner, but by the time that we arrived there he was of course dead. Yet even now the village was not destitute of ex-Liberal politicians. Sir John and Lady Horner had lived in the Park House until the early years of this century. Then they moved down to the present Manor House by the church. The Park was let to Mr Bates, the Chairman of the Cunard Line. Unfortunately, owing owing to an electrical mishap that house was burnt down during the First World War, and after the war Reginald McKenna, who had been Chancellor of the Exchequer in Asquith's Coalition Government and was then the head of the Midland Bank, got Lutyens to build him the present house. He and his wife were the kindest and most generous of neighbours but very different from one another. He was predominantly a man of facts and figures, and his conversation was almost exclusively of gold and inflation and the rate of interest. On the other hand Pamela McKenna, who was a niece of Lady Horner, was a musician and a romantic and almost extravagantly whimsy-whamsy. She was a great lover of animals and, discovering one day in her house a tapestry of a hunting scene, she was deeply distressed and gave orders that it be removed immediately. The next time that one visited the house one discovered that its place had been taken by a most grisly and realistic representation of the Massacre of the Innocents. I remember how at one time we had some trouble with our telephone which continuously kept giving little tinkling noises. I complained to the telephone people and asked that the defect be remedied. I also happened to mention my little trouble to Pamela McKenna. She was horrified. 'Oh, it's the little owls bouncing up and down,' she said. 'You must on no account interrupt them.'

Even after Mr Asquith's death the village was constantly visited by members of his family. Margot, his wife, was still alive, and the family used to take the near-by house of Babington, which was later to be the residence of Colonel Jennings, the father-in-law of my daughter. There she, along with all the members of the Bonham Carter family, used often to stay and I thus got the chance of making the friendship of Lady Violet Bonham Carter and of her children who were then still at school.

Mr Asquith was by no means a Catholic. He used in his old days to go and read the lessons at evensong in his parish church, but he did so primarily because of his liking for the beauty of the language of the Authorised Bible. At the time of his row with Cardinal Bourne over his refusal of permission for an outdoor procession of the Blessed Sacrament at the Eucharistic Congress, he said, 'These princes of the church have no message for me,' and I have no doubt that that was true. He had a great liking for guessing games and would set what he imagined to be most recondite conundrums for his guests. His favourite, to which he imagined that no educated person would know the answer, was 'What is the difference between the Virgin Birth and the Immaculate Conception?' His assumption of ignorance on this point is surely a very pertinent commentary on the eccentricity of culture among so-called intellectual liberals of that era.

No other member of the Asquith family has, I think, ever been at all bothered by the infections of Catholicism. But, largely under the influence of Hilaire Belloc, Katherine Asquith, soon after her husband's death, was received into the Catholic Church, and she and her three children have been brought up in that faith—the first Catholics, I should imagine, to have lived in Mells since the Reformation.

We had and still have many interesting neighbours. For all too short a time Compton Mackenzie pitched his all too peripatetic tent in the village of Horrington a few miles away. It was about the time when he was vigorously fighting the battle of Edward VIII against what he regarded as an establishment plan to force him off the throne. Leslie Hartley lived for a time in near-by Bath. He was driven to leave by an unfortunate lack of sympathy with a man and wife whom he had engaged to act as servants. Plucking up his courage, that mildest and least aggressive of men said to his servant, 'I am afraid that we are not very well suited to one another.' It was intended to be a prelude to his dismissal. However the manservant by no means took it as such. 'On the contrary,' he replied, 'I have never been better suited in my life,' and it was very evident from his conversation that he had no intention of moving. So Leslie himself had to go to London, leaving the man and his wife in possession of his house.

When I was a schoolboy I was of course introduced to the poetry of

Siegfried Sassoon, and I daresay shortly afterwards was told that he was the Literary Editor of the *Daily Herald*. I was brought up on him as one of the *enfants terribles* of the age. I did not see him again until in his old age he moved to Heytesbury near Warminster, and came over frequently to visit Katherine Asquith and Ronald Knox, who at that time lived in her house in the Manor. It would have been hard to foresee the change in a nature which some fifty years had brought. There was certainly no tinge of the revolutionary about him. If he had voted at all at elections I am sure that he voted Conservative but, to tell the truth, I never remember hearing him say any word about politics at all. The days of fox-hunting were of course behind him. His interest and poetry were entirely in things spiritual. His house was a large and, to be honest, not very attractive house and I could never see why he did not find something smaller to live in, for he spent the greater part of his time and all of the winter in bed. He used to beg his friends to see him, and we were always very glad to do so. But, as he was always in bed and his housekeeper would not disturb him by relaying telephone messages, and as he never answered letters, it was not very easy to make the arrangements. However, in the summer he rose from his bed and still, when well in his eighties, went over to Downside to play cricket for a team called the Ravens against the neighbouring villages. There was difference of opinion about his octogenarian cricketing. The local ladies all turned up and said to one another, 'Isn't it wonderful for Captain Sassoon to be still playing cricket at the age of eighty-three?' But I must confess that I once heard one of the lads of the village giving a less generous verdict. 'This bloody old fool,' he said. 'Can't catch our catches, can't run our runs. Slows up the whole game.'

Sassoon used to take his friends over with him to make up the team. I remember when my youngest son, then still a schoolboy, returned one day from such a match. I asked him how he had got on. He said that Siegfried had introduced him to a very old man to whom he had talked. I asked him what he had talked about. He explained that he had said how boring old people were who talked about the First War. I then asked what the old man had said. He quite agreed with me, answered my son, but I could not feel that the topic had been happily selected, for I knew that this 'old man' was in fact Edmund Blunden.

Another friend of Siegfried whose friendship he owed to the cricket field was Ralph Hodgson. I had of course been brought up on his poetry as I had been brought up on that of Siegfried himself. His life was a curious one. He had begun it by selling little cartoons of the players on the Canterbury cricket ground. Then he had become a missionary of a sort and gone out to Japan. There he had met an American lady to whom he proposed marriage. She accepted him. He then explained to her that his religious principles forbade him from earning any money to support a wife. The lady was apparently agreeable and they now live in a little house outside Chicago. She goes every day into the city to earn their living. He sits on a rocking chair on his veranda waiting for the end of the world through the dropping of an H-bomb which he is very reasonably convinced can not now be long distant.

I first heard the name Joseph Kennedy from Father O'Hara, as he then was, at Notre Dame shortly before the war. Father O'Hara was a good and kindly man, but, like many priests who are themselves unworldly, he had a simple-minded admiration for the success of all Catholic laymen. I do not think that he had ever anything to do with Boston, so I do not imagine that he had any very intimate acquaintance with the Kennedy family. But it was a feather in the cap for the Church that a Catholic—and above all an Irish Catholic—should have been appointed Ambassador in London. Father O'Hara boasted about it, and, when Joseph Kennedy did a hole in one in a golf match, it was yet a further triumph for the Church. Father O'Hara told me about it and how he had sent Mr Kennedy a letter of congratulations. Since I did not appear to be as well aware as a good Catholic layman should have been who Mr Kennedy was, he then proceeded to expand to me on his holiness, on the edifying regularity of his Catholic life and on the enormous size of his good family, satisfactory evidence that here there was no compromise with any evil practices of contraception.

Back in England I do not remember in the years before the war ever hearing anybody speak much of Joseph Kennedy. At the time of Munich there used to appear occasionally in the papers notes that Mr Kennedy had called at Downing Street on the Prime Minister. Somebody told me that he had said that he knew that the Prime Minister would not be able to spare the time to see him, but that he used to call and sit alone in the hall for thirty minutes. Then he would go away and give a notice to the papers that 'the American Ambassador called at 10 Downing Street'. This seemed a friendly enough little gesture, if not in itself of much value as evidence of Mr Kennedy's personal opinions.

I first heard criticism of him in the early days of the war from Douglas Jerrold. Why Douglas Jerrold disapproved of him I never discovered, for if Kennedy was opposed to the war he certainly was no more antagonistic about it than was Jerrold himself, and, after all, Jerrold was an Englishman and Kennedy was an American, the Ambassador of a neutral power. In any event it was not long before Jerrold's views were widely shared and it was common on every English tongue and on many American tongues to hear bitter attacks on the American Ambassador. I do not think that even today these attacks have altogether abated. Perhaps Edward Kennedy has given them a new lease of life. Myself, I did not think then, and I do not think now, that the attacks on the Ambassador were quite justified. He was attacked for advising Roosevelt that Britain would lose the war and for urging him at all costs to keep America out of it. In his judgement of the situation he was, most happily for us, proved wrong, but after the fall of France it was a long way from being a ridiculous opinion. It was the opinion which by far the greater part of the world outside England had formed. I was in America myself at the time that the Battle of Britain began. Public opinion there, as expressed through the newspapers, had no liking for Hitler. They did not want him to win, but they were generally of the opinion that, like it or not, he would in fact win. Kennedy's judgement was much the same. There is no reason to think that he liked Hitler, but, as Ambassador, it was his duty to appraise the situation. He formed the judgement that Hitler would win and advised the President accordingly. After our long centuries of survival, we in Britain refused to believe, even at the worst moments, in the possibility of a British defeat. Miraculously we proved right but few among us could give any coherent account for our wholly unreasonable faith and we could hardly expect Kennedy to share it. It is of course undoubtedly true that his belief in a British defeat was stimulated by his Irish blood. He was the descendant of generations which had lived for the blessed day of a British defeat and his ancestral prejudice doubtless helped him to expect Britain to be defeated in 1940.

It is true that Roosevelt came violently to detest Kennedy. Where did right lie in that quarrel? We now know from the papers recently revealed that Roosevelt, while promising that he had no intention of leading America into war, and while campaigning at his election on a promise to keep her out of the war, was all the time secretly working to bring America in. Naturally enough to English eyes such conduct appeared as rather a virtue than a sin, but it was not unnatural that to an American it should appear as almost treasonable. So my objections to Joseph Kennedy were not so much to his political opinions or his political conduct. He had, according to common gossip, amassed his gigantic fortune largely by foreseeing that prohibition would come to an end and by buying up enormous quantities of Scotch whisky which he then unloosed on the thirsty markets as soon as it was legal. If so, that was not perhaps a particularly apostolic activity (should anybody make himself enormously rich?) but it was not illegal or intrinsically sinful. But what I disliked, what his daughter described to me, and what indeed was fairly common knowledge, was his pursuit of and his demand for success carried to a pitch that was almost an insanity. In whatever activity a Kennedy engaged—whether it was playing in a football game or cheating in a history examination—he must win.

English opinion greatly exaggerated the fervour of Joseph Kennedy's Catholicism. His daughter Kathleen, known as 'Kick', told me that there was a considerable period of his life during which he did not practise his religion at all. It was that very remarkable man, Cardinal Cushing, who with some difficulty got him back to his duties. Nor was Kennedy so fervently Irish as English opinion thought. Irish Catholicism was to him not so much a source of spiritual comfort as a political base. For success in Boston politics it was very convenient to be able confidently to rely on the Irish vote, and he was of course careful not to compromise this, but of the way of life of the Irish in Ireland he knew little and cared little. Of Christianity's message of contempt for worldly success neither he nor, I suppose, any of his family had any understanding. They did not repudiate it, they were simply unaware of it. His sons turned out to be men of great charm and great generosity. They were willing to recognise and to honour demands that the rich should give of their superfluity to the poor, but I doubt if it ever occurred to them that there were dangers in being rich. Riches were to them without qualification an advantage.

I remember dining with their sister Kick Hartington and quoting in the course of an argument with her the biblical text about it being easier for a camel to pass through the eye of a needle than for a rich man to enter the Kingdom of Heaven. 'Oh, I don't agree with that,' said Kick, her eyes blazing with dissent. 'I don't agree with that at all.' 'It hardly matters whether you agree with it or not, Kick,' I answered. 'After all, you won't be running the Last Judgement, and these words have considerable authority behind them.' But to her they were plainly entirely novel and as plainly entirely nonsensical. Riches could buy their way into anything and as easily into the Kingdom of Heaven as into anywhere else.

Kick had married the Duke of Devonshire's son Lord Hartington. He was killed in the war and at its end she stayed on in London in a house in Smith Square. She was the most delightful of girls. It was my great good fortune that I got to know her well just after the war, and what I learnt about the Kennedy family I learnt mainly from her. I never remember having heard her attack her father directly, but I got the impression that there was not much sympathy between them. English aristocratic society was not a milieu in which Joseph Kennedy easily mixed, but he could appreciate success wherever he found it. Therefore he had a respect for a daughter who had the prospect of becoming a Duchess. (It is a curiosity that had Kick and her husband survived she would today be the Duchess of Devonshire and her husband England's leading freemason.) To marry the son of the Duke of Devonshire was a mark of success and, naturally, wives had to stay with their husbands. Therefore, as long as Lord Hartington was alive it was reasonable that she should remain in England. But that she should remain there as a widow and voluntarily—particularly in the England of post-war austerity—was, as she told me, in his eyes a proof of insanity. He knew that he had made himself unpopular in England and resented it that his daughter should so enjoy the country. She on her part thought equally insane his ruthless demand for success both for himself and for his children—a demand which she thought squeezed all pleasure and all reason for living out of life. They were at loggerheads. It could not be pretended that her reaction against the ruthless Kennedy pursuit of success in any way betokened a reaction towards deep religion.

Of one of her sisters, Eunice, who has now become Mrs Schriber, she told me that she thought that she would become a nun. Whether Mrs Schriber ever had any such intention I cannot say. Most certainly she did not fulfil it. In any event such projects were never in Kick's mind. She was a Catholic of a sort, willing to practise the religion to which she had been brought up so long as it imposed on her no great inconvenience. The Devonshire family would of course have been opposed to a Catholic marriage for their son, and she made no sort of bones about giving way to them on that point. When she became a widow she returned to religious practice of a sort but she once told me that she would never allow religion to become an obstacle to any future marriage which she might wish to contract. There was an eccentric aristocratic lady of the eighteenth century who had strongly Protestant views and who formed a religious congregation of her own which she christened Lady Huntingdon's Connection. In a spirit of good-humoured ribaldry I nicknamed the friends whom Kick collected around her 'Lady Hartington's Connection', but it was not, I am afraid, in any sincere recognition of the depth of her devotion. She could not in any sense be called 'devoted to religion', though she had a curious feeling that Catholics would disapprove of her conduct to an extent far greater, for better or for worse, than they in fact ever would. Alas, it was not to be long before she was killed in an aeroplane accident over France. Only the day before we had driven together on some errand in a taxi to St James Street. There we had bade each other Good-bye with no prevision that we would never meet again.

When I knew her her brothers had not begun their political careers. She was not, I suspect, especially close to them. Her influence, even if quite unmediated, had, I think, its effect in making them more pro-English than their father. I remember young John Kennedy who had not at the time been a candidate for any political post, coming over to stay with her and appearing at one of her parties. He was then a young man who handed round the sherry and, learning that I was an M.P., he asked me for advice on how to manage a political career. 'Of course you're established, but I haven't begun yet,' he said. I was under no illusion even then that he was doing more than make polite conversation.

There were of course times when it was convenient for the Kennedys to insist on their Catholicism and on their Irish origin, but in fact Irish Catholicism was to Joseph Kennedy primarily, as I say, a political base. The vast majority of Boston Catholics were from across the tracks rather than lace curtain—of small ambitions in general and of no ambitions at all in the intellectual field. If it had been Joseph Kennedy's ambition to bring up his sons merely to be members of that society he would have sent them to a Catholic parochial school or to the Christian Brothers and thence to the Jesuits at Boston College. Instead of that he sent them to the socially distinguished but very uncatholic Harvard. They were thus brought up in a milieu that was more English than Irish. The Kennedys, when their father had been forgotten, were generally well thought of in England, but English favourers did not perhaps sufficiently take in that the family were often suspect in American society on the ground that in their social tastes they were too little American and too much European, and particularly too English upper class. John Kennedy was always careful to be regular in his attendance at Mass. There were those who said that these attendances were made not so much out of conviction as of the sensible calculation that he was the Catholic candidate; those who thought that America should on no account have a Catholic President would vote against him anyway, and if he gave any colourable reason to think that he was a bad Catholic he would lose the Catholic vote and fall desperately between two stools. How far those were his motives I do not presume to say. His mother once asked a priest for some simple book which she might give her sons to teach them the rudiments of the Catholic religion. 'It must be very simple,' she said. 'They know absolutely nothing.' Robert Kennedy, by all accounts, at any rate towards the end of his life, was more deeply Catholic than his brother. Edward Kennedy over Northern Ireland has shown himself less anglo-phile. Certainly, as it turned out, Catholicism was no longer the utterly mortal handicap which Al Smith had found in it to be in 1928. On the other hand John Kennedy, though he was elected, was only elected by a very narrow majority and there is little doubt that his religion was to his electoral disadvantage.

By far the most impressive Catholic influence on his life was Cardinal Cushing, the Archbishop of Boston. Cardinal Allen, the great English Elizabethan ecclesiastic, once said, 'The man of apostolic life should despise riches but see to it that he has plenty of them.' I do not know if Cardinal Cushing ever heard of Cardinal Allen. I should think probably not, but he lived his life very exactly on that model. He had a very healthy lack of respect for his fellow bishops. Catholic bishops generally are very careful to give all their fellow bishops their full titles. Cardinal Cushing had no such inhibitions. Other bishops were addressed by their bald surnames—Spellman, McIntyre and the rest. Somebody was making a film of the novel *The Cardinal*. Cardinal Spellman, hearing of it, had assumed it would speak disparagingly of Catholics, and of bishops in particular, and at once planned to forbid all Catholics to go to it. Cardinal Cushing told me the story. 'Spellman,' he said, 'wanted to ban it, but I told him, "The Cardinal in this film is not a little guy like you. He's a great big guy, more like me." Then Spellman did not so much mind their going.' Certainly there was a remarkable contrast of habits of life of the Cardinal of Boston and the Cardinal of New York. Cardinal Spellman thought that a prince of the Church should live as a prince. Those who dined with him dined off gold plates. Those who dined with Cardinal Cushing were lucky if they got food at all. He usually forgot to eat and certainly in his closing years his stomach troubles were such that eating was neither a pleasure nor even much of a possibility for him. I wanted an interview with him once and was bidden for one o'clock. He had another visitor before me and another immediately after a quarter to two. As far as I could see he had no lunch at all that day or many other days. He was like Cardinal Allen in despising riches but seeing to it that he had plenty of them. His residence was simple to the verge of shabbiness. The wall-paper hung from the walls. He had the command of probably larger sums of money than any other Catholic prelate but none of that money was spent on himself. It all went on charitable works—perhaps to the poor

Catholics of Boston, perhaps to the yet poorer Catholics of South America. When the Vatican Council was summoned he soon got tired of it, left it and came back to Boston, saying that he lost many thousands of dollars every day that he was away from his episcopal see. Among the fortunes which he diverted to charitable purposes was that of the Kennedys. Judge Morrissey, who was John Kennedy's Boston agent, was the middleman who arranged its distribution. It was sometimes thought in England of Cardinal Cushing that he was a sort of court chaplain to the Kennedys. Particularly this was said when he refused to join in a cry of condemnation of Jacqueline Kennedy at the time of her marriage outside the Church to the divorced Onassis. This was, I fancy, an example of his compassion rather than of his approval. When penitents came to him for confession it was his custom to say that by coming to confession they had proved the genuineness of their contrition and to refuse to hear the details of what they had to say. I do not know if this was wise, but at least it gave evidence of a man who had no wish to sit in rigorous judgement over his fellows. Though he thought it his duty to champion the Kennedys nothing could be further from the truth than to think that he was blind to their shortcomings. I remember that he said only a few weeks before the President's death, 'Oh yes, of course I know him, baptised him, married him. Don't like him, of course—no heart.'

Christopher Dawson came out for a period of lecturing at Harvard. Cardinal Cushing thought it his duty to give a dinner in his honour. But Dawson was by then in poor health and had no appetite for social life. 'I got a very strong company for him,' Cushing explained to me, 'but it was a great failure. I couldn't get a word out of him. He was most disappointing. He spat his food out all over his beard, and when he had done that he thought he had done his stuff, and never said a word.'

This is no occasion to attempt a judgement on the policies of the Kennedys—what they achieved and what they might have achieved had they been spared. Surely never since the days of Atreus have such blows fallen upon a family. If Joseph Kennedy's prayer for success was an unworthy prayer, never has an ironic God answered that prayer more literally and more in a fashion in which he who prayed can have wished that it might not be answered. I, as it happened, was lunching at the British Embassy in Washington with David Ormsby Gore the week before the shot was fired in Dallas. The next week I flew back to England and it was while we were sitting at supper at home that my eldest son rang up from London with the news of the assassination. Never at any other time do I remember his ringing us up to report an event of public importance. The news had not been on the six o'clock news, so we had not heard it, but we should have heard soon enough in any event. We had lived through a century that has seen killing on a scale previously unknown to man but I do not think that there has been any other that has so struck the public throughout the world with the chilling fear of the end of things to come.

II
THE CHANGING CHURCH

How great have been the changes in the institution of the Catholic Church over the last half-century—since I became a Catholic! Fifty years ago being a Catholic meant 'accepting the Pope'. That was the test of membership. Those of us who were at all instructed knew of course that the definition of infallibility which emerged from the First Vatican Council very strictly circumscribed the Pope's authority. It was by no means a victory for the extreme Ultramontanes. But a custom had grown up among Catholics of thinking it a point of loyalty never to question any word that the Pope might utter. This special loyalty which was quite unknown throughout the greater part of the Church's history derived not so much from the definition as from a sentimental reaction against the indignities imposed on the old Pope Pius IX, during the imprisonment of his last years. It was in some ways a curious loyalty. We were all encouraged to say how wise were the words of the Pope and even to imagine that there was a special understanding of the workings of the world to be found in the officials of the Vatican Court, who, we were told, were 'so wise' but who were in fact for the most part far from peculiarly wise or well-informed men. They attached a childishly exaggerated importance to all honours or title, whether ecclesiastical or secular. I remember a Curial diplomat complaining bitterly and, as I thought, quite unnecessarily that insufficient distinctions in the British Honours list were given to Catholic men of letters. 'Why,' he asked, 'have they not received more knighthoods? Of course there's Compton Mackenzie, but then he's a civil servant. But why have they not given a knighthood to Graham Greene, and to WO?' I subsequently discovered that by 'WO' he meant Evelyn Waugh. Those of us who wished to be thought of as good Catholics accepted without question every word of Papal ruling on personal matters—on birth control, or the conditions of a marriage annulment. To his pronouncements on public affairs we were less attendant. Though we professed an intellectual allegiance, most of us were nationalists first and Catholics afterwards. Very few Catholics in any country paid much attention to Pope Benedict XV's plans for peace in the First World War. We in England, I think, did not attack these pleas. We ignored them. When Leo XIII issued his *Rerum Novarum* and subsequently Pius XI his *Quadragesimo Anno*, it was the custom proudly to claim that the Church knew the answer to the social problems but in practice to give our votes to one or other of the established political parties and to behave in very much the same way as our non-Catholic fellow citizens. Today the Popes do not fear to speak on peace and on the social problems and their words are on the whole more practical than those of their predecessors, for Leo XIII and Pius XI never rose above national limitations. They told us how power and wealth should be distributed within a nation. They never averted to the great and growing disproportion between the wealth of the have and the have-not nations. Today the Popes are as alive as any to the fact that social justice is a world-wide and international problem.

The fashion in ecclesiastical circles is to speak of the need for collegiality and for more power to the local national bishops—for more decentralisation. There may be fields where such policies are necessary. But on peace and on social teachings the record of the Popes has been better than that of local bishops who have all too often become mere servants of their national ambitions. There is a great danger in too much decentralisation. Between the wars Evelyn Waugh and I one day were confronted with an enthusiastic and pious young Catholic man of letters. He was strongly opposed to birth control and wished to found a magazine to propagate his convictions. He well understood that it might not have a very large circulation and was likely to lose money, but he was prepared in order to meet such a loss to forego the joys of a family. He asked us whether we would support him. Evelyn turned to me. 'I would sooner roger, wouldn't you?' he said. It would be less easy to find such enthusiasm today.

On personal matters the change has been great. It is not merely that fifty years ago birth control was unanimously repudiated by all practising Catholics and by many others and that today it is almost universally accepted by people outside the Church and by many within it. Fifty years ago all that the secularist claimed was freedom for himself to use such practices as he saw fit. If the Catholics chose to deny themselves those facilities and to produce gigantic families, that, thought the secularist, was their own problem. Today the traditional Catholic teaching

is under attack. Day after day we are told that the human race is threatened by the danger of the population explosion and that it is intolerable
if obstacles are put in the way of contraception. The Church's teaching is condemned not merely as an interference with private pleasure
and convenience but as a threat to human survival. How far these con-
demnations are justified I do not argue. It is possible that contraceptives
will be more widely adopted in the white Western countries than elsewhere and that a consequence of its preaching will be a shift of the proportion of the world's population so that the white proportion will be
much smaller than in the past. This, if it should prove to be so, will not
be altogether convenient. But while there doubtless have been some
alarmist exaggerations about the dangers of overpopulation, at the same
time there is an impressive array of men of the utmost integrity and knowledge who are frightened at the dangers. The danger cannot be merely
dismissed. But my concern here is not so much with settling the balance
of truth as with pointing out the fact that the situation is a real one.

Obviously there is no statistic which can tell us what is the number of
Catholics who deny themselves contraceptive practices in obedience to
the Pope's *Humanae Vitae*. As obviously, the number who defy that
teaching and think themselves in good faith in doing so and the number
of priests who countenance such belief is considerable. We are asked
'Are you in favour of birth control?' 'Are you in favour of abortion?'
These are not the real questions. It may be that the sexual act in marriage
is more satisfactory when it is undertaken without impediments and with
a full readiness to accept its consequences. But there obviously are certain
circumstances when, for medical or economic reasons, it is not possible
for the woman to have another child. What are the couple to do then?
The safe period is notoriously unsafe. Some couples may abstain without harm to themselves. To others an attempt at total abstinence would
be quite disastrous. Pope Paul in *Humanae Vitae* asserted that the use
of contraceptives will make it more likely that husbands will be unfaithful
to their wives. It is not easy to see why. It is at least as likely that the
refusal to use contraceptives will lead to infidelity. Yet the question is not
'Are you in favour of contraceptives?' but 'Are there absolutely no circumstances under which a contraceptive is at any rate the lesser evil—so
much so that the use of it can be condemned in all circumstances as a
mortal sin?'

In other matters the Church admits a certain degree of situation-
ethics. The Commandments tell us that we must not kill, and in general
this is the rule, but the moral theologians go on to tell us that there are

certain special circumstances—when a criminal with a weapon is attacking us or our family, when we are soldiers fighting in a legitimate army engaged in a just war, then to kill is no sin. It is only about contraceptives that no resort to this situation-ethics is admitted. The Church is not content with saying that contraceptives are in general to be avoided. It will not allow any consideration of special circumstances in which they may be thought the lesser evil.

The problems of abortion are up to a point similar to the problems of contraception. Both are disliked on the valid ground that human life is sacred and therefore any interference with it is undesirable. But on the one hand it is generally admitted—by the Church and by all others—that attention must be paid to quality of births and that a mere reproduction of the maximum quantity, whatever the circumstances, is not desirable. For that reason many people advocate both contraception and abortion under certain circumstances. But at the same time there is a difference between the two problems. One can hardly pretend that a baby that has not even been conceived has rights. As regards abortion, metaphysicians and theologians argue at what precise moment the soul can be said to come into the baby's body. I do not think that such attempted definitions are very valuable.

Surely we must agree that all conceived babies have certain rights and that they must not be destroyed merely for pleasure. Obviously, if a woman is not able or is not willing to have a baby it is much more sensible that she should see to it that she does not get pregnant and obviously it is much better that the abortion should be performed early rather than late in the pregnancy. But women are not always sensible. What is she to do when she has, however imprudently, got herself thus pregnant? A baby as yet unborn is not a complete person and therefore talk of its killing as an act of murder is a rhetorical exaggeration. The official teaching of the Church on abortion is very rigid. It will not admit it on any condition. To what extent Catholics either fifty years ago or today would accept the full doctrine it is hard to say. I think that all Catholics and many other people dislike abortion. They would not admit it for light reasons, but if a doctor were to say to a husband, 'I can either save your wife or save your child,' I do not know how many would say, 'Save the child.' I do not know how I myself would answer to such a dreadful question. Happily, like the vast majority of husbands, I have never had to face it. In past ages the danger of death in childbirth was very considerable. Owing to medical progress it is now fortunately very small. We are discussing not what is nor what should be Catholic doctrine. If a mother out of heroic piety chooses to sacrifice herself for her child there is no law to prevent her. The law does not compel the objecting doctor or nurse to take part in an abortion. What we are discussing is what the secular law in a pluralist society should consider as a criminal offence.

The Abortion Act has two parts. Its first concern is with what is called therapeutic abortion. I do not think that any serious Catholic opinion would have objected to an attempt to regulate the conditions under which abortion might be permitted by the secular law in a pluralist society in the case of a risk of grave injury to the mother. Life may be sacred but, if a life regrettably has to be lost, it is surely better to sacrifice the partial life of the child rather than the full life of the mother. But the Act also legislates for what it calls social abortion, and these clauses are much more debatable. It is a terrible and very serious thing for a mother to refuse the child which she has conceived. It is hard to believe that she can do such a thing, without at least running the risk of very grave psychological consequences. It is true that there may be social conditions under which a further addition to the family would create a very grave problem. But after all there is adoption. If it is not possible to accept another child into the family it is always possible to get it adopted. It may be a handicap for a child to be brought up as the child of adoptive parents. But is it a greater handicap than not to be born at all? It is of course arguable that, rightly or wrongly, a very large number of careless girls do have their misconceived children aborted and that it is much better, if they are going to have an abortion, that they should have it under properly regulated medical conditions than by an unregulated back-street operation, and if the result of the Act was that there were not more abortions but that the abortions took place under more satisfactory conditions, that would be a considerable argument for the change. But, even if the facts are difficult to establish, there is little reason to think that this is what is happening, though it is almost certainly true that the number of deaths in abortion operations has greatly decreased.

The abortion controversy arouses—perhaps inevitably—very considerable feeling. The advocates of freer abortion accuse its opponents of indifference to human happiness and to the problems of overpopulation. The opponents of abortion accuse the advocates of countenancing child murder. Happily I am saved from any temptation to discuss the problem in these unpleasantly emotive terms. The Abortion Bill was introduced and sponsored by Mr David Steel. Whatever truth there might be in the accusation against other supporters of abortion that they are the enemies of the Christian religion, anxious to undermine its claims, that accusation could certainly not be made against Mr Steel, the son of the distinguished Moderator of the Church of Scotland, who appears often on religious television programmes. I had had the great pleasure of his friendship before he took up this question and before I knew that he had any special views on it. It was generally admitted alike by those who supported him on the question and by those who differed from him that, whatever might be true of other people, he was able to maintain his side of the argument with perfect courtesy and without any introduction of personalities. When he had had to stand for re-election in his constituency I was most happy to write for him a letter of goodwill which he published in his election address prefacing it by a notice that our opinion did not coincide on this point. His constituency—Roxburgh, Peebles and Selkirk—is in a part of the country where I have no connections and I do not flatter myself that many, if any, voters cast their vote on account of my commendation, but I am very glad that his constituents returned him to continue his valuable career in Parliament.

Euthanasia is sometimes put on all fours with contraception and abortion. We are told by Cardinal Heenan and Malcolm Muggeridge, for instance, that the Abortion Act will undoubtedly lead to a legalisation of euthanasia. I do not, I will confess, well understand the political controversy about euthanasia. Many people—for instance the modern Japanese or the ancient Romans—have thought suicide to be permissible and under certain circumstances even laudable. In our modern society it is not difficult to find those who have abandoned religious belief who will defend it and even under certain circumstances practise it. I do not see how we can prevent them, or indeed how in a pluralist society it would be even right to try to prevent them by penal legislation. Few would defend what was until recently the law by which attempted suicide was treated as a crime. Certainly I do not think that any Catholic opinion objected to the removal of that law. Today Christians still think themselves obliged to obey the 'canon 'gainst self-slaughter'. Many others also obey it, but if any unfortunate person should wish to take his own life, how can he be prevented? Nor is there any great difficulty in taking a gross overdose of some prescribed tablets. But what I cannot see is what purpose is served by bringing doctors and their prescriptions and all the rigmarole of permits into the matter. The very notion of having to give such permits is enormously repugnant to doctors. It is generally admitted—even among Catholics—that in the case where the patient is suffering great and irremediable agony it is legitimate to give him drugs which will alleviate his pain at the expense of shortening his life. General opinion seems to be still opposed to any legalisation of euthanasia and indeed it is difficult to see any point in it. Catholic opinion certainly shares this opposition and I do not know that on this point there has been any great change over the last fifty years.

The Church is of course opposed to divorce, but here again the issue is not what should be the conduct of Catholics but what the law should permit in a pluralist society. There has been a great change. Fifty years ago the Church—not only the Catholic Church but also the Church of England—was still battling to impose the rules of the Church on all citizens as a part of the civil law. Every extension of divorce facilities was opposed by the Church authorities. Today the situation is different. Sensible secularists generally agree that the best basis for a happy life is a satisfactory marriage, that it is best for children to grow up within such a united family, and therefore they are not willing to encourage either arrangements or a climate of opinion in which stability of marriage is easily threatened. On the other hand secular opinion is not willing to say that marriage should be absolutely indissoluble—that there are never circumstances under which it is the lesser evil to admit that a marriage has irrevocably broken down and in which it is the lesser evil to permit a divorce with freedom to remarry. There is no example, I fancy, of any country which has absolutely forbidden divorce under any circumstances unless it accepted the unquestioned discipline of the Christian code. Therefore in a pluralist society it is common sense to make divorce difficult, in every way to encourage the stability of marriage, but at the same time to admit divorce as an exceptional remedy and Christian opinion both in the Roman Catholic and in other Churches has come to accept this—to impose the discipline of indissoluble marriage on its own members but no longer to oppose reasonable facilities for divorce under the civil code. Italy's refusal of such facilities is hardly an encouragement to morality.

It is the same with homosexual legislation. Fifty years ago it was common to meet people who in private condemned the laws treating homosexual acts as penal offences as absurd, but it was generally thought that public opinion should not tolerate their modification and that it was out of the question that any legislator would ruin his career by proposing such a modification. The opposition of all ecclesiastics to any such proposals for a modification would be taken for granted. Today the Church authorities have in no way abated their teaching that the commission of homosexual acts is a sin. They may not be exactly a sin 'crying to heaven for vengeance', but the possession of predominantly homosexual affections is at any rate a grave misfortune, condemning the possessor to be tortured by desires for a companionship which the object cannot in his nature reciprocate. The story of homosexual love affairs is littered with misery. Yet again today most people—and among them most ecclesiastical leaders—recognise that the solution for these twisted tragedies is not to be found in the crude verdicts of a court of law and have agreed to the repeal of the laws. Indeed it is a curiously ironical commentary on the modern movement of ecumenism that almost the only point on which all religious leaders are able to find themselves in total agreement is on the repeal of the laws against homosexuality.

Christianity's interest in these problems of contraception, abortion and euthanasia derives of course from its belief that life is sacred—that though we may have the right to dispose of other objects as we see fit, God has kept in His own hands the decision when we shall live or die and we do wrong if we take this responsibility from Him. This conviction is surely a just conviction, if not an absolute truth, and if we allow ourselves to become careless about killing one another we soon get a labefaction of all morality. For this reason it is right that Christians should be at least very hesitant to support capital punishment and particularly hesitant to support it for any crime other than murder. On such a principle it might be argued that war ought to be especially hateful to all Christians. It should be hateful for two reasons—firstly, because it involves killing and, secondly, because whatever the theoretical possibility—

> To honour, while you strike him down,
> The foe that comes with fearless eyes—

it is not in practice possible to have war without having hatred. The teaching of Christianity bids us that we love our enemies and contains its precepts against the use of violence, and among the early Christians many like St Chrysostom interpreted its teaching as forbidding a Christian from serving in the army. So long as the Christians were a small and insignificant minority they were able to interpret this obligation simply by looking to general moral principles. When by the fourth century they had become an important and influential part of society other considerations had to be taken into account. Doubtless life was sacred. It was important not recklessly to sacrifice it. But was it always true that a policy of absolute non-resistance was the best way to save life? The army stood out along the frontiers. The barbarians confronted it. Was it the Christian duty that all the Christian soldiers should with-draw? Would not that let the barbarians in? Might not the result of that well be that many more lives were lost than if the barbarians had been resisted and repelled along the frontiers? So the general Christian mind rejected absolute pacifism. There were occasions, it thought, when war was perhaps the lesser evil. But, saying this, it by no means said that the Christian was entitled to take part in any war in which he found his country to be engaged. On the contrary St Augustine and others laid down very rigid rules which must be satisfied before a Christian could say that a war was a just war and with a good conscience take part in it. It is a sad truth that, though those rules still stand, the whole history of the last fifteen hundred Christian years have been filled with wars, a very large proportion of which have been plainly for quite insufficient reasons. Yet it would be very difficult to think of any instance in which the national ecclesiastical leaders have condemned any war in which the secular government of their country was engaged. Benedict XV in the 1914 war was an almost unique exception. Forty years ago I was brought up in an atmosphere in which it was the custom to speak with verbal respect of the Pope's person but in which neither in England nor in any other country did the most loyal of Catholics pay the smallest attention to what he had to say on such a topic.

The modern Popes, John XXIII and Paul VI, have spoken for peace as bravely as Pope Benedict. Alas, they have not brought us peace. The world is very far from being at peace. But it is arguable—perhaps owing to the unique personal popularity of Pope John—that more attention is paid to their words by Catholics and non-Catholics alike than was ever paid before to their predecessors'. Whereas in 1914 public opinion among both Catholics and non-Catholics replied to Pope Benedict's efforts for peace by bidding the Pope to mind his own business, now they are inclined to ask, even if not with much hope, Cannot your Pope do some-thing about it? In the 1914 war Catholics in every country almost without exception lamely took their nation's side. In America the bishops, though like most Irish Catholics they had opposed America's entry into the war until it happened, gave their affidavits that this was a just war and on their affidavits Catholics were refused to be allowed to plead con-cientious objection. Today, Catholics like the Berrigan brothers are at least as prominent as any in their opposition to the war in Vietnam. At the foundation of the League of Nations, the Pope, owing to the demands of anti-Papal Italy, was excluded from membership. Pope Paul is welcomed as an honoured guest before the United Nations in New York.

It is much the same with industrial problems. It is sometimes an accusation against the Church that it is solely interested in the affairs of the next world—with 'pie in the sky'—whereas ordinary men and women are mostly interested in making a living in this world. The accusation against true Christianity is not just. Christians who are bidden to pray 'Our Father which art in heaven' are equally bidden to pray 'Give us this day our daily bread'. Other religions may be entirely interested in the God who reigns in heaven. Christianity is the religion of man's heavenly Father but it is also the religion of God who became Man. His kingdom may not be of this world and true reality may be elsewhere. But our life here is our testing ground and our religion forbids us from thinking that it is unimportant. Nevertheless it is true that the Church, frightened by the persecutions of the French Revolution, was after 1815 too timorous to say very much in the way of positive social teaching and resigned itself to the complacent defence of established governments—to the alliance of Throne and Altar. Its main teaching on riches was that it was an act of great wickedness under any circumstances to take away from the possessor of property that which he possessed. If we consider the lessons that the Gospels had to teach us about riches and rich men, it was odd to find this principle thus paraded as a main teaching of Christianity. It is Christian teaching that all souls are equal in the sight of God. That does not, it is true, imply that they need be equal to the last sixpence in their incomes. Such absolute equality could only be imposed, if at all, by an absolute tyranny that would be worse than the disease. But people have roughly the same physical needs and appetites. The first business of an economic system is not to guard the rich in their riches but to see to it that nobody is in penury, and, if sacrifices are necessary, those sacrifices should be required of the rich who have a superfluity. Christianity and common sense are united in teaching that destitution is surely a very great evil but that above the level of sufficiency riches are of little assistance either to virtue or to happiness. It is as strange that politicians should make the object of their policy to increase as much as possible the Gross National Product, and as strange that the nineteenth century should have thought to invoke the name of Christ to defend such men in their riches, as it is that the ecclesiastics of the Inquisition in the Middle Ages should have thought it right to burn in order to impose their beliefs. Yet I can think of a Catholic friend of great piety and generosity who yet considers it a main task of his life to devise curious ways by which he can outwit the Inland Revenue. It is odd. The Church has perhaps now swung to an opposite extreme. In the nineteenth century it was at fault in committing itself too completely to the support of the monarchical system. Now it is in danger of allowing itself to become too committed to parliamentary democracy, careless that the one form of government is likely to prove as ephemeral as the other. Cardinal Suenens tells us that 'the renewal of community in the Church, which ultimately derives from faith, naturally finds its place within the progress of a world moving more and more in the direction of democracy'. Is it not all too likely that in a generation's time, when Parliaments will perhaps have fallen in their turn into discredit, these words too will sound extremely dated?

The great social problems of the nineteenth century were the problems created by the new industrialism, and it so happened that the industrial revolution took place almost entirely in countries—mainly in England—where the Catholic population was negligibly small. Therefore all through the bulk of the nineteenth century if one were to ask, 'What does the Papacy think of the new social problems created by industrialism?' the only possible answer was that the Papacy, absorbed in the defence of the Papal states in Italy, did not think of them at all. It was not a very satisfactory answer, and of course at the end of the century, in 1891, Pope Leo XIII gave a more positive answer. When I became a Catholic it was on Pope Leo's *Rerum Novarum* that I was instructed. Pope Pius XI's *Quadragesimo Anno*, repeating such teaching, was still to come. As a disciple of Belloc's and Chesterton's distributism I was of course a ready disciple of Pope Leo. How far his teaching was generally known and followed among Catholics or among non-Catholics I am uncertain. Today the present Pope, John XXIII in *Mater et Magistra* and Paul IV in *Populorum Progessio* have reiterated the Papal teaching, perhaps improving it in so far as they no longer lay down as an absolute requisite that under no circumstances must the wealth of owners be confiscated even though it is manifestly in the public interest to do so. Does the Catholic or the non-Catholic world pay any more attention to these Popes than to their predecessors? Perhaps a little, not so much because Popes are now more highly thought of as because the programmes of the regular political parties are less believed, but it cannot be pretended that even now the importance of Papal teaching over practical politicians is very large. Catholics, it is true, are much more keenly interested in social problems than they were fifty years ago. Much of that interest is good and healthy, but the danger today is that a number of Catholics seem to consider the Church solely as a social agency—a sort of subsidiary of Marxism. The Church has her social teaching. She is not indifferent to such problems. But her most fundamental teaching is not with the things of this world at all, and the danger of some modern Catholics is that they will overlook the supernatural altogether.

The ceremonies of the Church are of course very different from what they were fifty years ago. Fifty years ago we told ourselves that the Church was the Latin Church. Its ceremonies were in Latin and Catholics boasted that it was an international institution—that one could go into church in any country in the world and find there the same Latin Mass being celebrated. We could never have foreseen that in a generation's time the ceremonies of the Church would be in the vernacular and that all the order of the Mass would be changed. On the controversies of liturgical reform I hold a middle course, disliking the extremists on both wings. Brought up and accustomed to Latin, reasonably familiar with the language, I would have been content enough, had the whole business of the Church been arranged for my convenience, that we should have gone on with the old ways to which I was accustomed. I wished for no change. I regretted even the changes which Pius XII introduced when he abolished the old Holy Week Tenebrae. On the other hand, we have lived into an age where, rightly or wrongly, Latin is no longer the universal language of education. The young city boy or girl, attracted to the Church, went to Mass and heard there an abracadabra of Latin that was quite without meaning to them. I have little patience with those extravagant reactionaries who accuse the new Mass of having abandoned the notion of sacrifice. Yet, while I do not grudge the revisers the Mass in English and welcome the dialogue, I wish that, while they were about it, they could have found rather more dignified English for their version and that there could have been less chopping and changing. I do not like it that every time one goes to Mass one finds a different rendering, which is almost what seems to be happening today. One reads from time to time—happily more often in other countries than in England—of ecclesiastical practices where priests, without any sort of authority from the Vatican Council or their bishop, have celebrated the Sacred Mysteries with antics of mere buffoonery. I remember a priest in California who said his Mass in English with great reverence but when at the end he came to the words where in Latin he would have bade us '*ite missa est*' he said in English, 'All right, boys, you can relax now.' A certain reverence is owed to the past even if we do not concede its divine authority.

The question of liturgical reform is of course mixed up with the question of ecumenism. Under the teaching of John XXIII we have come to be much more conscious of the evil of denominational division than was the habit of the past and much more conscious of the scandal given to those outside religion by the sight of these divisions of Christians with one another. One of the reasons for these liturgical reforms is the hope that we shall be able to re-word our worship so as to make it less difficult of acceptance by those of other denominations. The ideal is obviously worthy. Faced as we are by Christ's prayer 'that they may be all one', we should indeed be guilty if we allowed ourselves to be divided by a merely unnecessary difference of phraseology, and the ecumenical movement has certainly had a considerable degree of success. The dialogue of courtesy has been substantially won— everywhere, except perhaps in Northern Ireland. Members of different denominations are able to meet together on terms of easy friendliness that would have been quite unthinkable fifty years ago. We have from time to time our joint meetings and joint services and this is surely all to the good. But can we go further, or have we now reached a sticking point? Obviously we cannot claim that there has been any real reunion until free joint communion is permitted, and that up to the present has not been achieved.

Again, fifty years ago, and indeed very much later than fifty years ago, we would all have told one another that not only had that not been achieved but that it was quite idle even to think of its achievement as possible. Roman Catholics, we said, believed in transubstantiation. Others, whatever their beliefs, did not believe in transubstantiation. Roman priests claimed to be priests in virtue of their possession of apostolic succession. Pope Leo had told us that we could not accept the claims of Anglicans to possess that succession. So there was no more to be said. We must agree to differ.

Today the problem, though not solved, is at any rate changed. Roman Catholics are now no longer nearly so insistent on transubstantiation as they were. All that Christ promised, they say, was his Real Presence in the sacrament. How He might be present no one could say. Indeed His presence was so great a miracle that any attempt of human language to describe it must necessarily be inadequate. The word 'transubstantiation' is a word in terms of a particular metaphysical system. In such a context it is perhaps as satisfactory as can be found. But it can have no claims to be utter and absolute truth. All that we can say about the nature of the sacrament is the old sixteenth-century jingle:

> His was the Word. He spake it
> He gave the bread and brake it
> And what his Word did make it
> I do receive and take it.

All that we have a right to insist upon is the Real Presence and many Anglicans and Lutherans of course believe in that as much as do Roman Catholics.

There remains the question of the validity of orders, but what certainty can we have that orders were handed down in an unbroken line from bishop to bishop through all the dark years of the first millennium? Even if the sacrament should be administered by someone who is not a validly ordained priest, is there so great a harm in that? 'Where two or three are gathered together, there am I in the midst of them,' whether they be validly ordained or not. It is of course sometimes objected that if we admit non-Catholics to the Eucharist we shall have there partaking of it persons of a wide variety of beliefs as to what the Eucharist means. But already people of a wide variety of beliefs kneel together at the Anglican altar rail, and I do not know that anyone is the worse for that. Of course I am under obedience. It is not for me personally to do anything that I have not got authority's permission to do, but I am free to welcome every extension of permission as a good thing.

Other things have been brought into question that no one would have thought possible to question fifty years ago. Should priests be allowed to be married? Should women be allowed to be priests? Should the rules of mixed marriages be revised? My instincts are not in favour of married or female priests—perhaps through a mere prejudice of conservatism—but they are matters which would not affect my personal conduct and upon which I claim no right to express an opinion. What fun it would be if among early Christian literature we only had the Epistle of St Peter's Wife. 'Can't you remember that my mother is ill—with a fever. Out again, I suppose—with those Apostles—the third time this week. I have heard quite enough about them.' She would be as tired as Dante's wife would be of hearing about Beatrice.

The great changes in the Church certainly date from the Papacy of John XXIII and from the Second Vatican Council. When John was elected his name was not well known to most of us and it was generally thought that the Cardinals had elected a safe old man who would hold the seat for a short time and do nothing very notable. I happened to be lunching on the day of his election with Peter Tapsell, a progressive young Conservative Member of Parliament with no especial pro- or anti-Catholic prejudices, and he deplored the election as evidence of how the old men were determined to keep the government of the world in their own hands and refused to recognise that a younger generation had grown up since the war. I was inclined to agree with him. But in that judgement it was of course soon to be proved that, like all the rest of us, I was in error. John was to do more than any of his predecessors to throw open the windows of the Vatican to the world. Whereas it had often been thought of many of his predecessors that they were greatly interested in defending their own co-religionists but less concerned with the fate of those outside their flock—whereas such an explanation had for instance been given of Pius XII's allegedly insufficient concern for the fate of the Jews in Germany—John was able to persuade the world that he was afire with love for all mankind irrespective of race or creed—a man sent from God, whose name was John.

Opinions on his experiment still differ. He spoke to all men. Conservatives were very content with things as they were and have not been able to see what purpose has been served by such reckless invitations to every irresponsible critic to challenge the foundations of the faith. Beyond question the invitation has had some frightening consequences. The Church in its material organisation is today in great danger. People still go, it is true, to church—in as great or almost as great a number as they ever did. Yet in family after family—often in the most regular and devout of families with generations of faithful Catholicism behind them—one hears stories of a member who has abandoned his faith. Converts are fewer. There is a frightening abandonment of vows by priests—whether because of an objection to celibacy or for another reason. In every religious order there is so serious a shortage of novices that it is not easy to see how they will be able to carry on in a few years' time when the older Fathers have died off and there are no young men to take their places. It is easy for the timorous to make out their case that the whole experiment of the *aggiornamento* has been a gigantic mistake. On the other hand John from his residence in Bulgaria and France had come to the Papacy with a wider experience of the world than most Curialists. He was a man not only of great love but also of great courage, ready to defy the dead weight of official opinion. He had clearly formed the impression that the faith of too many Catholics was formal, wooden and monotonous—that without renewal the Church as an effective institution would come to an end. It needed violent action to be made real.

> Now, Lord, some piercing pleasure take
> And stab my spirit broad awake. . . .

It must be uncertain how far he foresaw all the consequences that would follow from his great invitation to adventure. It is certain that some of the more extravagant of adventures that have followed would be ones of which he would not have approved. But it is also certain that he knew that such a calculated *bouleversement* would not be without its casualties. He called for the experiment because the world needed to recapture the surprise at the Christian Gospel which in rule and regulation and conformism it had so largely lost. The Christian Gospel was a gospel to be preached to all the world—not merely to be retained for the faithful. We were called on not merely to keep to but to re-examine our faith. I do not think that it is true, as is so often said, that the present is an age that is not interested in religion. I think that there is more discussion of religion than there has been for a long time—some of it valuable, some of it, of course, naïve and ridiculous. The policies of repression which Pius X imposed upon the faithful led us not so much to a rescue and purification of religion as to a decline in the interest in it. If any expression of opinion other than that dictated by ecclesiastical authority was going to lead him who expressed it into trouble, the safest plan was to say nothing and not to think about religion at all. In such a world 'he who could hold his tongue could hold anything'. Today we are invited to re-examination. All things are under challenge—most of all the institutions of established religion. Our interests, as Blougram says, are 'on the dangerous edge of things'. It is better so. If it survives that re-examination religion will emerge from it doubtless having suffered grave casualties as all armies do in a battle, but emerge the better for the re-examination. John has taken us on from an age of power, worship and triumphalism to an age much more like that in which Christ preached his original gospel among hostile unbelievers.

I joined the Church fifty years ago because I had been able to persuade myself that Catholics were better than other people. That as a generalisation I can no longer believe. I have no wish to indulge in any of the lamentations of a Baron Corvo and say that they are worse, but, if we look for instance to Northern Ireland where a higher proportion of the population, both Catholic and Protestant, are church-going than anywhere else in the world and yet such atrocities are committed that defy belief, one can hardly claim that going to church and professing a faith automatically makes people better than those who do not practise. Yet even among less spectacular sinners genuine faith does not always lead to virtue. We all know of pious people of perhaps slight unbalance who in their rigour of devotion forget the ordinary duties of unselfishness and kindness and are so keen to be on their knees that it never occurs to them to help in their home with the washing-up. As Byron truly said:

These vegetables of the Catholic creed
Are apt to run exceedingly to seed.

It is not surprising that sinners sin and the respectable citizen is
perhaps often a more satisfactory citizen but not necessarily more attuned
to the reception of God's grace. There are many to whom the acid test
is 'Are Catholics better than other people?' If we can answer 'Yes', they
think that then perhaps the Church's claims can be considered. If the
answer is 'No', then in the opinion of such people the whole case automatically collapses. Whereas fifty years ago I believed in Christ because
of the Church, today I believe in the Church because of Christ. I am
not greatly interested in the achievements of Catholics. I am more deeply
interested in more fundamental points. Is religion at all true? Are the
claims of Christ valid?

On these points, as I have said, there are arguments on both sides. It
is of course true that there is some unifying force which keeps the world
together and a pantheist describes this by saying that God is in everything. So He doubtless is, but a God in everything does not help us. It
makes little difference if God is everything or if He is nothing. Panthe-
ism is little more than a polite atheism. Obviously God is in a sense in
everything. In some mysterious way He must be responsible for evil and
ugliness. Yet He is more present in the good and the beautiful which are
according to His plan than in that which is in conflict with it. There is a
God, but He is a God who is in some way hidden from us—a Deus
Absconditus. There is much in life where His finger does not show itself.
I think kindly of Humanists and am all in favour of cooperating with
them in worthy social activities, but I cannot think their position very
rational. There are difficulties about believing in God, but the difficulties
about believing in Man seem to me much more formidable. If God became Man it is reasonable to think Man of importance. If he did not,
there seems no intrinsic reason to believe the human race very valuable.

Some of the most common arguments for the existence of God—such
as the argument of the First Cause—are not very compulsive. As St
Thomas says, in itself a universe that was created and a universe that
always existed are equally inconceivable. I prefer the argument of Pascal,
'thou wouldst not be seeking me if thou hadst not found me'. Unlike
Shakespeare's Richard III, I am not 'myself alone'. I am of the company
of man, the animal unique among all creatures. Throughout the ages
there has been a *consensus universalis* to God's existence and I think it
wiser and more reasonable to be with the general opinion. '*Credo ut*

intelligam,' said St Anselm. Yet why, if God made the Word, did He not make it a bit better? One sees of course the argument that the scene of things has been marred by Man's sin. But there are many evils in the world that have nothing to do with human sin. Why does He permit earthquakes? Why does He permit cancer? Again what of animals? If it is to be argued that the scheme of creation does not make sense unless I survive my death, why is that not equally true of my cat who now lies sleeping at my feet? For what purpose was he created? Has he got free choice? Has he got a soul? The book of Genesis says that he was created to serve me. That may in a measure be true of him, but the vast majority of animals clearly in no way serve man. What are they for?

Of course a man can live without religion as he can live though he be colour-blind or tone-deaf. But can he live a full life without it, without ever meditating on the answer to the ultimate mysteries? The Christian religion gives dignity to Man and gives meaning to life. If it is true, love is not a merely pleasurable appendage. It is the lord of the world—the love, as Dante put it, which moves the sun and the other stars. We cannot perhaps prove that but we can at least hope.

Has it your vote to be so if it can?

It is, it is true, in some ways difficult to believe, but as Bishop Blougram truly said, it is at least as difficult not to believe.

> Just when we are safest there's a sunset touch,
> A fancy from a flower-bell, some one's death,
> A chorus-ending from Euripides,
> And that's enough for fifty hopes and fears.
> All we have gained then by our unbelief
> Is the life of doubt diversified by faith
> For one of faith diversified by doubt.
> We called the chess-board white—we call it black.

The most difficult of all the teachings of religion is that there can be some efficacy in prayer. It is a curiosity that all religions and all forms of religion should be united in accepting that difficult teaching. Where on so much else there is diversity, on that there is a strange and impressive unanimity.

We are told, of course, that mankind has indeed through the ages adhered to religion, but that now we have for the first time come to an age where man no longer needs or at least no longer accepts religion, 'an age simply atheist', said Newman. For two reasons I am not greatly disturbed by that argument. In the first place it does not seem to me to be in the least true. It is probably true that there has been a great decline in institutional religion. This loss of faith has spread down from the middle-class agnostics of Victorian times to the ordinary inhabitants of the villages. A generation ago the churches in towns were often fairly empty, but in the country people still went to church and, whatever their secret questionings, they did not publicly confess them. In our day in our village the Anglican church is ill-attended. My wife was challenged by a former excellent keeper of the pub who, as he filled up the car with petrol, expostulated to her, 'An eddicated woman like you, you can't believe in them things like the Virgin Birth.' 'Of course I'm not a Christian, madam,' said the most saintly odd-job man to her. 'At any rate you behave like a Christian,' she replied. 'That's as may be, madam,' he answered, 'but I'm not a Christian.' The confessing village atheist is a novelty. A generation ago I would have divided the world into those who had observed the difficulties and contradictions in the gospel stories and by consequence rejected them, and those who accepted the gospels but had not adverted to their difficulties. It would have hardly occurred to me that heuristic examination had ever led not to a rejection of faith but to a deeper faith. Doubtless this was a folly, but it was a folly for which, prior to the Vatican Council, official Catholic teaching gave me much excuse. I could not have pretended—at any rate before Pius XII— that the ecclesiastical authorities gave much encouragement to biblical criticism or thought it likely that the effect of it would be to strengthen faith.

Yet though it is true that people no longer go to church as they did in the past, the belief or half-belief that forces from outside can act on this world—the belief in omens, talismen, astrology and all forms of super- stition—seems to me greater today than it has been in the past. Even the pop world is invaded by exercises in religiosity which, whatever their value or their sincerity, are at any rate evidence that religion of a sort is a box-office attraction as it would not have been in the days of my early life. A strong official religion, for better or for worse, is a discourage- ment of irresponsible religious debate. Weaken the official Church and you throw open the doors to all manner of speculation. It may be more nearly true as Chesterton said that 'he who does not believe in God will believe in anything'. Furthermore, even if I admitted that the charge of irreligion in the modern world was true, I would not be greatly impressed by it. Perhaps the modern generation has more defiantly and consciously than any of its predecessors set out to build a civilisation wholly independent of the grace of God. And what sort of success has it had? Within two generations it has succeeded in bringing the human race more nearly to self-destruction than ever previously in its history. I can never understand the ambition of Bishop Robinson for a religion that is up-to-date and acceptable to the twentieth century. It is surely the business of religion not to be in the fashion but rather to insist on the truths that are at the moment overlooked and out of fashion. The irreligion of the modern world, if the fact be conceded, is surely most adequate evidence in favour of Man's incapacity to manage the world unaided.

Yet of course the fact of a general consent of mankind to the existence of preternatural powers beyond this world, the fact that men so commonly, throughout all pre-Christian history, looked for the coming of a special voice from God—most notably with the Jews looking for Messiah—by no means proves that the claims of Christ were valid. The Jews are so often blamed because, as is alleged, they were looking for Messiah, but failed to recognise him in Christ. But the Jews when they were looking for Messiah never thought that they were looking for a Being with all the claims which the Christians were to make for Christ. There was never any suggestion that Messiah would be God. And the fact that Messiah was promised did not in any way prove that anyone who claimed to be Messiah was genuine in his claims. On the contrary, as Gamaliel tells us to have happened, it was only too probable that impersonators would take advantage of the expectation to make false claims. What reason was there to think that Christ was not one of such false claimants?

Let us imagine that we were told that in our village, say, the son of the local garage owner was a very remarkable boy. We would accept evidence if it were provided that he was a great teacher, a great prophet, perhaps in a way a great saint. If it was in our habit to use such language, we might even admit that he was a prophet of God—in the sense that Mahomet was a prophet. But if we were told, No, he was more than that. He was the Son of God—not in the general sense that all creatures are the Sons of God but in a sense special and unique, the Creator of the Universe—we would dismiss the claim as insane and without consideration of the evidence. Nor is it surprising that many of those to whom Christ first preached did this—not surprising that the strictly monotheistic Jews rejected the claim as a blasphemy. I remember a young friend of mine who has an erratic mother who has made claims of such a sort about a certain priest. I commented that the claim was evidence of insanity. He had no sympathy with his mother's obsession, but he replied, 'No more insane than you are for your beliefs about Christ.' What is surprising about the Christian claim is rather that there were some who did not reject it, that those extraordinary claims found their disciples, that within three centuries they had conquered the Roman Empire.

Clearly the divinity of Christ is not capable of absolute demonstration. The fact that over the ages so many men and women of ability and integrity have examined the case without favour and been unable to accept it is proof enough of that. Indeed it is hard to see what evidence could be absolutely conclusive for such enormous claims as His. Supposing that we accept the evidence for the Resurrection as conclusive, that may prove that Christ was the most remarkable of men—that He in some special way spoke for the people of God. It can hardly prove that He was the Son of God. What could prove such an enormous claim? Indeed at first sight it is more natural to dismiss the claim as so extravagant as to be almost insane.

The essence of the Christian claim is that it is historical. Plenty of other Eastern religions—that of Osiris in particular—have offered mythical tales as symbolical of the way in which God created Man and tales which were not very dissimilar to the claims of the Christians. But these religions merely asserted, 'This is the sort of way in which things must happen. Otherwise they do not make sense.' The Christians made the historical claim 'This is the way things did happen. They happened on a hill and in a tomb in Jerusalem when Tiberius was on the Roman throne and Pontius Pilate was Procurator of Judaea.' What is the reason for thinking that those things ever did happen?

Substantially our sole evidence for Christ's life is the Four Gospels. Of course we have no right without examination to say that what the Gospels tell us is true. What we have a right to say is that what they tell us was what the early Christians believed to be true about the life of Christ. These were the documents which out of a variety of other documents the early Christians selected as their documents in the case. So, whatever their exact dates, whatever the names of their authors, whether we agree with Belloc's firm assertion or prefer Clutton Brock's more tentative doubts, we can say that these events represent what the early Christians believed about Christ, that they believed that He existed, was crucified and rose again from the dead, that they believed this with such profound and unquestioning sincerity that it wholly transformed their lives and made them, who had before the Crucifixion shown themselves to be timorous and unworthy men, able to confront and defeat the Roman world.

To appeal back to the Gospels as the authority on what the early Christians believed about Christ is admittedly not without its difficulties. The modern man so commonly says that he cannot accept Christ's claim to divinity but that he accepts the obligation to obey Christ's ethical maxims. But what were Christ's ethics? We think that He taught us to love all mankind, including our enemies, and to do unto others as we would that they should do unto us—and so He did. But He also taught many other things—lessons of most violent denunciation of his enemies that by no means suggest a 'Jesu meek and mild' of the pious hymn. We find the Pharisees greeted with unbridled abuse as whited sepulchres and a generation of vipers. We find the rascally economic behaviour of the unjust steward commended. We find Christ boasting that He had brought not peace but a sword into the world. We find His disciples specifically told they should hate their wives and their parents. It is hardly possible to make sense of the record without an authority to interpret it. Again, as everyone knows, the Gospels differ from one another on a number of points. So far as they differ on the mere wording of some saying or event, this is no great difficulty. Written in different cities—Antioch, Caesarea, Alexandria—such incidental difficulties are only to be expected. But there are of course more important difficulties. There is no reason to think that the story of the Virgin Birth was known either to Mark or John, or indeed to St Paul. More important is the uncertainty among the Evangelists concerning the Ascension, whether it took place in Galilee or at Jerusalem or whether it took place at all. Yet the real issue is the issue of the Resurrection. It is of course true that the Evangelists differ from one another about very many of the details of the Resurrection. It is important that they are all agreed, and all early Christians seem to be agreed, that the Resurrection happened. On that, as Paul says, their faith stood or fell. Now at first sight of course their claim that a crucified man rose again from the dead would have been merely absurd—to be instantly dismissed hardly with examination. There are two reasons which lead to me accept it. First, if Christ had not risen, then His body must still have been in the Tomb. All that Christianity's enemies had to do was to lead men to the Tomb and show him still there and the whole story was exposed. It is strange that there is no hint of this simple device being employed. Secondly, between Good Friday and Whitsunday the disciples had obviously received some psychological experience which had entirely transformed their natures, causing those who on Maundy

Thursday had been so craven and hopeless to become the fearless confronters of the world. They thought that the experience was not so much the experience of having found the empty tomb as the positive experience of seeing the Risen Lord. This, which we may call the detective side of the Resurrection, has its value and it is indeed important that critics should understand that something clearly happened at the beginning of the Christian era and on Easter Sunday morning and that it is by no means so easy to give an account of those events other than the Christian account as is commonly imagined. Still it would be hardly sufficient, if that were all the story. We have the beautiful teachings of Christ—the Sermon on the Mount and the parables—but they in themselves are hardly sufficient to prove Him Almighty God. No one claims that Shakespeare was Almighty God because he was a great poet.

What for my part wins my acceptance is the record of Christians through the ages—the record of the early Christians born into a world to which such tales were utterly fantastic and within three or four hundred years conquering the Roman world not so much by their dialectics as by their example of pure sincerity—even to death and torture—to the faith and person of Christ—to the example of the saints through the ages. The majority of Christians throughout the ages have by no means been saints. All too many of them have been most unedifying people. Of all too many it is possible to wonder in what way the faith which they professed with their lips has at all influenced their lives. Still every age has produced a number of men and women whose life has been entirely inspired by the love of Christ, a Mother Teresa or a John XXIII in our own time. In spite of all the virtues of the old pagans, sanctity, the devotion to the person of God, did not exist in the world before Christ. Christ has brought into the world a new sort of man and woman—the saint in whom He lives—and even the ordinary worldly man, dying with all his sins, is anxious in the hour of death

> Through blurred and glazing eyes to see
> A Female figure and a Child.

I can only account for it by thinking as other men have thought before me that He was not as other men.

Fifty years ago, as I have said, I became a Catholic. I accepted Christ because I adopted the Catholic Church and would then have argued that Catholics were the superiors of other people. I would no longer be prepared to take such a ground. I think that the supreme proof of Christ's Divinity is the existence of saints, and that there could hardly have been saints if there had not been a company in which they lived and that, though in the interdenominational debate all the points are by no means to the one side, yet on the whole the Roman Catholic Church has the better of that argument. We are members of a company. Nothing is clearer in the Gospels than that Christ intended us to be so and founded a company. Yet, though I think that there could hardly have been saints without such a company I certainly would not argue that it is only within the visible Roman Catholic Church that sanctity is to be found. I am more inclined to sympathise with an announcement in the *Connaught Times* about a lady who has recently changed her religious allegiance. 'The Hon. Mrs —— has renounced the errors of the Church of England and embraced those of the Church of Rome.'

CHAPTER SEVEN
Second Childishness and Mere Oblivion

Yet the main difference between one's Catholicism of today and one's Catholicism of fifty years ago is unconcerned at all with the changing habits of the world but a change that must be inevitable in everybody's life. As I have said, when I became a Catholic I obediently accepted what the Church taught about life after death, but it did not greatly interest me. It was not one of the important suasions which led me to accept the Church, for death seemed to me so distant then that I did not feel it as a reality. I thought of myself as in practice immortal. Whatever might be due to happen in the world I always thought of myself as being there to see it happen. At the age of over seventy things are very different. I am not, as far as I know, threatened with death tomorrow, but my health is not robust and in the nature of things there cannot be many years before me.

In face of an affliction in youth, if one enjoys reasonable health, one wonders and frets how long it will be before one is well again. In old age one begins to wonder whether recovery is worth while—worth while to recover, not to enjoy a prospect of infinite good health but for the doubtful comfort of a few more years or months. One merely recovers in order to be ill again. The final victory of death is inevitable. One is fighting a certainly losing battle. I do not particularly wish to die. I do not welcome death. The pretended triumph of Abt Vogler—

> Grow old along with me
> The best is yet to be—

seems to be nonsense. Nevertheless, whether we like it or not, there death is. The unbeliever may denounce the Christian promises as a fraud but he does not thereby escape the grave. We may wish for life but it is idle to waste time in cavilling at the inevitable. We have no alternative and, in great contrast to my mood in youth and to the mood of most people in youth, in old age death, so far from being unthinkable, becomes the great subject of curiosity. Miss Muriel Spark wrote a whimsical book called *Memento Mori* in which she imagined a number of old people being rung up by Death on the telephone and told that they were about to die. If she had made Death ring up a number of people in their twenties, the conceit would have had great point, but I cannot imagine anybody in the seventies, whether called by Death on the telephone or not, who does not have the prospect of death constantly in his or her mind. Death's reminder seemed very unnecessary. They say that the modern man shrinks from talking or thinking about death as much as the Victorians shrank from talking or thinking about sex. I do not know if that is true. Certainly for myself no other subject any longer excites my curiosity and there is nothing much else about which I am willing to talk with any interest. Its promises of a future life, far from being an uninteresting irrelevance, are what the Christian religion is not indeed solely but what it is predominantly about.

Of course many Christians—and many early Christians in particular —have thought that they lived in the latest hour—the *novissima hora*— and would themselves see the consummation of things. All Christians indeed say in their creeds that they believe in the world to come and I know of no reason why the end should not come at any minute—in the twinkling of an eye, as St Paul thought. But we cannot easily believe in it. We may faintly accept Teilhard de Chardin's Omega Point, but we cannot easily believe in the imminent coming of the last day. We take it for granted that the world will go on as it always has gone on, but a man who was alive at the time of the Incarnation might quite reasonably have said, 'The World has gone on without an Incarnation for all these thousands of years. Is it likely that it would happen precisely now?' Yet I must confess—perhaps it is a confession of little faith—that I would be surprised if the world came to an end before my death and, if it did so, I think that it would be more likely to be through Man's folly than through God's direct intervention.

Yet there are advantages in old age which I had not at all foreseen. It is a sorrow to me that I can no longer play games and, if ever I see some young men knocking the ball about on a tennis court, I sigh that I can no longer join with them. But apart from that the compensations are about equal to the disadvantages. I have little money and little capacity for making money, but I am greatly surprised and relieved not only at the things on which I cannot spend money but at how little I any longer wish for such things. In my days I have been a wide traveller over the world. Now it is no longer possible for me to take large and complicated journeys. But I find that not only can I not travel, but I have no wish to do so. I have no wish to leave my village. I hardly ever leave it, and the thought of going to London, to say nothing of a foreign journey, is repugnant to me. I used to be a hearty eater. I remember one day when I was working on the land in Sussex during the First World War that they, by mischance, brought out an extra packet of sandwiches at lunch time. I managed to scoff it and I remember reflecting that I could not imagine a circumstance under which I would be offered more food than I would be glad to consume. For many years after that I remained a hearty trencherman, but now in my old age the very sight of a well-piled plate fills me with revulsion and I eat very little. Throughout all my years of vigour I have been a hearty drinker. Now my wife and I keep a bottle or two in the house and pour from it when a friend is good enough to call on us, but when there are no guests we never drink any alcoholic drink, being content, as Winston Churchill said of Stafford Cripps, 'to drink only water and very little of that'. I am very deaf and that has admittedly its disadvantages, but it has also great advantages. How many of the things that are said are worth hearing? To the one side of our house is a constantly blasting quarry, to the other a road down which lorries ceaselessly trundle. To others the noise is intolerable. I happily am unable to hear it. I cannot stand up for long nor endure large companies. I am grateful when one or two friends call upon us, but the days are past for going to large parties. Thus it will be seen that not only are most of the things that cost much money no longer possible for me, but—what I had never foreseen—far from missing them my appetite for them has wholly gone. I prefer not having them to having them.

I say that speculation about death wholly occupies my attention. What happens at death? Are the Christian promises true? Since the beginning of time men have occupied themselves with the greatest of all debates. The two cases are fairly evenly balanced. On the one hand is it to be believed that man had these intimations of immortality if they did not correspond to something? Without survival all our obstinate conceptions of honour are of little meaning since it is obvious that in this world happiness is by no means always the reward of virtue. On the other hand, if we survive what survives? It is obvious that this body which we now possess does not survive. It is very certainly eaten by worms. Is it just our soul—the *animula vagula blandula*—which survives? If so, what does that mean? Can such survival of the disembodied soul be properly called our survival? What evidence is there for it? Christianity of course promises much more—promises in the most mysterious article of the creed the resurrection of the body. And, if we can accept that, our fears can be at rest and the debate is ended.

Most people, Christian or not Christian, have had some sort of belief in a future life and I find it hard to believe that as with Pascal and the existence of God or Kant and the categorical imperative, anyone would ever have thought of such a notion if it had not corresponded to some reality. Some say that such notions are the mere product of wishful thinking—that man invents for himself such a future because he cannot bear to face the horror of annihilation. But the future life of many— whether Calvinists among Christians or the adherents of various pagan faiths—have by no means been always pleasant or comfortable.

> All the days and nights of Sramandazi
> Are not worth an hour of yonder sun.

I believe in a future life because I believe that we must be ruled by a God of reason and because this life manifestly does not explain itself. There must be a compensation elsewhere for the many injustices and absurdities of this life. But, if you ask me how the future life works, I must of course confess complete ignorance and enormous curiosity. It seems that we have a resurrection body that is, in some way that we cannot begin to understand, ourselves and yet not ourselves—much as, I imagine, Christ's Resurrection Body was. It was indeed flesh and blood but yet something more than the disciples who had daily walked with him had known, so that even those who knew Him best—Mary Magdalene and Peter—did not at first recognise Him though, having once recognised Him, they had no doubt that it was He. I attach, I fear, little importance to the pictures of Dante as pictures of reality or to the meticulous details which some theologians have given of the minutiae of indulgences. Such minutiae have no authority in any recorded teaching of Christ and no inherent probability. They express themselves in a time-sequence of days and years which can clearly have no meaning in another world.

I have only once met an educated Catholic who pretended to accept the details of official Catholic teaching about our life after death. Evelyn Waugh, at any rate in certain moods, professed to accept such literalism. He argued that he indeed accepted the teaching of the Church that some might be saved on account of 'invincible ignorance'. Such teachings, he said, might perhaps excuse a few poor Eskimos who had never heard nor had the chance to hear of Christ. It was absurd to think that they could possibly excuse the ordinary educated Englishman who had gone through his life in the modern world not bothering to discover the truth. Sir John Betjeman was once so ill-advised as to send him a Christmas card. In reply he received a postcard which merely said, 'Hell yawns—and this goes for Penelope, too.' Towards the end of the war I wrote a book called *Death of a Gentleman*, one of the characters of which was an Anglican clergyman whom I intended to be pious, kindly and well instructed. Evelyn wrote me a generally friendly letter about it but added, 'But I have one complaint and that a serious one.' He admitted that such a clergyman would go to heaven if he existed but complained that I had seriously misled my public in pretending that such virtuous Anglican clergymen did exist. I remember one day hearing him develop his thesis in a flat which Douglas Woodruff then owned in Park West. He explained how all non-Catholic clergymen would certainly go to hell. 'You think Bishop Hollis is in Hell, don't you?' he said to me of my father. I answered a little angrily that I most certainly did not, and Father Martin D'Arcy who happened to be present afterwards spoke with some reprehension of Evelyn's habits of speaking lightly of the fate of departed souls. Indeed I would hardly have tolerated such talk from anybody else, but I knew well that it was his habit to use such language, scarcely himself knowing how much he meant it seriously.

For Blougram he believed, say, half he spoke.

It is possible that there may be real extreme wickedness by which a few souls utterly shut themselves off from all love—sell themselves, as the phrase goes, to the devil. If love is the law of God an utter lack of love must be deserving of His condemnation. Such a man perhaps cannot be saved because if he does not love at all there is nothing in him to save. On the other hand I cannot believe that any normal man or woman whom we meet walking the streets, a mixture like most of us of good and bad, a mixture of love and of the lack of it, is deserving of hell. I have never myself met an utterly wicked man. God would surely frustrate His own purposes if He created man in His own image and redeemed them only in order that the majority of them might be lost.

I do not think the death of religion very probable. Society does not, as is sometimes said, advance in a straightforward line of progress, nor can I find Teilhard de Chardin's prognosis that we are advancing in this dispensation to a final Omega Point at all convincing. If evolution is the law of the universe and man its prime product then it would seem to me reasonable that the future would consist of the further evolution of man into some superman beyond himself, but that apparently is not Teilhard's expectation. Man is a final form. His future evolution is to be a moral progress towards a consummation of unity. Of that I would say, first, that it does not seem to me a process that should properly be called evolution, secondly that there is absolutely no reason to think that it is happening. Man advances not in a straight line but by oscillation. First we have too much rigidity and, finding that intolerable, demand permissiveness. Then we find that permissiveness too boring with the great misery which it brings and there are demands for a return to tradition and discipline. I have little doubt that we shall see such a return and that people will return to worship because it is a natural need of man without which he is only half a person and because they have learnt from experience of the hollowness and misery of a life in which it has no place.

But, though I find it hard to be afraid of hell, I equally cannot believe that most of us have lived such lives that we are fit to go immediately into the awful presence of God and to meet the Beatific Vision. It is as if a man should be required to wash his face before he presents himself to an important host. So I do not doubt that Purgatory exists—the place for face-washing before we are admitted to Beatitude, even though the Bible has very little to tell us about it. But how Purgatory exists, in what form we survive, I neither know nor can imagine and am in great curiosity to discover. It is, I admit, an oddity that the barrier of communication should be so absolute between the living and dead. But so it is. I do not find any special cogency in the professed revelation of spiritualists, and perhaps it is better that we do not know. In Ronald Knox's *Other Eyes Than Ours* the spiritualists pretend to know all about the arrangements of the next world and to know that it is much the same as our own. The consequence is that people commit suicide for the most trivial of causes—cut their throats because bores are coming to tea.

As I say, I believe without hesitation in Purgatory and am more doubtful about hell. The only reason why I am hesitant about complete repudiation is the fact that there are some strange and violent threats in the Gospels of which at any rate the apparent meaning is that we cannot be indifferent to the threats of what the Mass calls 'final damnation'. Whoever has the arranging of the Last Judgement it will not be me. So it is of little importance what I may think about it. My friend Smitt-Ingerbretsen was the Chairman of the Religious Committee of the Norwegian Government. It fell to him to give advice to the King what doctrine the King as head of the State Lutheran Church should pronounce about hell. His natural instinct was to be liberal, but then he reflected on the possibility that, if he denied all possibility of damnation, 'my constituents, they will go to the Last Judgement, and they will say, "Mr Smitt-Ingerbretsen said it would be all right," and Almighty God, He will say, "Who the hell is Mr Smitt-Ingerbretsen?" and I shall look a bloody fool'. He was a very sensible man.

Index

Acton, Harold, 47
Adenauer, 164
Agar, Herbert, 72
Agnew, Alan, 183
Alfonso, King, 78
Alington (Headmaster of Summerfields), 18, 19, 46
Allison, Jim, 52
Allen, Cardinal, 101–2, 202
Allen, 'Gubby', 19
America, visits to Universities in the '20s, 68–70, 74, 75, 77; efficiency of, 70–1; isolationism of, 71, 72–4, 80–1, 140; and Trade Unions, 75, 78; and Prohibition, 79–80; and racialism, 77–8, 86; and religious attitudes, 84–87, 121–2; in 1935, 119–22, 130–4; and anti-Semitism, 134; attitude to European War, 140–6
Amis, Kingsley, 123
Ampleforth, 103, 115
Arnold, Matthew, 69
Asquith, Anthony, 20, 193
Asquith, H. H., 20, 44, 45, 66, 193–4
Asquith, Katharine, 193–6
Asquith, Margot, 194
Astor, Jakie, 190
Attlee, Clement, 170, 174, 182–3, 184–6, 191
Australia, arts in the '20s, 88, 97; religious attitudes, 89, 91–4, 98–9; politics of, 89–93; C. H.'s affection for, 94–6
Axbridge, 1–2

Baldwin, 159, 167

Balliol, 38–67
Baring, Maurice, 88
Barkley, William, 44
Barnes, Mgr (Oxford Chaplain), 48, 51, 52, 63
Barry, Kevin, 90
Bassett, Fr Bernard, S.J., 189
Bates College, Augusta, 68–9
Bates, 194
Bath and Wells, Bishop of, 2, 14
Beaumont College, 115
Beck, Archbishop, 177
Beck (U.S. Attorney General), 73
Beechman, Alec, 43, 44
Bell, Clive, 159–60
Bell, Col Howard, 159
Bell, Kenneth, 51
Belloc, Hilaire, 45, 51–3, 58, 59, 60, 104, 109, 133, 134, 136, 173, 180, 195
Benedict XV, Pope, 91
Bennett, Jill, 62
Berry, Pamela, 179
Betjeman, Sir John, 26, 151, 185, 190–2
Betjeman, Penelope, 192, 233
Bevan, Aneurin, 182, 183
Bevin, Ernest, 180, 183
Bird, Kenneth (Fougasse), 188–9
Birdwood, Lord, 149–50
Birkenhead, Lord, 52, 73, 179
Bismark, 138
Blougram, Bishop, 53, 58, 232
Boenhoffer, 62
Bonham-Carter, Lady Violet, 189, 195
Boothby, Lord, 165
Boswell, 162
Bottomley, Horatio, 27

Bourne, Cardinal, 195
Bowra, Sir Maurice, 42, 191
Bracken, Brendan, 180
Bradman, Sir Donald, 97
Bretton Woods Agreement, The, 165–166
British Council, The, 98, 163
Brock, Clutton, 53
Brooke, Rupert, 47
Brown, Dr McAfee, 117
Bryan, William Jennings, 86
Buchman, Frank, 81–2
Bulganin, 189
Butler, Bishop Christopher (former Abbot of Downside), 192
Butler, R. A., 175

Cabot Lodge, Henry, 74
Capital Punishment, 166–8, 173–4
Carnegie Foundation, 120
Carson, 170
Casti Connubii, 121
Catholicism, 10, 12–14, 51, 53, 59, 61–4, 66–7; author's conversion to, 51, 55–60, 62, 64–7, 125–6, 172, 204, 219–27; in America, 84–7, 121–2; and schools, 175–6; changes and reforms, 204–28; and birth control, 48–9, 209–11; and euthanasia, 209, 211; and abortion, 206–9, 211; and ecumenism, 214–18; and death, 228–34; and Stonyhurst, 107–10, 111–13; and politics, 173–5; and Abyssinian War, 126–7; and Nazis, 128; and anti-Semitism, 134; and Spanish Civil War, 136, 139
Chamberlain, Neville, 125, 130, 137, 138–9, 145
Chapman, Abbot, 13
Cherwell, 43
Cheshire V.C., Group-Captain, 1
Chesterton, Cecil, 180
Chesterton, G. K., 44, 45, 52, 59, 60, 188, 222
Christian Science, 188–9
Church, Dean, 9
Churchill, Randolph, 179
Churchill, Sir Winston, 150, 154, 156,
164–5, 169, 174, 177–8, 180, 184–5, 189, 190, 230
Collins, Michael, 170
Collis, Jim, 81
Coolidge, 176
Cooper, Lady Diana, 148
Cooper, Duff, 145
Coote, Colin, 188
Corlie, Fr, 104
Cosgrave, 130
Costello, Declan, 169, 183
Council of Europe at Strasbourg, 62, 163–4
Craigavon, Lord, 171
Cripps, Sir Stafford, 166, 178, 181, 182, 230
Crutwell, 46

Dad's Army, 148
Daily Express, 44
Daily Telegraph, 188
Dalton, Hugh, 166, 182
D'Arcy, Fr Martin, 111, 114, 232
Darling, Sir William, 174–5
Darrow, Clarence, 85–6
Darwin, Charles, 86
Davis, John W., 76–7
Dawson, Christopher, 203
de Broke, Lord Willoughby, 152
Decline and Fall, 47
Delargy, Hugh, 174
Delmas, Chaban, 164
de Valera, 150, 169–70, 184
Devizes, 159–60
Donovan, General, 152
Douglas, Lord Alfred, 20
Douglas, Lord Archibald, 20
Douglas-Home, Sir Alec, 47
Downside, 12–13, 103, 173
Dragon School, 19
Dreyfus Case, 134
du Bos, Charles, 136
Duhig, Archbishop, 93

Ede, Chuter, 182
Eden, Anthony, 148, 180, 189
Edinger, 38

Edward VII, 91
Einstein, 138
Elliott, Sir Walter, 181
Eton, 2, 8, 17–18, 24,–38 53, 54, 69, 104,
    106, 108, 147, 188; religion at, 27–9,
    34–5, 36–7; snob appeal of, 24–6;
    'Pop', 25–6; discipline at, 29, 30–1,
    33–4, 117; fagging at, 29–30; homo-
    sexuality at, 37–8, 115
Evans, John, 20
Evatt, 90

Fagan, Vincent, 124, 130, 137, 140
Farnell, Dr, 48
Fisher, Archbishop of Canterbury, 4
Fitzgerald, Desmond, 129, 113, 170
Flying Inn, 60
'Fougasse', *see* Bird, Kenneth
Foster, John, 164–5
Franco, 136, 139
Fry, Sir Geoffrey, 167
Fulford, Roger, 154

Gaitskell, Hugh, 184
Gandhi, 179
Gardiner, Lord Gerald, 48
Garman, S.J., Fr, 108
Geary, Wade, 51
George III, 102
Gilroy, Cardinal, 93
Gladstone, 9, 165
Glastonbury, 14
Goering, 141
Goudge, Dr, 9
Goudge, Elizabeth, 9–10
Greenwood, Arthur, 182
Grey, Sir Edward, 140
Grigg, John, 129
Guardian, The, 1, 188
Guedella, Philip, 44
Gurian, Waldemar, 16–19, 142, 145
Gwynn, Dennis, 129
Gwynn, Stephen, 129

Haile Selassie, 126
Hailsham, Lord, 69
Harding, 76

Harford, Sir Arthur, 188
Hartington, Lord, 199–200
Hartington, 'Kick', 199–201
Hartley, L. P., 54, 195
Harvard, 74
Head, Anthony, 163
Headlam, Tuppy, 28
Heald, Lionel, 150
Heath, Edward, 187
Heenan, Cardinal, 134, 209
Herbert, A. P., 51, 82
Herschel, 134
Hinsley, Cardinal, 156
Hitler, 82, 92, 129, 131–2, 134–5, 136,
    138–9, 141–5, 198
Hodgson, Ralph, 196
Hollis, Christopher, childhood in
    Somerset, 1–10; at Eton, 2, 17–18,
    24–38, 41, 61, 101, 134; own religious
    environment, 2–9, 21–3, 27–31, 35–7,
    50, 60–2, 83–7, 229–31; in Wells,
    2–10, 11, 12, 13, 14; early attitudes
    to Catholicism, 7, 14, 49, 57, 61–4,
    83–7; attitudes to general Christian
    tenets, 8, 9, 11, 12, 23, 27–31, 35–7,
    52–3, 54–5, 204–27; relationship with
    father, 9, 13, 57–9, 66; in Leeds, 10–
    15; and the Jews, 14, 134–5, 220–7;
    at Summerfields, 16–24; and Orwell,
    17–18; at Balliol, 38–75, 191; and
    Evelyn Waugh, 43, 46, 65, 117, 149,
    231–2; and the Oxford Union, 43–5,
    53, 68–70, 75; conversion to Catholi-
    cism, 51, 55–60, 62, 64–7, 125–6, 172,
    204, 219–27; and Belloc, 51–3, 58, 60;
    and Douglas Woodruff, 59–60, 70,
    76–7, 83, 129; and the Council of
    Europe, 62, 163–5; and Ireland, 66,
    169–71; and America in the 20's, 68–
    88; in 1935, 119–42; and Moral
    Rearmament, 81–3; and Australia,
    88–100; and Archbishop Mannix,
    91–4; and John Betjeman, 97, 151,
    185, 190–3; and Sir Robert Menzies,
    96, 99; and Stonyhurst, 100–18; at
    Notre Dame University, Indiana,
    119–42; and build-up to World War

II, 130–46; and the Home Guard, 147–50; in the RAF, 150–7, 158; as an MP for Devizes, 158–87; and capital punishment 166–9; 173–4; and Catholic hierarchy, 172–5; and Malcolm Muggeridge, 187–90, 209; at *Punch*, 187–91; and Asquith family, 193–5; and Parliamentary colleagues, 177–87; and Siegfried Sassoon, 195–196; and Kennedy family, 196–202, 203; and birth control, 48–9, 206–7, 209, 211; and abortion, 207–9, 211; and euthanasia, 209, 211; and Catholic attitudes to social problems, 211–214, 228; and recent liturgical reforms, 215–19; and Christian attitude to death, 229–34

Hollis, Bishop (father), 1–2, 6, 8, 10, 12, 13–14, 17, 57–8, 66–7, 232

Hollis, Bishop Michael (brother), 1

Hollis, Mrs (mother), 7, 100

Home Guard, The 147–50

Hoover, President, 131

Horner, Sir John and Lady, 145, 193, 194

Hughes family, of New South Wales, 90

Hughes, Billy, 90, 92

Humanae Vitae, 206

Hurd, Sir Percy, 159

Huxley, Aldous, 29, 45

Inge, Dean, 48, 190

Innitzer, Cardinal, 142–3

Ireland, situation in the 20's, 66, 90, 93; Catholicism of, 87; Irish boys at Stonyhurst, 105; nationalism of, 105, 122; settlement of, 129–30; Declaration of Republic, 169–71

Jardine, Douglas, 19

Jennings, Col, 195

Jerome, Silas K., 82

Jerrold, Douglas, 197–8

Jesuits, The, 101, 107–17

Jews, and anti-Semitism, 134–5; religion of 14, 220–7

John, Augustus, 111–12

John, Henry, 111–12

John XXIII, Pope, 212, 215, 217–18, 226

Johnson, Dr, 87, 142, 157, 182

Jowett, 51

Joyce, James, 113

Kelly, Archbishop of Sydney, 93

Kennedy, Edward, 198

Kennedy, Jacqueline, 203

Kennedy, John F., 133, 201–4

Kennedy, Joseph, 197–200

Kennedy, 'Kick', *see* Hartington

Kennedy, Robert, 202

Kennington, Eric, 153–4

Kennion, Bishop, 3

Kettle, 109

Kiesinger, Herr, 164

King, Fr Leicester, 167

King, Fr Michael, 118

Kingsley, 57

Knox, Bishop, 67

Knox, Mgr Ronald, 42, 44, 67, 180, 196, 233

Koening, General, 164

Kruschev, 189

Lambton, Cecily, 193

Lancing College, 47

Lavery, Lady Hazel, 40, 46, 129

Lavery, John, 129

Law, Toby, 163

Lawrence, D. H., 45

Lawrence, T. E., 154

League of Nations, 73–4, 79, 125, 131, 135

Lee, Bishop, 172–3

Leeds, 10–12, 14–15, 158

Leeds Grammar School, 10–11, 16–17

Leo XIII, Pope, 56, 205, 214

Lindsay, Kenneth, 69

Lindsay, Norman, 88

Little Learning, A, 46

Lloyd George, 152

Londonderry, Lady, 129

Longford, Lord, 185

Loom of Youth, The, 32

Low, 97
Lutyens, 194
Lyttleton, Edward, 29
Lyttleton, George, 38

Macaulay, 64
MacAuley, James, 98
MacDonald, Malcolm, 70, 76
MacDonald, Ramsay, 184
Mackenzie, Compton, 195, 204
Macmillan, Harold, 20, 180
MacQuarie, Governor, 97
Mangon, Fr Richard, 105
Mannix, Archbishop, 91–4, 99
Marconi Scandal, The, 180–1
Marjoribanks, Edward, 69, 73, 74
Marlborough College, 3, 43, 159
Marshall Aid, 165
Martindale, S.J., Fr, 59, 114
Mathews, Ronald, 54, 64
Maud, Lord Recliffe, 101
Maudling, Reginald, 154
Maxwell-Fyfe, David, 43
Maynooth College, 99
McAdoo, 76, 77
McCausland, Connolly, 171
McKenna, Reginald, 20, 194
McIntyre, Cardinal, 202
McNaghten, Hugh, 8
Mein Kampf, 128
Mells, Somerset, 42, 193–6
Mencken, H. L., 85
Mendes France, 164
Menzies, Sir Robert, 96, 99
Meredith, 54
Moore, George, 91
Moreton, Fr, 12
Morissey, Judge, 203
Morrell, Lady Ottoline, 45–6
Morrison, Herbert, 153, 164, 182, 183–4
Morrison, 'Shakes', Speaker of the House of Commons, 181
Mosley, Oswald, 137
Muggeridge, Malcolm, 82, 186, 188–9, 209
Murray, Basil, 46
Murray, Gilbert, 46

Murphy, Fr, 98–9
Mussolini, 87, 125, 126, 130–1, 135, 136–8, 156

Newman, Cardinal, 9, 54, 103, 107, 110, 126, 183
New Statesman, 52
New Zealand, 88
Nichols, Beverley, 43
Nicholson, Harold, 55
Non abbiamo bisogno, 137
Notre Dame University, Indiana, 119–142; standard of education at, 123–4; discipline at, 124; football at, 123–4; Irishness of, 123–4, 130, 140

O'Hara, Cardinal, 119, 197
O'Neill, Terence, 99, 172
Oratory, The 103
Orwell, George, 17
Oxford, and the 'new psychology', 39; state of permissiveness of, 40–1, 44–50, 63; Dons, 42; Union, 42–5, 53, 60, 68–9, 75, 158, contemporaries, 46–8; and sex, 47–50; religious attitudes of, 50–3, 58–9, 60, 62–3, 65
Oxford, Lord, 194
Oxford Movement, The, 2, 8

Pannico, Archbishop, 93–4
Parliament, 158–70
Parnell, 90
Paul VI, Pope, 99, 206, 212
Petre, Maud, 58
Pius IX, Pope, 126, 204, 214
Pius X, Pope, 219
Pius XI, Pope, 121, 205
Pius XII, Pope, 175, 215, 222
Porter, Dr, 29
Portrait of the Artist as a Young Man, 113
Pound, Ezra, 133
Powell, Enoch, 181
Public schools, views on, 24–5, 32–3
Punch, 187, 188, 189, 193

Quadragesimo Anno, 121, 205, 214

Quennell, Peter, 47

R.A.F., The, 150–5, 158
Ramsay, Abbot, 12
Redmond, John, 89–90
Redmond, Willy, 89–90
Rerum Novarum, 205, 214
Reynaud, Paul, 164
Rhodes, Cecil, 57
Robinson, Armitage, 12–13
Romulo, Carlos, P., 121
Roosevelt, Mrs Eleanor, 133
Roosevelt, President, 78, 120–1, 122, 131–2, 133, 140, 198
Rossall School, 101–2
Runciman, 20
Russell, Bertrand, 45, 148–50
Russell, Conrad, 148–50
Ryan, Mgr, 171

Salisbury, Lord, 112
Samuel, Lord, 180
Santa-Maria, 90
Sassoon, Siegfried, 45, 196
Scott-James, Anne, 116
Showan, Percy, 151
Shriver, Eunice, 200
Silverman, Sidney, 166, 168
Simon, Gilbert, 65–6
Simon, Sir John, 65–6
Sinclair, Sir Archibald, 154
Sinn Fein party, 124
Smith, Al, 76, 77, 80, 202
Smitt-Ingerbretsen, 233
Smuts, Field-Marshal, 153
Spaak, Henri, 184
Spark, Muriel, 229
Spellmann, Cardinal, 186, 202
Stalin, 142
Stanley, Oliver, 180
Stansgate, Lord, 152, 153
Steel, David, 208–9
Stevenson, Adlai, 68
Stokes, Dick, 174
Stonyhurst, 100–18, 135; treasures of, 102; history of, 102–3; religious atti-

tudes of, 106–13; discipline at, 107–8, 113–14, 117
Stopes, Dame Marie, 48
Stormon, Fr, 99
Strachey, John, 147, 177
Strickland, Lord, 127
Suenens, Cardinal, 214
Summer Fields, 4, 14–24, 193
Sunday Express, 163
Sutherland, Dr Halliday, 48
Syllabus Errorum, 129

Tablet, The, 159
Tapsell, Peter, 217
Teilhard de Chardin, 232–3
Temple, Archbishop, 156
Thackeray, 188
Times, The, 133, 153
Tomlinson, George, 182–3
Travers, Ben, 150–1
Tweedsmuir, Lord, 136

Urquhart, 'Sligger', 48, 51, 52, 101, 110

Vassall, 133
Vatican II, Council, 135
Vidler, Dr Alec, 188
Vile Bodies, 47

Ward, Wilfred, 172
Washington, Booker, 78
Watson, Fr Sam, 112
Waugh, Alec, 32, 46
Waugh, Evelyn, 43, 46, 65, 82–3, 117, 125, 147, 149, 180, 186, 204, 205, 231, 232
Waugh in Abyssinia, 125
Waverley, Lord, 152–3
Weber Orlando, 119, 131–2
Weld, Fr, 104
Weld, Thomas, 102
Wells, H. G., 21
Wells, 2–5, 8–9, 10–11
Wells Theological College, 2–5, 8, 12, 21, 66
Wesley, Charles, 87
Williams, Dr, 16, 18, 20, 21, 23
Wilson, Harold, 48

Wilson, Sir Henry, 105
Wilson, Dr McNair, 135
Wiseman, Cardinal, 56, 177
Wodehouse, P. G., 149
Woodrow Wilson, 73–4, 76
Woodruff Douglas, 44, 59, 70, 76, 77, 129, 232

Woolf, Leonard and Virginia, 52
Wright, 99
Wyndham-Lewis, Percy, 137
Wynne-Wilson, Bishop, 3

Yale, 75–6
Young, G. M., 159